1001 HuMOROuS ILLuSTRATiONS FOR PUBLIC SPEAKING

1001 HuMoRouS iLLuStRaTiOnS FOR PUBLIC SPEAKING

MICHAEL HODGIN

ZondervanPublishingHouse
Grand Rapids, Michigan

A Division of HarperCollinsPublishers

1001 Humorous Illustrations for Public Speaking
Copyright © 1994 by Michael Hodgin
All rights reserved.

Requests for information should be addressed to:
Zondervan Publishing House
Grand Rapids, Michigan 49530

Library of Congress Cataloging-in-Publication Data

1001 humorous illustrations for public speaking : fresh, timely, and compelling
   illustrations for preachers, teachers, and speakers / edited by Michael Hodgin
     p.   cm.
   Includes indexes.
   ISBN 0-310-47391-8 (pbk.)
    1. Public speaking. I. Hodgin, Michael, 1953–   . II. Title: One thousand one
  humorous illustrations for public speaking.
PN4121.A15   1994
081–dc20   94-32880
                                                    CIP

Cover design by Tammy Johnson
Cover illustration by Bruce Day
Interior design by Sue Koppenol

Printed in the United States of America

     98 99 00 01 02 /❖DH/ 10 9 8

Special thanks to those who helped prepare this book for publicaton:

Rose,

Renae,

Ryan,

Michelle,

Angie,

Jan,

Teresa

& Deb

Contents

Preface   9

Permissions   10

Illustrations Topically Arranged   11

Index of Subtopics   374

Alphabetical Index of Titles   382

Numerical Index of Titles   389

List of Sources   397

Preface

There is one essential difference between a good speaker and a great speaker: The message of the great speaker is alive in the mind of the listener. There are various ways to infuse one's message with life–inflection, tone, enthusiasm, eye contact, and such. But there is one particular ingredient in the recipe of a great message that is universal. Great speakers strategically place illustrations into their messages that will connect with their listeners.

For the past fourteen years Saratoga Press has provided public speakers with the resources needed to turn good messages into great messages. The subscribers to two monthly resource letters, *Parables, Etc.* and the *Pastor's Story File*, never run out of the ammunition they need to win the communications battle. And their source of illustrations is unique: Most of the illustrations come from the subscribers themselves. Every month we glean a new harvest of illustrations, the cream of a crop that has already been tested and proved successful in bringing the message to life.

Of all the types of illustrations we publish–jokes, quotes, anecdotes, poems, and so on–the ones that consistently illustrate best are those containing humor. Humor gets the listener's attention. It takes the listener by surprise. It amuses and entertains. And while this is happening, the message is getting heard. Now, with the publication of this book, the best of our humorous illustrations are all neatly packaged in a ready reference that should serve its users for years to come.

The compiler is grateful to the following publishers for permission to quote from their publications:

Preaching Magazine, P.O. Box 7728, Louisville, Kentucky 40257-0728, for illustrations #679, 748, and 976.

Sunshine Magazine, Sunshine Press, East Route 16, Litchfield, Illinois 62056, for illustrations #98, 764, 874, and 927.

See also the List of Sources, pages 397–411.

1

TOPIC: Ability

More Light Bulbs

How many people does it take to screw in a lightbulb in the basement of the White House?

Answer: None, they prefer to work in the dark.

How many Harvard MBAs does it take to screw in a lightbulb?

Answer: Only one. He stands still and holds onto the bulb, and the world revolves around him. *(You may substitute Princeton M.Div.s, or whatever group you want to persecute that particular day.)*

Dates & Places Used:

2

TOPIC: Acceptance

Infatuation or Love

Infatuation is thinking he's as sexy as Robert Redford, as smart as Henry Kissinger, as noble as Ralph Nader, as funny as Woody Allen, and as athletic as Jimmy Connors.

Love is realizing he's as sexy as Woody Allen, as smart as Jimmy Connors, as funny as Ralph Nader, as athletic as Henry Kissinger, and nothing like Robert Redford, but you'll take him anyway!

Dates & Places Used:

3

TOPIC: Acceptance

Unconditional Love

Maxie Dunnam tells the story of an elderly man who began spending a significant amount of time with an elderly woman. Neither had ever married and each had lived alone for many years. Gradually the old gentleman recognized a real attachment to her but was shy and afraid to reveal his feelings to her. After many days of anxiety and fear, he finally mustered up the courage to declare his intentions. He went over to her home and in a nervous frenzy blurted out, "Let's get married!!"

Surprised, she threw up her hands and shouted, "It's a wonderful idea, but who in the world would have us?"

Dates & Places Used:

4 TOPIC: Acceptance

Let Them Go

An astronomer at Harvard once was giving a lecture entitled, "The Expanding Universe." In it, he pointed out that there are galaxies greater than our Milky Way speeding outward, moving away from us faster than the speed of light. This means that we're actually losing them. They're falling off the edge of the universe, so to speak. It is a mind-boggling thing to think about. In the question-and-answer period that followed the lecture, a woman who appeared to be terribly upset by this revelation, asked anxiously, "Professor, what are we going to do about all of those galaxies we're losing?" To which the learned professor quietly replied, "Let them go, Madam. Let them go!"

Dates & Places Used:

5 TOPIC: Accidents

Body Designs

Some believe the shin was invented for finding furniture in the dark. Others find the little toe much more effective for such activity.

Dates & Places Used:

6 TOPIC: Accomplishments

A Paneful Target

As a young man, Jack (Guelker) had purchased archery equipment and could hardly wait to try it out. Knowing that bales of hay would provide an excellent backdrop for a target, but having none readily available, he chose to use more obtainable facilities. Several sheets of insulation board leaning against an old out-building seemed to provide the perfect substitute. After centering the target over the boards, he stepped off the required distance to practice shooting. He strung the bow, carefully fitted an arrow onto the bowstring, drew the arrow and fired. Although the arrow struck the target, the instantaneous sound of breaking glass was the first indication that the target area might not have been a good choice. In the springtime, however, it had seemed the best place to stack all twenty of the storm windows from the house. The arrow had passed through the target, the insulation boards, and the entire stack of glass windows, breaking every one.

There are times that the results of our best-aimed intentions are not what we plan them to be, but what we least expect. Proper planning involves looking beyond the obvious and checking for the possibilities of broken glass.

Dates & Places Used:

7 TOPIC: Accountants

Accountant's Maxim

When you make the mistake of adding the date to the right side of the accounting statement, you must add it to the left side too.
Dates & Places Used:

8 TOPIC: Action

Carry-Outs

Preacher to the congregation: "Crying babies and disruptive children, like good intentions, should be carried out immediately."
Dates & Places Used:

9

TOPIC: Activity

But Hurry

This is the age of the half-read page and the quick hash and the mad dash; the bright night with the nerves tight; the plane hop and the brief stop; the lamp tan in a short span; the big shot in a soft spot; and the brain strain and the heart pain; and the cat-naps 'til the spring snaps; and the fun is done.

Dates & Places Used:

10

TOPIC: Advertising

Modern Marketing

A local farmer had come to the conclusion that the local car dealer had profited greatly by all the add-on options that increased the price of cars sold to the hapless farmer. Then one day the car dealer informed the farmer that he was coming around to buy a cow. In a spirit of justice, the farmer attached the following price information to the cow: Basic cow $500.00, Two-tone exterior $45.00, Extra stomach $75.00, Product storing compartment $60.00, Straw chopper $120.00, Four spigots at $10.00 each $40.00, Cowhide upholstery $125.00, Dual horns $15.00, Automatic fly swatter $38.00, Fertilizer attachment $185.00; Total $1,233.00

Dates & Places Used:

11

TOPIC: Advice

Two Different Words

A grandmother who was concerned about her granddaughter's vocabulary frequently advised the child concerning her chosen words. On one such occasion, Grandma said, "Dear child, I would like you to do something for me. Would you please promise not to use two words? One is swell, and the other is lousy." The girl replied, "Sure, Grandma. What are the two words?"

Dates & Places Used:

12 TOPIC: Advice

Surrendered Advisor

There was a pious old gentleman of an earlier generation who used to get up regularly at prayer meeting in his church to pray: "Use me, O Lord, use me—in some advisory capacity!"

Dates & Places Used:

13 TOPIC: Advice

Overly Helpful

Three men were about to be executed by the guillotine. One was a Frenchman, one was an Englishman, and the other was an American. The Frenchman went first. He was asked if he wanted to wear a hood over his head. He declined and said he was not afraid. He was placed under the guillotine, with his neck on the block. He looked up bravely at the sharp blade that was about to fall. The rope was pulled, but nothing happened. His executioners believed this was an act of God, and they freed him. The same process was repeated with the Englishman. He refused the hood, was set into place, and the rope was pulled. Again, nothing happened. This too was interpreted as an act of God, so they freed the Englishman as well. Now it was time for the American's execution. "Do you want a hood?" He refused, "Nope. I am just as brave as those other two guys." They laid the American face up in the guillotine and were about to pull the rope when the American stopped them. "Hey, wait just a minute. I think I found the problem with your guillotine."

Dates & Places Used:

14

TOPIC: Advice

Free Advice

Receiving advice is like getting kissed on the forehead. It doesn't hurt, but it doesn't help much either.

Dates & Places Used:

15

TOPIC: Affirmation

Better Than Nothing

A true story: A father (Kenneth Fox of Warrenville, Illinois) was filling in as mother while his wife was at the hospital. He was trying to be a good mother for his two kids, ages 10 and 15. After several days he needed a little affirmation and started fishing for a compliment, observing, "I'm doing pretty well as a mother, don't you think?" His older son said, "You're doing fine, Pop. I like the way you do this cold cereal." The 10-year-old girl added, "Well, at least you are better than nothing."

Dates & Places Used:

16

TOPIC: Age

Only the Tough Grow Old

A group of senior citizens at a retirement home were having a high old time discussing their various aches, pains, and ills. One had arthritis, another indigestion, someone else ulcers, still another insomnia, and on and on it went. Finally an eighty-year-old man said—"Think of it this way, my friends—it just proves that old age isn't for sissies!"

Dates & Places Used:

17

TOPIC: Age

Long-Term Driving

A little boy was riding along with his father from New Mexico to Colorado. They were traveling 250 miles to go fishing. Every fifty miles the excited son asked his father if they were almost there. The father answered that they had quite a distance to travel yet. So the son waited for a few more minutes and asked his father again.

"Sorry, son, we have another hundred miles yet."

After fifty more miles the son asked, "Daddy, am I still going to be four years old when we get there?"

Dates & Places Used:

18

TOPIC: Age

The Young Get No Respect

Police were called to help restore order at the Presbyterian Home for the Aged, the scene of a week-long revolt. Three militant octogenarians were arrested after a scuffle in the north parlor. These three who were arrested were identified as leaders of the activist group that seized control of the parlor three days earlier and locked the matron in the closet.

One reason given for the protest: "We have a bunch of young whippersnappers running things around here, and we don't trust anybody under sixty-five." Another reason from another of the activists: "What is the sense of living a long time if some fifty-year-old kid is going to tell you what to do?"

Dates & Places Used:

19

TOPIC: Age

Middle-Aged Action

You have reached middle age when you try to find out where the action is so you can go somewhere else.

Dates & Places Used:

20

TOPIC: Age

Healthy Circulation

The denunciation of the young is a necessary part of the hygiene of older people and greatly assists in the circulation of the blood.
Dates & Places Used:

21

TOPIC: Age

Counting the Years

A friend and I took my little daughter, Ellen, to a movie for her birthday. After we left the theater, while I was bundling up Ellen against the cold wind, my friend asked her how old she was.

"I can't tell you," Ellen said. "I have my mittens on!"
Dates & Places Used:

22

TOPIC: Age

Stay Young

You can stay young indefinitely if you eat wisely, get plenty of sleep, work hard, have a positive mental outlook, and lie about your age.
Dates & Places Used:

23

TOPIC: Age

Open to the Future

A woman in a convalescent home was given a party to celebrate her one-hundredth birthday. Her pastor came to offer his congratulations. Later, the pastor said, "Her mind was keenly alert. When I arrived, she was completely caught up in the excitement of the birthday party."

A reporter had come to interview her. And when he asked that high-spirited, one-hundred-year-old woman, "Do you have any children?" she replied, without hesitation, "Not yet!"

Dates & Places Used:

24

TOPIC: Age

More to Keep Quiet About

As people grow older, they generally become more quiet.
But of course, they have more to keep quiet about.

Dates & Places Used:

25

TOPIC: Age

Really Fast

Forget about jets, racing cars, and speed boats.
Nothing goes as fast as middle age.

Dates & Places Used:

26

TOPIC: Age

Age Discrimination

A while back, *Fortune* magazine did their cover story on Warren Buffet of Omaha, Nebraska. The magazine tells the amazing tale of one of our country's most successful billionaires. He has been an enormous success as he has invested in all kinds of companies in the process of building the conglomerate, Berkshire Hathaway. He has been referred to as "The Wizard of Omaha." He looks for strong companies that are well positioned in the market. He seeks to take over these companies. Then he leaves the management of these acquired companies in place, rather than replacing them, as do many other corporate chairmen.

One of the companies he owns is Nebraska Furniture Mart, which was founded by Rose Blumkin. He keeps in touch with the local managers in many different ways, usually informal, such as by phone, or by means of periodic meetings over a meal. The following is *Fortune's* description of Buffet's dealings with the Blumkin family, prior to the family's splitting into competitive factions. The Blumkin family (or as Buffet refers to them, "the amazing Blumkins") meet for dinner every few weeks at an Omaha restaurant. The Blumkins attending usually include Louis, 68, and his sons: Ron, 39; Irv, 35; and Steve, 33.

The matriarch of the family and chairman of the Furniture Mart is Rose Blumkin, who emigrated from Russia as a young woman, started a tiny furniture store that offered rock-bottom prices. Her motto is "Sell cheap and tell the truth." She built this furniture store into a business that last year did $140 million in sales. At age 94, she still works seven days a week in the carpet department.

Buffet says in his new annual report that she is clearly gathering speed and "may well reach her full potential in another five or ten years. Therefore, I've persuaded the Board to scrap our mandatory retirement-at-100 policy. And it's about time," he adds. "With every passing year, this policy has seemed sillier to me."

Perhaps he jests, true, but Buffet simply does not regard age as having any bearing on how able a manager is. Maybe because he has bought so many strong managements and stuck with them, he has worked over the years with an unusually large number of older executives and treasured their abilities. Buffet says, "Good managers are so scarce I can't afford the luxury of letting them go just because they've added a year to their age."

Dates & Places Used:

27 TOPIC: Age

Individualism

The famous actress Sarah Adler was never willing to accurately admit age. On one such occasion a newspaperman asked her to tell her age. Without hesitation, Sarah replied that she was sixty-eight.

The reporter objected, "But, Madam Adler, how can you be sixty-eight? I just asked your son his age, and he said that he is sixty."

Sarah replied, "My son lives his life and I live mine."

Dates & Places Used:

28 TOPIC: Aging

Aging Poem

I can live with my arthritis,
And my dentures fit me fine.
I can see with my bifocals,
But I sure do miss my mind.

Dates & Places Used:

29 TOPIC: Aging

You Know You're Older

You know you're getting older when: Everything hurts, and what doesn't hurt, doesn't work. The gleam in your eyes is from the sun hitting your bifocals. You feel like the morning after, and you haven't been anywhere. Your little black book contains only names ending in M.D.

You get winded playing chess. Your children begin to look middle-aged. You join a health club and don't go. You decide to procrastinate, but never get around to it.

Your mind makes contracts your body can't meet. You know all the answers, but nobody asks you the questions. You look forward to a dull evening at home. You're turning out lights for economic rather than romantic reasons. Your knees buckle and your belt won't.

The best part of your day is over when the alarm goes off. Your back goes out more than you do. A fortune teller offers to read your face. The little gray-haired lady you help across the street is your wife. You've got too much room in the house and not enough room in the medicine cabinet. You sink your teeth in a steak, and they stay there.

Dates & Places Used:

30 TOPIC: Aging

Jump Start

A wealthy retiree goes into a chic club with a stunningly beautiful young woman on his arm. The old fellow turns up his pacemaker and they start to dance. The band plays an up-tempo tune. He turns up his pacemaker again and keeps dancing. Then the band starts really cooking and plays an even faster number. He turns up his pacemaker even faster, still dancing. Then, suddenly, the old guy slumps over on the floor. The bartender comes over and asks, "Want me to call the paramedics?" The girl responds, "No, just call the Auto Club. I think we can jump start him."

Dates & Places Used:

31 TOPIC: Aging

Time for Teeth

A couple had been married for fifty years. "Things have really changed," she said. "You used to sit so close to me."

"Well, I can remedy that," he said, moving next to her on the couch.

"And you used to hold me tight."

"How's that?" he asked as he gave her a hug.

"Do you remember you used to nuzzle my neck and nibble on my ear lobes?"

He jumped to his feet and left the room. "Where are you going?"

"I'll be right back," he said. "I've got to get my teeth!"

Dates & Places Used:

32

TOPIC: Agreement

Too Late

Sign on the desk of an airline executive in Chicago:
"Don't bother to agree with me, I've already changed my mind."
Dates & Places Used:

33

TOPIC: Anger

All About Bees

Bees fly thousands of miles to gather enough nectar to make a pound of honey. Then someone comes along and steals it from them. Maybe this explains why bees have such lousy dispositions.
Dates & Places Used:

34

TOPIC: Anger

A Honking Parent

Shouting to make your kids obey is like using your horn to steer the car,
    and you get about the same results.
Dates & Places Used:

35

TOPIC: Anger

Regretful Speech

Speak when you're angry, and you'll deliver the best speech you'll ever regret.
Dates & Places Used:

36

TOPIC: Anniversary

Two Cards in One

A man entered a stationery store and asked the clerk for a "birthday-anniversary" card. The clerk replied, "We have birthday cards, and we have anniversary cards. Why not take one of each?" He said, "You don't understand. I need a card that covers both events. You see, we're celebrating the fifth anniversary of my wife's thirty-fourth birthday."

Dates & Places Used:

37

TOPIC: Anniversary

Stages of a Cold

A husband's reactions to his wife's colds during the first seven years of marriage: 1ST YEAR: "Sugar Dumpling, I'm really worried about my baby girl. You've got a bad sniffle and there's no telling about these things with all the strep going around. I'm putting you in the hospital. I know the food's lousy, but I'll be bringing your meals in from Rozzini's. I've already got it all arranged with the floor superintendent." 2D YEAR: "Listen, Darling, I don't like the sound of that cough and I've called the doctor to rush over here. Now you go to bed like a good girl, just for Pappa." 3D YEAR: "Maybe you'd better lie down, Honey. Nothing like a little rest when you feel lousy. I'll bring you something. Have we got any canned soup?" 4TH YEAR: "Now look, Dear, be sensible. After you feed the kids, do the dishes and mop the floor, you'd better rest." 5TH YEAR: "Why don't you take a couple aspirin?" 6TH YEAR: "If you'd just gargle or something instead of sitting around barking like a seal all evening . . ." 7TH YEAR: "For Pete's sake, stop that sneezing. What are you trying to do, give me pneumonia?"

Dates & Places Used:

38

TOPIC: Anniversary

Tired of You

A golden anniversary party was thrown for an elderly couple. The husband was moved by the occasion and wanted to tell his wife just how he felt about her. She was very hard of hearing, however, and often misunderstood what he had to say. With many family members and friends gathered around, he toasted her: "My dear wife, after fifty years I've found you tried and true!" Everyone smiled approval, but his wife said, "Eh?" He repeated in a louder voice, "AFTER FIFTY YEARS I'VE FOUND YOU TRIED AND TRUE!" His wife harumphed and shot back, "Well, let me tell you something—after fifty years I'm tired of you, too!"

Dates & Places Used:

39

TOPIC: Apologies

Clout—Who Has It?

In the classified section of a newspaper an ad appeared that read: "I would like to announce that the ad I put in this newspaper last Saturday was in error. I will be responsible for any debts incurred by my wife. And I will start paying as soon as I get out of the hospital."

Dates & Places Used:

40

TOPIC: Apology

Art of Apology

It takes real talent to be able to apologize in a manner that makes the offended person feel guilty.

Dates & Places Used:

41

TOPIC: Appearances

Not As They Seem

A True Story: A mother was shopping at a mall with her three-year-old daughter, who was growing weary of the outing. To renew her interest in shopping, the mother asked if she would like to visit the toy store that was just ahead. The daughter responded enthusiastically and took off toward the toy store as fast as her little feet could carry her. To keep up with her child, the mother broke into a trot. As the mother approached the racing child, she said, "I'm going to beat you to the store!" The girl looked around and screamed, "Don't beat me, Mommy! Don't beat me!" The startled mother looked around and realized that everyone in the mall was watching with shock and fear for this poor child. Now what?

Dates & Places Used:

42

TOPIC: Appearances

Life's Deeper Meaning

Tom Mullen illustrates a twentieth century preoccupation with trying to find a deeper meaning in life at the very beginning of his book, *Laughing Out Loud and Other Religious Experiences:*

An engineer, a psychologist, and a theologian were hunting in the wilds of northern Canada. They came across an isolated cabin, far removed from any town. Because friendly hospitality is a virtue practiced by those who live in the wilderness, the hunters knocked on the door to ask permission to rest. No one answered their knocks, but, discovering the cabin was unlocked, they entered. It was a simple place—two rooms with a minimum of furniture and household equipment. Nothing was surprising about the cabin except the stove. It was large, pot-bellied, and made of cast iron. What was unusual was its location: it was suspended in midair by wires attached to the ceiling beams. "Fascinating," said the psychologist. "It is obvious that this lonely trapper, isolated from humanity, has elevated his stove so he can curl up under it and vicariously experience a return to the womb." "Nonsense!" replied the engineer. "The man is practicing the laws of thermodynamics. By elevating his stove, he has discovered a way to distribute heat more evenly throughout the cabin." "With all due respect," interrupted the theologian, "I'm sure that hanging his stove from the ceiling has religious meaning. Fire LIFTED UP has been a religious symbol for centuries." The three debated the point for several minutes without resolving the issue. When the trapper finally returned, they immediately asked him why he had hung his heavy potbellied stove by wires from the ceiling. His answer was succinct: "Had plenty of wire, not much stove pipe!"

Dates & Places Used:

43

TOPIC: Appearances

Bubble Gum Return

A department store floor manager noticed a young boy staring intently at the handrail of an escalator. The manager walked over to him and asked, "Son, are you all right?" The boy nodded yes without looking up. "Can I help you?" he asked. The boy shook his head no and continued to look at the handrail. "Well, young man, do you want me to explain to you how escalators work?" The lad replied, "No, Mister. I'm just waiting for my bubble gum to come back!"

Dates & Places Used:

44

TOPIC: Appearances

Identity Crisis

Early one morning a woman made a mad dash out of the house when she heard the garbage truck pulling away. She was still in her bathrobe. Her hair was wrapped in big curlers. Her face was covered with sticky cream. She was wearing a chin-strap and a beat-up old pair of slippers. In short, she was a frightful picture. When she reached the sidewalk, she called out, "Am I too late for the garbage?" And the reply came back: "Nope, hop right in."

Dates & Places Used:

45

Liberace's Line

"Go ahead and stare. I don't dress this way to go unnoticed."
Dates & Places Used:

46

Talk to George

A hobo knocked on the door of an English inn called George And The Dragon. A woman opened the door. He asked, "Could I have a bite to eat?" The woman screamed at him, and began to curse and malign him and finally slammed the door in his face. He knocked again and the woman opened the door. "Now could I have a few words with George?"
Dates & Places Used:

47

Genetic Apparel

As seven-year-old Sally stood in front of her parents who were lined up before a cash register in a supermarket, a midget-sized adult person crossed nearby. Sally overheard her mother tell her father in an audible whisper, "It's the genes that make the difference." A few days later in school some little boy asked the teacher why some people did not grow like everyone else and remained midgets. Before the teacher could answer, Sally, raising her hand and standing at the same time, proudly thought she knew the answer: "It's because they wear tight blue pants."
Dates & Places Used:

48

Careless Appearance

A woman seeking a divorce complained that her husband was careless about his appearance. He hadn't shown up in two years.

Dates & Places Used:

49

Chasing Shadows

Max was a handsome Irish setter that my brother's family had agreed to "baby-sit" for the weekend. I was visiting that weekend and was keeping an eye on Max while the family ran some errands.

It was a bright, hot, Georgia afternoon. Max was resting in my brother's large, fenced-in backyard. I was sitting on the back steps, petting Max and admiring his beautiful, long-haired, wine-colored coat, when all of a sudden Max leaped up and tore out after some creature that had caught his eye.

As he ran, I looked out ahead of him, and sure enough, there was his prey, the shadow of a bird that was flying over the yard. As the shadow neared the end of the yard, it "flew" into the shadow of a tree that reached out onto my brother's property. When the two shadows met, the bird's shadow disappeared. But that's not how Max was interpreting the experience. He was still almost at a full run for a mature but somewhat inexperienced Irish setter when he reached the tree's shadow. The abrupt disappearance of his prey was quite confusing for Max.

There he was–every muscle in his body tense, claws dug into the dirt, tail high and wagging with excitement and anticipation, ears forward, tongue out and panting, eyes wide open and searching everywhere in the immediate area for his illusive game. That is just the way we are when we fall for the deception of the enemy: so willing and determined to expend any amount of energy for something that looks real or right, that calls on our natural abilities in just the right way ... but there is no substance, only shadow.

The obvious difference between Max and us is that one hopes we don't keep chasing shadows all day long, or life long.

By the end of the afternoon, Max was exhausted. Isn't that what chasing shadows does to all of us?

Dates & Places Used:

50 ◆ TOPIC: Appearances

First Impressions

A policeman arrived at the scene of an automobile accident and saw a horrible sight smashed against the inside of the windshield of one of the cars. The policeman quickly called for help and then rushed to the car.

The officer asked the man in the front seat, "How bad are you hurt, sir?"

The driver responded, "I'm not hurt at all, but this pizza sure made a mess."

Dates & Places Used:

51 ◆ TOPIC: Application

Applied Learning

"Son, don't give me any of those fancy pamphlets. Why, I don't farm half as well as I know how to now!"

Dates & Places Used:

52

TOPIC: Appointments

Never Too Early

Bob called his wife from work in the middle of the afternoon. "I'm able to get two tickets for the show we wanted to see. It's playing now. Do you want to see it?"

"Oh, yes!" she answered excitedly. "I'll get ready right away."

"Do that," Bob said, "the tickets are for tomorrow night."

Dates & Places Used:

53

TOPIC: Appreciation

A Good Day

"I know it's going to be a good day when all the wheels on my shopping cart turn the same way."

Dates & Places Used:

54

TOPIC: Appreciation

Almost Expressed Thanks

In Vermont a farmer was sitting on the porch with his wife. He was beginning to realize how much she meant to him. It was about time—for they had lived together forty-two years, and she had been such a help, a very willing worker.

One day as they sat together, he said, "Wife, you've been such a wonderful woman that there are times I can hardly keep from telling you."

Dates & Places Used:

55

TOPIC: Aptitude

It's a Gift

Sugar Ray Leonard was speaking at Harvard: "I consider myself blessed. I consider you blessed. We've all been blessed with God-given talents. Mine just happens to be beatin' people up."
Dates & Places Used:

56

TOPIC: Archaeologists

Valued Wives

Agatha Christie once said, "An archaeologist is the best husband a wife can have: the older she gets, the more interesting she is."
Dates & Places Used:

57

TOPIC: Art

Abstract Art

Abstract art is a product of the untalented sold by the unprincipled to the utterly bewildered. (*Al Capp*)
Dates & Places Used:

58

TOPIC: Art

A Point of Reference

Picasso once asked his friend Rodin if he liked Picasso's latest painting that was yet unsigned.

Rodin studied the painting from all directions and, only after careful deliberation answered Picasso, "Whatever else you do . . . sign it. If you do that . . . we will know which way to hold it."
Dates & Places Used:

59

The Man We Want

Adrian Rogers tells of Mike Kollin, former linebacker of the Miami Dolphins. His former coach, Shug Jordan, asked him if he would do some recruiting. Mike said, "Sure, coach. What are you looking for?" "Well Mike, you know there's that fellow, you knock him down, he just stays down?" Mike said, "We don't want him, do we, coach?" "No, that's right. Then there's that fellow, you knock him down and he gets up; you knock him down again and he stays down." Mike answered, "We don't want him either, do we, coach?" Coach said, "No, but Mike, there's a fellow, you knock him down, he gets up. Knock him down, he gets up. Knock him down, he gets up. Knock him down, he gets up." Mike said, "That's the guy we want, isn't it, coach?" The coach answered, "No, we don't want him either. I want you to find that guy who's knocking everybody down. That's the guy we want!"

Dates & Places Used:

60

TOPIC: Assistance

Can't Be Helped

Two Cub Scouts, whose younger brother had fallen into the lake, rushed home to mother with tears in their eyes. One of them sobbed, "We try to give him artificial respiration, but he keeps getting up and walking away."

Dates & Places Used:

61

TOPIC: Association

The Company You Keep

General William Westmoreland was once reviewing a platoon of paratroopers in Vietnam. As he went down the line, he asked each of them a question: "How do you like jumping, son?" "Love it, sir!" was the first man's answer. "How do you like jumping?" he asked

the next. "The greatest experience in my life, sir!" exclaimed the paratrooper. "How do you like jumping?" he asked the third. "I hate it, sir," he replied. "Then why do you do it?" asked Westmoreland. "I want to be around guys who love to jump."
Dates & Places Used:

62

TOPIC: Assumptions

Assumptions Cost

A tough store manager was walking through the packing room one day when he saw a young man lounging on a shipping crate, whistling and relaxing. He asked how much he was paid. The young man answered, "$120 a week." At that, the manager paid the man $120 and said, "Here's a week's pay. Get out!" The man-ager immediately found the department head and demanded to know who had hired this sloth. He replied, "We didn't hire him. He was just picking up a package."
Dates & Places Used:

63

TOPIC: Assumptions

Wrong Machine

We find ourselves operating on assumptions from time to time that prove to be all wrong from square one. Like the new sales-man who was carrying an important-looking document and walked over to an office employee who was standing by the paper shredder. He asked, "Can you show me how to operate this machine?" The other man said, "Sure, just flick this switch to turn it on, then put your paper in that slot. That's all there is to it." The salesman said, "Thanks." He followed the instructions, then turned and asked, "Now, how do you set it to make three copies?"
Dates & Places Used:

TOPIC: Assumptions

Just Counting

A cluster of small boys, obviously without the price of admission, milled about near one of the entrance gates to a football stadium. An observer said to the ticket-taker in a voice resonant with authority, "Let these kids in and tell me how many there are." The boys filed in and scampered delightedly into the crowd. As the last one entered, the ticket-taker said to the observer, "Thirty-four." The man nodded. "Right you are," he said, as he walked back into the crowd outside the gate.

Dates & Places Used:

TOPIC: Assumptions

Worst-Case Scenario

Fear is the wrong use of imagination. It is anticipating the worst, not the best that can happen. A salesman, driving on a lonely country road one dark and rainy night, had a flat. He opened the trunk; there was no lug wrench. He headed into the driving rain toward a dimly lit farmhouse. Surely the farmer would have a lug wrench he could borrow, he thought. Of course, it was late at night—the farmer would be asleep in his warm, dry bed. Maybe he wouldn't answer the door. And even if he did, he'd be angry at being awakened in the middle of the night. The salesman, picking his way blindly in the dark, stumbled on. By now his shoes and clothing were soaked. Even if the farmer did answer his knock, he would probably shout something like, "What's the big idea waking me up at this hour?" This thought made the salesman angry. What right did that farmer have to refuse him the loan of a lug wrench? After all, here he was stranded in the middle of nowhere, soaked to the skin. The farmer was a selfish clod—no doubt about that! The salesman finally reached the house and banged loudly on the door. A light went on inside, and a window opened above. A voice called out, "Who is it?" His face white with anger, the salesman called out, "You know very well who it is. It's me! And you can keep your

blasted lug wrench. I wouldn't borrow it now if you had the last one on earth!"
Dates & Places Used:

---

66 TOPIC: Attendance

What Doesn't Count

Going to church doesn't make anybody a Christian any more than taking a wheelbarrow into a garage makes it an automobile. *(Billy Sunday)*
Dates & Places Used:

---

67 TOPIC: Attendance

Faithful to the End

The church choir director was frustrated with the sporadic attendance of all the choir members for rehearsals for the Christmas Choral Concert. At the final rehearsal he announced: "I want to personally thank the pianist for being the only person in this entire church choir to attend each and every rehearsal during the past two months." At this, the pianist rose, bowed, and said, "It was the least I could do, considering I won't be able to be at the Christmas Choral Concert tonight."
Dates & Places Used:

---

68 TOPIC: Attendance

Power of Television

The Reverend Harold Bales, pastor of the First United Methodist Church in Charlotte, North Carolina, devised a test to reveal whether someone is watching too much television. Here is the nub of the matter. You know that you are watching too much TV if:

A. You can name all the characters on "As the World Turns" but can't remember the names of the Twelve Disciples.

B. You can anticipate in advance the outcome of a "Falcon Crest" episode but can't remember how the New Testament ends.

C. You can recognize the local TV news reporter on the street but wouldn't know your next-door neighbor if you saw her standing on the porch.

D. Your cable TV bill is more each month than your contribution to your local church.

E. You find yourself following, in your personal file, a script you've seen on your favorite soap opera.

Dates & Places Used:

69 ◆ TOPIC: Attendance

Established or Stuck

D. L. Moody told a story of a man who was asked by his ten-year-old son, "Daddy, why don't you ever go to church with us?" The father replied, "I don't need to go to church, son. My faith is established." Later that same day the man drove his horses out of the barn and hitched them to the buggy. As he and his son drove out of the yard, the horses became mired in a mud hole. The man tried in vain to extricate them, whereupon the boy observed: "They're not going anywhere, Daddy. I believe they're established."

Dates & Places Used:

70 ◆ TOPIC: Attendance

Sporting Excuses

Here's an old classic entitled "Pastor Quits Sports: Twelve Reasons Why Local Clergyman Stopped Attending Athletic Contests." Every time I went, they asked me for money. The people with whom I had to sit didn't seem very friendly. The seats were too hard and not comfortable. The coach never came to call on me. The referee made a decision with which I could not agree. I was sitting with some hypocrites who came only to see what others were wearing. Some games went into overtime, and I was late getting home. The band played some numbers that I had never heard before. The games are scheduled when I want to do other things. My parents took me to too many games when I was growing up. Since I read a book on sports, I feel that I know more than the coaches anyhow. I don't want to take my children, because I want them to choose for themselves what sport they like best. On the bottom of the page was this one line postscript: "With apologies to those who use the same excuses for not coming to church."

Dates & Places Used:

71 TOPIC: Attitudes

Perspective

If a man has limburger cheese on his upper lip, he thinks the whole world smells.

Dates & Places Used:

72 TOPIC: Attitudes

Reality and Otherwise

Former NBA center and coach Johnny Kerr said his biggest test as a coach came when he coached the expansion Chicago Bulls and his biggest player was 6–8 Erwin Mueller: "We had lost seven in a row, and I decided to give a psychological pep talk before a game with the Celtics," Kerr said. "I told Bob Boozer to go out and pretend he was the best scorer in basketball. I told Jerry Sloan to pretend he was the best defensive guard. I told Guy Rodgers to pretend he could run an offense better than any other guard, and I told Mueller to pretend he was the best rebounding, shot-blocking, scoring center in the game. We lost the game by 17. I was pacing around the locker room afterward trying to figure out what to say when Mueller walked up, put his arm around me and said, 'Don't worry about it, coach. Just pretend we won.'"

Dates & Places Used:

73

TOPIC: Attitudes

Clear Coffee

A man stopped at a cafe for a break in his trip. He sat down to order a cup of coffee. He was looking for a bit of conversation with the waitress when she brought the coffee. He said to her, "It sure looks like rain, doesn't it?" And she responded snappishly, "I can't help what it looks like; we sell it for coffee."

Dates & Places Used:

74

TOPIC: Attitudes

Wake Up Grumpy

"Did you wake up grumpy this morning?" "No, I let him sleep in."

Dates & Places Used:

75

TOPIC: Attitudes

Condensed Viewpoint

Sally says to Charlie Brown, "We have to write a short piece for school that expresses our personal philosophy. So far I've written, 'Who cares?' and 'Forget it.'" Charlie Brown says, "How about 'Why me?'" Sally says, "That's good, I'll fit it in." ("Peanuts")

Dates & Places Used:

76

TOPIC: Attitudes

Planning for Misery

A friendly waitress couldn't get a smile out of a certain customer. The woman was dour, depressed, and dejected all

through her dinner. And the food was delicious! As the woman paid her bill and was leaving, the waitress said, "Have a nice day!" And the woman responded snappishly, "I'm sorry, but I've made other plans!"
Dates & Places Used:

77 TOPIC: Attitudes
Greatest Pitcher

A boy, playing baseball alone, was heard to say, "I'm the greatest hitter in the world." He tossed the ball into the air, swung and missed. "Strike one!" Undaunted, he picked up the ball, threw it into the air and said to himself, "I'm the greatest baseball hitter ever," and he swung at the ball again. And again he missed. "Strike two!" He paused a moment to examine his bat and ball carefully. Then a third time he threw the ball into the air. "I'm the greatest hitter who ever lived," he said. He swung the bat hard again, missed a third time. He cried out, "Wow! Strike three—what a pitcher! I'm the greatest pitcher in the world!"
Dates & Places Used:

78 TOPIC: Auditors
Bayonet the Wounded

Auditors are the people who go in after the war is lost and bayonet the wounded.
Dates & Places Used:

79 TOPIC: Authority
Initial Taste of Power

A first-grade boy was told by his mother to return home directly after school was dismissed, but he arrived home from school late almost every day. He was sometimes as much as twenty minutes late. His mother asked him, "You get out of school the same time every day. Why can't you get home at the same time?" He said, "It depends on the cars." "What do cars have to do with it?" The youngster explained, "The patrol boy who takes us across the street makes us wait until some cars come along so he can stop them."

Dates & Places Used:

80

TOPIC: Authority

Assistance or Respect

A young second lieutenant at Fort Bragg discovered that he had no change when he was about to buy a soft drink from a vending machine. He stopped a passing private and asked him, "Do you have change for a dollar?" The private said cheerfully, "I think so. Let me take a look." The lieutenant drew himself up stiffly and said, "Soldier, that's no way to address an officer. We'll start all over again. Do you have change for a dollar?" The private came to attention, saluted smartly, and said, "No, sir!"

Dates & Places Used:

81

TOPIC: Authority

Communication Flow

Alain C. Enthoven was one of McNamara's "Whiz Kids" in McNamara's early days in the Defense Department. Strong in physique and intellect, Enthoven was an economist who earlier, at RAND, specialized in strategy and strategic weapons. Enthoven did not lack self-confidence. He once visited U. S. Air Force Headquarters in Germany. He was met by an assortment of generals with decades of accumulated experience and yards of ribbons. Enthoven, fresh-faced and youthful, listened with growing impatience as the number one general outlined plans for briefing the visitor. Finally Enthoven interrupted. "General," he

said, "I don't think you understand. I didn't come for a briefing. I came to tell you what we have decided."
Dates & Places Used:

TOPIC: Awards
Oblivious Award

It seems this particular fellow frequently came home drunk, and he was so far gone that he would fall into bed fully clothed, pass out, and then snore loudly all night long. Finally, his wife was losing so much sleep because of his snoring that she went to her doctor and said, "Doc, I can't take it any longer. If you'll only tell me how to keep him from snoring, I'll pay you anything." The doctor said there was no problem at all. He could give her the answer and he wouldn't even charge her. He told her that whenever her husband passed out and started to snore she was to take a ribbon and tie it around his nose, and his snoring would stop. Well, that night her husband came in as usual, fell across the bed fully dressed, passed out, and started snoring. The wife got up, pulled a blue ribbon from her dresser, and tied it around his nose. Sure enough, the snoring stopped. Next morning, the wife, fully refreshed, was preparing breakfast and asked her husband, as he was awakening, "Honey, where were you last night?" The husband, still fully clothed, looked in the mirror and seeing the blue ribbon around his nose, replied, "I don't know, but wherever I was, I won first prize!"
Dates & Places Used:

TOPIC: Banks
The Good with the Bad

A farmer who had experienced several bad years went to see the manager of his bank. "I've got some good news and some bad news to tell you. Which would you like to hear first?" he asked.

"Why don't you tell me the bad news first and get it over with?" the banker replied. "Okay. With the bad drought and inflation and all, I won't be able to pay anything on my mortgage this year, either on the principle, or the interest." "Well, that is pretty bad." "It gets worse. I also won't be able to pay anything on the loan for all that machinery I bought, nor on the principle or interest." "Wow, is that ever bad!" "It's worse than that. You remember I also borrowed to buy seeds and fertilizer and other supplies. Well, I can't pay anything on those items either, principle or interest." "That's awful and that's enough! Tell me what the good news is." "The good news," replied the farmer with a smile, "is that I intend to keep on doing business with you."

There's some rather profound theology in that story, provided we reverse the subjects. The good news of the Gospel is that, in spite of our total moral bankruptcy, God keeps on doing business with us.

Dates & Places Used:

84

TOPIC: Banks

Sign in a Bank

Don't kiss our girls. They're tellers!

Dates & Places Used:

85

TOPIC: Banks

Uncertain Accounting

A teacher was having trouble with his bank. Neither the bank's accuracy nor its mode of expression lived up to his standards. The last straw arrived in the form of a letter from the bank. The letter read: "Your account appears to be overdrawn."

The teacher wrote back, "Please write again when you are absolutely certain."

Dates & Places Used:

86

TOPIC: Baptism

Immersed in the Scenery

A party of clergymen was attending a conference in Scotland. Several of them set off to explore the district. Presently they came to a river spanned by a temporary bridge. Not seeing the notice that said it was unsafe, they began to cross. The bridgekeeper ran after them to protest.

"It's all right," declared the spokesman, not understanding the reason for the old man's haste. "We're Presbyterians from the conference."

"I'm no' caring aboot that," was the reply. "But if ye dinna get off the bridge, you'll all be Baptists!"

Dates & Places Used:

87

TOPIC: Beauty

Ugly to the Bone

"Beauty is skin deep, but ugly goes clean down to the bone." *(Charles Swindoll)*

Dates & Places Used:

88

TOPIC: Beauty

Superbowl Wisdom

During the boredom of Superbowl XXIV, the announcers had to come up with some pretty good filler stories. One that was particularly good was told of a San Francisco player. The day before, it was told, he was watching the floats being pulled by tractors. His remark went something like this: "Look at those beautiful tractors! It's a shame they're being wasted on those floats." So beauty IS in the eye of the beholder.

Dates & Places Used:

89

TOPIC: Beauty

Not Ready for Aging

In the cartoon *For Better or Worse*, a mother is looking into the mirror and carrying on a conversation with herself. She says, "My face is changing. It's not the same—definitely not the same—different. It's older. Maybe if I parted my hair on the side. Maybe if I were to rub a little more moisturizer around each eye. A little different colored blush perhaps? Nope, this is it. I look older and there's nothing I can do about it. I remember my mother's face looking like this. I remember how the lines crept around her mouth and her eyes. Yes, it's my turn now to take on that look of the mature, older woman." She gazes intently into the mirror, and then shouts for all to hear, "And I'm not ready!"

Dates & Places Used:

90

TOPIC: Betrayal

Lost in Translation

Some years ago the people of Texas were being plagued by a Mexican bandit who continuously slipped across the border and robbed their banks. His name was Jorge Rodriguez. He had become bolder and more successful, and yet they could never capture him before he hightailed it back across the border to his hideout in the mountains of Mexico. These Texans hired a well-known detective to get back their money. The detective tracked Jorge to a small Mexican town. He walked into a saloon, and, lo and behold, there in the corner was the man he was after, Jorge Rodriquez. "Aha!" he said, "I found you!" and he pulled out his gun. "Where have you hidden the millions you have stolen from our banks in Texas? Tell me, or I'll blow you away!" At this point another man, Juan Garcia, who was also in the saloon, stepped up to the detective and said. "Sir, you cannot talk to Jorge like this. He doesn't understand a word of English. He has no idea what you just said. Would you like me to translate for you?" The detective said, "Yes, of course. Tell him to confess to me where the money is or I'll kill him." So Juan Garcia turned to Jorge and jabbered away at him for a few moments in Spanish. There was much gesturing and chattering, and Jorge told Juan in Spanish that if he would take the man to the well that was just a mile out of town, climb down into the well and remove the third brick, there he would find over three million dollars in gold. When Jorge was finished speaking, Juan, the helpful translator, turned around to the detective and said, "Senor, he says that he has absolutely no idea where the gold is. I'm sorry."

Dates & Places Used:

91 ◆ TOPIC: Bible

Reading Priorities

G. K. Chesterton and several other literary figures were asked one evening what book they would prefer to have with them if stranded on a desert isle. One writer said without hesitation: "The complete works of Shakespeare." Another said, "I'd choose the Bible." They turned to Chesterton. "How about you?" And Chesterton replied, "I would choose *Thomas's Guide to Practical Ship Building.*"

Dates & Places Used:

92 ◆ TOPIC: Bible

Ignorance

The following story is told of Harry Cohn, for many years head of Columbia Movie Studios: In the early days Harry's brother came out from New York and was criticizing the way Harry did things. They got into a heated argument. Harry: "I bet you don't even know the Lord's Prayer." Brother: "What's that got to do with anything?" Harry: "I just bet you don't know the Lord's Prayer." Brother: "Well of course I do: Now I lay me down to sleep, I pray the Lord my soul to keep. If I should die before I wake, I pray the Lord my soul to take." Harry: "Oh! Well, I apologize. I really didn't think you knew it."

Dates & Places Used:

93

TOPIC: Birth

Making a Baby Brother

Dear God, my name is Robert. I want a baby brother. My mother said to ask my father. My father said to ask you. Do you think you can do it? Good luck, Robert.

Dates & Places Used:

94

TOPIC: Birth

The Stork Babies

A little boy asked his mother where he came from and also where she had come from as a baby. His mother gave him a tall tale about a beautiful white-feathered bird. The boy ran into the next room and asked his grandmother the same question and received a variation on the bird story. He then scampered outside to his playmate with the comment, "You know, there hasn't been a normal birth in our family for three generations!"

Dates & Places Used:

95

TOPIC: Blessings

To Get or Not to Get

If you don't get everything you want, think of the things you don't get that you don't want.

Dates & Places Used:

96

TOPIC: Blessings

Thoughtful Thanks

It was Thanksgiving season in the nursing home. The small resident population were gathered about their humble Thanksgiving table, and the director asked each in turn to express one thing for which they were thankful. Thanks were expressed for a home in which to stay, families, etc.

One little old lady in her turn said, "I thank the Lord for two perfectly good teeth, one in my upper jaw and one in my lower jaw that match so that I can chew my food."

Dates & Places Used:

TOPIC: Bloopers

Saturday Night Live

Late one Saturday night I was in church at the pulpit, practicing my sermon and adjusting the brand-new sound system. I was enjoying myself so much I did a little singing, which was not typically my practice.

After the "concert" I decided to record my singing and sermon, then sit down and enjoy the fruits of my labor. This I did. As I listened to the unfamiliar sound of my own voice, I noticed that not all of the sound was coming from the speakers in the auditorium. I walked around inside the church building, trying to locate the sound. I returned to the auditorium without finding the sound.

Then it hit me. We had installed wiring to outside speakers. The whole neighborhood had been listening to my Saturday night performance. I hope they liked it.

Dates & Places Used:

TOPIC: Bloopers

Bottom Dollar

A little girl walked into a small grocery store and placed an earthen jar on the counter, asked for two dollars' worth of honey. Soon the jar was filled. She picked up the jar and started for the door. The storekeeper stopped her and asked her if she had forgotten to pay for her honey.

"No sir, I thought you got the money," the startled youngster replied. "My mother put it in the jar."

Dates & Places Used:

99 TOPIC: Bloopers

Foot-in-Mouth Disease

Scott Widmer, Methodist pastor from Morgantown, Pennsylvania, relates this true foot/mouth incident: It was more embarrassing than hilarious at the time. I was using John Wesley's Covenant Renewal Service on New Year's Eve, one line of which goes: "Let us bind ourselves with willing bonds to our covenant God." The way it came out was, "Let us bind ourselves with willing blondes."

Dates & Places Used:

100 TOPIC: Bloopers

Ever Draw a Blank?

I suppose one of the recurring fears of anyone who has to speak in public is the phenomenon of going blank at the critical moment. I'm sure we've all done it at one time or another. Roger Smith, from Seattle, Washington, relates the following story:

We were traveling one summer in the Pocono Mountains and, like a good Presbyterian family, attended church while we were on vacation. One lazy Sunday we found our way to a little Methodist church. It was a hot day and the folks were nearly passed out in the pews. The preacher was preaching on and on until, all of a sudden, he said, "The best years of my life have been spent in the arms of another man's wife." The congregation let out a gasp, came to immediate attention, and the dozing deacon in the back row dropped his hymnbook. Then the preacher said, "It was my mother." The congregation tittered a little and managed to follow along as the sermon concluded. I filed this trick away in my memory as great way to get the congregation's attention back when it has been lost.

Sure enough, the next summer, on a lazy Sunday, I was preaching and the flies were buzzing around and the ushers were sinking lower and lower in their seats in the back row until I could hardly see them. Then I remembered our experience in the Pocono Mountains, and I said in a booming voice, "The best years of my life have been spent in the arms of another man's wife." Sure enough, I had their attention. One of the ushers in the back row sat up so fast he hit his head on the back of the pew in front of him. I had them. But you know something, I forgot what came next. All I could think to say was, "And for the life of me, I can't remember her name!"

Dates & Places Used:

TOPIC: Bloopers

101

Bring Out Your Bibles

Some of our best stories originate from our most trying experiences. Such is the case with the following:

We had scheduled a teenage girl from the church to play her accordion on a Sunday morning just before the sermon. She was scheduled to play "How Great Thou Art." This young woman was the only one from her family who attended church and was not always predictable. At the appropriate time she walked to the front of the church with her accordion and played a lovely rendition of "How Great Thou Art." It was beautiful! It really set the mood for the rest of the service. I was ready to approach the pulpit with added enthusiasm for the majesty of our great God.

Then it happened. At the conclusion of her song, the young lady announced that this is what the accordion is really for . . . and she played "Roll out the Barrel" with all the gusto and volume she could muster from that accordion. By the end of her unscheduled song the atmosphere had changed from that of a vibrant worship service to that of a beer party.

And now it was my turn. I calmly walked to the pulpit without a clue as to what I would do. But it was my turn. I thanked this teenage girl for that fine rendition of "How Great Thou Art." I told the congregation that I enjoyed the song so much that I would like to turn to hymn number 87 and have the congregation sing that song before I began the message. The congregational singing helped immeasurably to return the mood of our service to worship and adoration.

That evening, I was given a poem entitled, "Semper Paratus" (Latin for "Always Ready"). It was written that afternoon by Norma Vincent, a woman in the church who had witnessed the ordeal that morning. In the tradition of the great hymn writers, she had taken this old tavern song and transformed the words to a Christian hymn. She had begun the song, "Bring out your Bibles."

The gates of hell will not prevail! *(Michael Hodgin)*
Dates & Places Used:

102

TOPIC: Boredom

Boring Sermons

If some sermons were for sale, they should be labeled: Dry Goods and Notions.
Dates & Places Used:

103

TOPIC: Boredom

A Long Film

Director Billy Wilder was asked how he liked a new film. He replied, "To give you an idea, the film started at 8:00 P.M. I looked at my watch at midnight, and it was only 8:15."
Dates & Places Used:

104

TOPIC: Bosses

Cry-Babies

Our friend Lynda Pearce says she never regrets taking a couple years off to care for her new baby.

"I thought the crying and whining would drive me crazy at first," she explains, "but my boss eventually calmed down."
Dates & Places Used:

105 TOPIC: Bosses

A Brief Message of Hot Air

A note was hung on the hot air hand dryer in the restroom at work: "Push here for a word from the boss."
Dates & Places Used:

106 TOPIC: Bribes

Friend for Sale

A farmer was detained for questioning about an election scandal. "Did you sell your vote?" the attorney asked. "No sir, not me," the farmer protested. "I voted for that there fella 'cause I like him." "Come now," threatened the attorney. "I have evidence that he gave you fifty dollars for a vote." The farmer said, "Well now, it's plain common sense that when a fella gives you fifty dollars you like him."
Dates & Places Used:

107 TOPIC: Budgets

Choose Any Two

Husband to wife as they plan a budget in the current inflationary times: "Let's start with the basic necessities—food, clothing, and shelter. We have a choice of any two."
Dates & Places Used:

108

TOPIC: Camp

Purpose of Poison Ivy

At a summer religious camp for children one of the counselors was leading a discussion on the purpose God has for all of his creation. They began to find good reasons for clouds and trees and rocks and rivers and animals and just about everything else in nature. Finally, one of the children said, "If God has a good purpose for everything, then why did He create poison ivy?" The discussion leader gulped and, as he struggled with the question, one of the other children came to his rescue, saying, "The reason God made poison ivy is that He wanted us to know there are certain things we should keep our cotton-pickin' hands off of."

Dates & Places Used:

109

TOPIC: Change

If God Were Alive

A long-time member of St. John's church scolded the new pastor for his radical new ideas and changes: "Reverend, if God were alive today, He would be shocked at the changes in this church!"

Dates & Places Used:

110

TOPIC: Change

It Won't Happen!

Speed: "What can be more palpably absurd than the prospect held out of locomotives traveling twice as fast as stagecoaches?" (*The Quarterly Review*, 1825)

Television: "While theoretically and technically television may be feasible, commercially and financially, I consider it an impossibility, a development of which we need not waste time dreaming." (*Lee Deforest, scientist and inventor, 1926*)

Transportation: "As a means of rapid transit, aerial navigation could not begin to compete with the railroad." (William Baxter, Jr., *Popular Science*, 1901)

Automobiles: "The ordinary 'horseless carriage' is at present a luxury for the wealthy; and although its price will probably fall in the near future, it will never, of course, come into as common use as the bicycle." (*The Literary Digest*, 1889)

Dates & Places Used:

111
TOPIC: Character

How to Live

So live that you wouldn't be ashamed to sell the family parrot to the town gossip.

Dates & Places Used:

112
TOPIC: Cheating

Teacher Jargon

Teachers never seem to put down kids anymore. A young lad had a teacher's notation on his report card saying that he was very adept in the creative use of visual aids for learning. His father called up his teacher and said, "What does that mean— 'the creative use of visual aids?'"

Teacher: "That means he copies from the kid in the next seat."

Dates & Places Used:

113
TOPIC: Cheating

Esoteric Cheating

In Woody Allen's movie *Annie Hall*, Woody has his protagonist say: "I was thrown out of New York University for cheating on a

metaphysics test. The professor caught me looking deeply into the soul of the student seated next to me."
Dates & Places Used:

114

TOPIC: Children

Prejudice Unites

A first-grader went on her first day to a newly integrated school at the height of the segregation storm. An anxious mother met her at the door to inquire, "How did everything go, Honey?"

"Oh, Mother! You know what? A little black girl sat next to me!"

In fear and trepidation, the mother expected trauma, but tried to ask calmly: "And what happened?"

"We were both so scared that we held hands all day."

Dates & Places Used:

115

TOPIC: Children

Growing Objects

If a growing object is both fresh and spoiled at the same time, chances are it's a child.

Dates & Places Used:

116

TOPIC: Children

Sinning Is the Best

Students of a Sunday school class were asked to write down what they liked best about Sunday school. One little boy, who also happened to be the pastor's son, thought for a moment and remembered all the songs the class had sung during the year. His spelling was not as good as his memory, for he wrote, "The thing I like best about Sunday school is the sinning."

Dates & Places Used:

117

TOPIC: Children

Corn on the Palm

On Palm Sunday, I took my three-year-old nephew to church. When the ushers walked down the aisle with armloads of palms, Mike cried out, "Oh boy, corn on the cob!"

Dates & Places Used:

118

TOPIC: Children

Catholic Grocery Beads

A Baptist child attending a Catholic school was asked by his father about his first day of school.

"It was OK, Dad," he replied, "but I wish I had a set of grocery beads like the other kids."

Dates & Places Used:

119

TOPIC: Children

The Left Hand of God

The story is told of a little girl and her mom discussing the morning Sunday school class. The child told her mom that they talked about Jesus going up to heaven and that he is now sitting beside God. As they continued to look at the Sunday school paper, the mother noticed a picture of a rainbow. She said, "Look at that beautiful rainbow that God painted for us!" The little girl replied, "And just think, Mommy, God did it all with his left hand." The mother replied, "What do you mean? Can't God use both His hands?" The girl stated, "Of course not, Mom, my Sunday school teacher said that Jesus is sitting on His right hand."

Dates & Places Used:

120

TOPIC: Children

The Mouth of Babes

My sister and her children moved to my city not long ago and began attending church for the first time in their lives. They particularly loved the singing and the communion service. One day while babysitting, I fixed them their favorite lunch of burritos and apple juice. As I left the room, I heard four-year-old Alisha begin to celebrate communion with her lunch items. She seemed to have memorized the words of institution quite well, except when it came to the cup. She was heard to say, "And Jesus took the cup, and he blessed it, and he gave God thanks for it, and he said, 'Fill it with Folgers and wake 'em up!'" What wonderful theology!

Dates & Places Used:

121

TOPIC: Children

History Revisited

Here is a list of some answers turned in by students of history to their teachers:

David was a Hebrew king in the Old Testament who was skilled at playing the liar.

Solomon, his son, had 500 wives and 500 porcupines.

Without the Greeks we wouldn't have history.

Socrates died from an overdose of wedlock.

The Greeks invented the Olympic Games where they hurled biscuits and threw the java.

The Romans were called Romans because they never stayed in one place very long.

Nero was a cruel tyrant who tortured his subjects by playing the fiddle to them.

Then came the Middle Ages when King Alfred conquered the dames.

The Magna Carta proved that no man should be hung twice for the same crime.

The Renaissance was the time when Martin Luther was nailed to the church door. He died a terrible death, being excommunicated by a papal bull.

Gutenberg invented the Bible and Sir Walter Raleigh invented pipe tobacco.

The government of England was a limited mockery.

Henry VIII found walking difficult because he had an abbess on his knee.

Queen Elizabeth was the Virgin Queen. When she exposed herself before the troops, they all shouted, "Hurray!" Then her navy went out and defeated the Spanish Armadillo.

A great writer was John Milton. He wrote "Paradise Lost." Then his wife died and he wrote "Paradise Regained."

Christopher Columbus discovered America while cursing the Atlantic.

When the Pilgrims landed, they were greeted by Indians who came down the hill rolling their war hoops before them and carrying their porpoises on their backs.

Meanwhile in Europe, gravity was being invented by Isaac Walton. It is chiefly noticeable in the autumn when the apples are falling.

Queen Victoria was the longest queen. She sat on a thorn for 63 years.

The First World War was caused by the assignation of the Arch-Duck by a surf. This ushered in a new error in the annals of human history.

Dates & Places Used:

TOPIC: Children

122

Children's Paraphrase

A Church of England publication listed the following children's answers to church school questions:

- Noah's wife was called Joan of Ark.
- Henry VIII liked Wolsey so much that he made him a cardigan.
- The fifth commandment is: Humor thy father and mother.
- Lot's wife was a pillar of salt by day, but a ball of fire by night.
- Mary was the mother of Jesus, and sang the Magna Carta.
- Salome was a woman who danced naked in front of Harrods.
- Holy acrimony is another name for marriage.
- Christians can have only one wife. This is called monotony.
- The Pope lives in a vacuum.
- Paraffin is next in order after seraphim.
- Today wild beasts are confined to Theological Gardens.
- The patron saint of travelers is St. Francis of the seasick.
- Iran is the Bible of the Moslems.
- A Republican is a sinner mentioned in the Bible.

- Abraham begat Isaac, Isaac begat Jacob and Jacob begat twelve partridges.
- The natives of Macedonia did not believe, so Paul got stoned.
- The First Commandment: Eve told Adam to eat the apple.
- It is sometimes difficult to hear what is being said in church because the agnostics are so terrible.

Dates & Places Used:

TOPIC: Children

123 Kid's Concerns

Here are some letters kids wrote to their ministers:

Dear Minister: I know that God loves everybody, but he never met my sister.

Dear Minister: I would like to bring my dog to church on Sunday. She is only a mutt, but she is a good Christian.

Dear Minister: I like to read the Bible, but I would read it more if they put it on TV.

Dear Minister: Please say a prayer for the President, even if he is a Republican.

Dear Minister: I would like to go to heaven someday because I know my big brother won't be there.

Dear Minister: I'm sorry I can't leave more money in the plate on Sunday, but my father didn't give me a raise in my allowance. Could you give a sermon about a raise in my allowance? It would help the church get more money.

Dates & Places Used:

TOPIC: Children

124 Children Ask God

Dear God, Do you get your angels to do all the work? Mommy says we are her angels, and we have to do everything. Love, Maria.

Dear God, when you started the earth and put people there and all the animals and grass and the stars, did you get very tired? I have a lot of other questions too. Very truly yours, Sherman.
Dates & Places Used:

125

TOPIC: Christians

Mother Knows

A small boy sat with his mother in church, listening to a sermon entitled, "What Is a Christian?" The minister punctuated his talk at several key intervals by asking, "What is a Christian?" Each time, he pounded his fist on the pulpit for emphasis. At one point, the lad whispered to his mother, "Momma, do you know? Do you know what a Christian is?" "Yes, dear," the mother replied, "now try to sit still and listen." As the minister was wrapping up the sermon, once again he thundered, "What is a Christian?" and pounded especially hard on the pulpit. At that, the boy jumped up and cried, "Tell him, Momma, tell him!"
Dates & Places Used:

126

TOPIC: Christians

Ever Met a Christian?

A father was teaching his son what a Christian should be like. When the lesson was over, the father got a stab he never forgot. The little boy asked, "Dad, have I ever met one of these Christians?"
Dates & Places Used:

127

TOPIC: Christmas

Day After Christmas

'Tis the day after Christmas and inside and out,
The holiday carnage lies scattered about.

And Ma with a wet towel atop of her head
And aspirin tablets has crawled into bed.
The kiddies, God bless 'em, are raising a din,
With thundering drums and shrill trumpets of tin.
While Pa, like a schoolboy, forgetting his years,
Is all tangled up in the bicycle gears.
Old Duffer, the dachshund, delightfully smug,
Lies gnawing a carcass upon the new rug.
And Muffet, the kitten, despaired of a lap,
On the dining room table is taking her nap.
Plaid neckties and pink socks and what-nots galore
Await their exchange at the five-and-ten store.
While tidbits and knick-knacks of leftover sweets
Must furnish the menu for future-day eats.
'Tis the day after Christmas, and once every year
Folks willingly pay for their holiday cheer.
With toothaches from candy and headaches from bills,
They call up the doctor and order more pills.

Dates & Places Used:

128 TOPIC: Christmas

A Fertile Nativity

Walter Lauster tells of a personal experience: I was sitting in my office on the first Saturday of December. Outside in the court-yard of our church the men of the church were in the process of building the stage for a live nativity scene. Since my door was open, I heard two children discussing the process. One asked of the other, "What is this going to be?" Answered the other, "Oh, they are building a live fertility scene."

Dates & Places Used:

129 TOPIC: Christmas

Round John Virgin

A kindergarten Sunday school teacher had her class draw a nativity scene. One youngster had done a very fine job in drawing the baby in a manger, with Mary and Joseph and the animals; but the teacher noticed with anxiety that he had drawn a little fat man right beside the manger. She asked, "Jimmy, that isn't Santa, is it?" Jimmy answered indignantly, "Of course not, that's Round John Virgin."

Dates & Places Used:

130 TOPIC: Christmas

Don't Turn Off Jesus

The highlight of the Christmas play was to show the radiance of Jesus. An electric light bulb was hidden in the manger. All the stage lights were to be turned off so that only the brightness of the manger could be seen. At the appropriate time all lights went out! Silence was broken when one of the shepherds said in a loud stage whisper, "Hey! You turned off Jesus!"

Dates & Places Used:

131 TOPIC: Christmas

Christmas Lore

A tramp stopped at a Catholic rectory shortly before Christmas and told the priest, "Father, I've been floating around long enough. Could I join your church and settle down?" The priest replied, "Why, yes. But first, let's find out how much you know about the Bible and the Christian faith."

With Christmas coming soon the priest naturally asked, "Where was Jesus born?" The tramp replied, "In Pittsburgh." The priest shook his head and the tramp tried again: "In Philadelphia."

Again the priest shook his head, and not wishing to embarrass the tramp anymore, said slowly, "Jesus was born in Bethlehem." Quickly the tramp declared, "Oh, yeah! I knew it was someplace in Pennsylvania."

Dates & Places Used:

132

Christmas Caution

In the rush of last-minute Christmas shopping, a woman bought a box of fifty identical greeting cards. Without bothering to read the verse, she hastily signed and addressed all but one of them.

Several days after they had been mailed, she came across the one card that hadn't been sent, and she looked at the message she had sent. She was horrified to read: "This card is just to say . . . a little gift is on the way."

Dates & Places Used:

133

TOPIC: Christmas

Wrong Checks

"I'm sorry you don't like my Christmas gift," the aunt said to her nephew, "but I asked if you preferred large checks or a small checks."

He replied, "I know, but I didn't think you meant neckties."

Dates & Places Used:

134

TOPIC: Christmas

Let's Get Practical

And then there was the wife who said to her husband, "This year let's give each other more practical gifts like socks and fur coats."

Dates & Places Used:

135

TOPIC: Christmas

Mouse's Bathing Suit

An elephant was thoroughly enjoying himself as he splashed about in the river. A mouse was perched on the sandy shore. It was obvious that he was disturbed about something. The mouse yelled at the elephant, "Come out of the water at once." The elephant laughed and said, "Why should I come out?" The mouse was not about to be humiliated by this mountain of flesh. He kept yelling and yelling.

The elephant realized that if he wanted any peace and quiet he had better come out of the water. Slowly the elephant lumbered out of the water and stood towering over the mouse. "Now, why did you want me to come out of the water?" The mouse looked up and said, "I wanted to see if you were wearing my bathing suit."

It is easier for us to understand how an elephant could wear a mouse's bathing suit than it is for us to understand the awesome mystery of the incarnation—God's Word became flesh. He wore our suit of flesh.

Dates & Places Used:

136

TOPIC: Christmas

The Plot Thickens

A small boy was bitterly disappointed at not being cast as Joseph in the school Nativity play. He was given the minor role of the innkeeper instead, and throughout the weeks of rehearsal he brooded on how he could avenge himself on his successful rival.

Came the day of the performance. Joseph and Mary made their entrance and knocked on the door of the inn. The innkeeper opened it a fraction and eyed them coldly. "Can you give us board and lodging for the night?" pleaded Joseph, who then stood back awaiting the expected rebuff.

But the innkeeper had not pondered all those weeks for nothing. He flung the door wide, beamed genially and cried, "Come in, come in. You shall have the best room in the hotel."

There was a pause, then with great presence of mind, the youthful Joseph said to Mary, "Hold on. I'll take a look inside first." He peered past the innkeeper, shook his head firmly and announced, "I'm not taking my wife into a place like that. Come on, Mary, we'll sleep in the stable."

The plot was back on course.

Dates & Places Used:

Bike Before Christmas

'Twas the night before Christmas, when all through
our house
Not a creature was sleeping, not even my spouse.
The stockings were hung by the chimney with screws.
(If you can't find the nails, what else do you use?)
The children were restless, awake in their beds,
While visions of spanking them danced in our heads.
I worked in my bathrobe. My husband, in jeans,
Had gone down to the den with directions and dreams
To assemble a bike that came in small pieces
With deflated tires and fenders with creases.
Soon down in the den there arose such a clatter,
I sprang from my task to see what was the matter.
Away to my husband I flew like a flash;
He was shuffling through cardboard; his actions
were rash.
The bike on the rug by this now-flustered dad
Soon gave me a hint as to why he was mad.
He needed a kickstand. It had to be near.
I shuffled some papers—he saw it appear!
We twisted the screws; we were lively and quick,
And we soon knew assembly would be quite a trick.
Fast as eagles in flight the pieces were found,
And he whistled and shouted for parts all around:
"Now socket! Now pedal! Now tires! Now brakes!
On handles! On kickstand! On horn! . . . oh . . . but wait!"
In the top of the toolbox, he fumbled around;
"I need two more screws!" he said with a frown.
And like all good parents determined to please
When they meet with an obstacle late Christmas Eve,
We shouted and yelled some complaints to each other.
There was never more frustrated father and mother!
And then, in a panic, we heard on the stairs
The prancing and hopping of feet . . . 'bout two pairs!
I opened the door and was turning around,
When kids burst from the hall with a leap and a bound.
They were dressed all in flannel, from their necks
to their knees,

And their nightgowns were soiled with sugar and cheese!
Excuses poured forth from each pair of lips;
They stood in defiance with hands on their hips.
Their eyes were wide open, and each little child
Jumped when I yelled with a voice hardly mild.
They were frightened but cute, though much bigger than elves,
And we laughed when we saw them, in spite of ourselves.
A wink of the eye and a pat on the head
Soon let them both know they had nothing to dread.
They saw not a thing but went straight to their beds,
And we finished the bike and put bows on the sleds.
Then wheeling the bike by the tree (out of sight),
My hubby announced we should call it a night.
He sprang to his bed, to the clock gave a whistle,
As the time had flown by like a large Titan missile.
But I heard him exclaim as he turned out the light,
"Merry Christmas, my dear, but next year NO BIKE!"

Dates & Places Used:

138 TOPIC: Christmas

Personal Touch

A couple heard the doorbell ring and went to open the door.
Their neighbors were at the door and explained their visit.
"We're saving postage by hand-delivering our Christmas cards
this year, and dropping in for a bit of lunch and a cup of coffee."

Dates & Places Used:

139 TOPIC: Christmas

Fresh Perspective

A young man not known for his intelligence tried out for the football team. The coach told him frankly that he didn't think he was
smart enough to play football. The young fellow pleaded; so the
coach agreed to give him a test. He even let him take the test home
to think about it. There were just three questions on the test:

"First: How many seconds are there in a year? Second: What two days of the week begin with T? Third: How many D's are in Rudolph the Red-Nosed Reindeer?"

The fellow returned early the next morning. The first answer was reported to be "twelve seconds." The puzzled coach asked how he figured that. The fellow said, "Yeah, there's twelve seconds in the year, coach—January 2nd, February 2nd, March 2nd, and so on." The coach said, "That's not exactly what I had in mind, but I'll accept that." The young man answered the second question: "The two days of the week that begin with 'T' are Today and Tomorrow." The coach was impressed, though that wasn't what he had in mind. Then he asked how many "D's" are there in Rudolph the Red-Nosed Reindeer? The young man brightened and said "Oh, I know that one—there's 138." He started counting on his fingers, chanting the familiar Christmas tune, "De De, De De, De De De, De De De De De De."

Dates & Places Used:

TOPIC: Christmas

The Modern Scene

In a cartoon by Guindon a weary woman shopper is shown resting for a moment with her arms filled with packages. She is in the middle of a very busy department store filled with other Christmas shoppers, and she is explaining the whole Christmas scene to her small son as follows: "No one is quite sure how Christmas worked out like this, dear. Theologians are working very, very hard on that question right now."

Dates & Places Used:

TOPIC: Church

Football Fans and Church

Note the contrasts between the average football fan's worship of a pigskin oval and the average Christian's worship of God:

1. Football fans often pay a hefty sum to park their cars and walk a long distance to the stadium. The churchgoer expects free and convenient parking close to the building or he will not attend.

2. Football contests are noisy with loud cheering and the enthusiasm of the fans. The churchgoer sits in grim silence, showing no emotion. He objects to loud organ music and extra volume from the choir and complains ad nauseam after the service.

3. Football stadium seats are narrow, backless, and assigned. The churchgoer hates a hard pew and insists on a particular seat.

4. Football games always last more than three hours, and if they go into overtime, fans consider it a bonus. The churchgoer expects worship to take an hour, and if a pastor does not confine himself to that limit, he may come under pointed rebuke from the faithful.

5. Football fans fail to let any climate influence their attendance at games. The churchgoer needs only a few drops of inclement weather to provide an excuse for his absence at worship.

6. Football tickets for professional team games are expensive. Many fans think nothing of paying in excess of fifty dollars to see their favorites play. Added to that is the cost of the ubiquitous program and the exorbitant costs of refreshments. The churchgoer objects to the mere mention of money, and an appeal for extra offerings evokes inward and frequently outward groaning, fulfilling the line in a well-known song, "When we asunder part, it gives us inward pain."

Are those who worship at the shrine of the oval sphere more devoted to their "religion" than those who profess to follow Jesus Christ? It causes one to pause and ponder.

Dates & Places Used:

142 TOPIC: Clarity

Communicating Jargon

A memo at a certain company showed a tongue-in-cheek attempt at clear communication on the part of the service and sales department. It went something like this, so we're told:

From: Marketing . . . To: Sales . . . Subject: Marketing Forecast

Sales and income figures show an easing up of the rate at which business is easing off. This can be taken as ample proof of the government's contention that there's a slowingup of the slow-down. Now, to clarify that, it should be noted that a slowingup of the slowdown is not as good as an upturn in the downturn. On the other hand, it's a good deal better than either a speedup of the slowdown or a deepening of the downturn. Also, it suggests that the climate is about right for an adjustment of the readjustment to rate structures. Now, turning specifically to rates. We find a very definite decrease in the rate of increase. This clearly shows there should be a letting up of the let-down. Of course, if the slow-down should speed up, the decrease in the rate of increase rates would turn into an increase in the rate of decrease. And finally, the inflation of the recession would turn the recession into a depression while a deflation in the rate of inflation would give the impression of a recession of the depression.

Dates & Places Used:

143 TOPIC: Clarity

To the Point

Communication should be crisp and to the point. Such was a sign seen in Chicago: WARNING! GUARD DOG ON DUTY—SURVIVORS WILL BE PROSECUTED! That communicates. No one wants any part of that fence, that dog, that yard, or that house. To be effective communicators, we should always be just that clear, though not necessarily that threatening.

Dates & Places Used:

144 TOPIC: Clothes

In Front of Ourselves

We are physically made so that we can walk more easily forward than backward. It is easier to manipulate our hands in front of us than behind us. A little girl discovered this principle when she was trying to button the buttons on the back of her dress. The

frustrated little girl exclaimed, "How can I button these buttons when I am in front of myself?"
Dates & Places Used:

TOPIC: Clothes

Family Resemblance

When my three-year-old son was shown a portrait of his five older brothers, taken when they were much younger, he pointed and said, "Those guys are wearing my clothes!"
Dates & Places Used:

TOPIC: Clothes

Clothes Make a Church

A Methodist church tried to get a man to attend, but he never did. "Why don't you come?" the minister asked, and the man finally admitted it was because he didn't have proper clothes. So a member of the congregation took him to a clothing store and got him a nice suit, shirt, tie, and shoes.

But on the following Sunday, he still did not show up. So the minister visited him again and asked why he didn't come.

"When I got dressed up in my new suit," the man explained, "I looked so good I decided to go to the Episcopal church."
Dates & Places Used:

TOPIC: College

Bearded Christmas

On Christmas Eve a pastor was talking with a woman after the service. She told her pastor that earlier that evening she met a bearded fellow carrying a large sack over his back.

The pastor told the woman that he did not like the emphasis on Santa Claus.

She explained, "It was my son home from college."

Dates & Places Used:

148

TOPIC: College

Finally Alone

It was midnight after registration day at the college when the policeman noticed a couple in a lingering embrace in the campus parking lot. Mildly surprised at the scene before the school year had even begun, he approached the car.

"Sorry, officer," the driver explained. "We just left our youngest son, our baby, there in the dorm. It's the first time Mother and I have been alone for twenty-seven years."

Dates & Places Used:

149

TOPIC: College

The State of Education

Now that loafers and buckle shoes have gained in popularity, colleges no longer must conduct classes in remedial shoe-tying for incoming freshmen.

Dates & Places Used:

150

TOPIC: Comfort

Misdirected Comfort

A hospital administrator was startled to see a patient fleeing down the hall out of the operating room, his loose hospital gown flapping in the breeze behind him. He stopped the patient and said, "Do you mind telling me why you ran away from the operating room?" The patient looked at him with startled eyes and said,

"It was because of what the nurse said." The administrator said, "Oh, what did she say?" "She said, 'Be brave! An appendectomy is quite simple.'" The administrator said, "Well, so what? It is quite simple. I would think that would comfort you." The patient said, "The nurse wasn't talking to me; she was talking to the doctor."
Dates & Places Used:

151 TOPIC: Commitment

A Fish Story

There was a man who always seemed to bring home a boatload of fish. It was uncanny, and people wondered how he could be so successful. The game warden heard of this man's great success and asked to go with him. The two men started early one morning and went across the lake to a secluded area. The warden noticed that the fisherman did not have a fishing pole, just a net and a rusty old tackle box. When they got to the appointed place, the fisherman opened the box and pulled out a stick of dynamite, lit it, and tossed it into the water. It blew up and the fish rose to the surface. The fisherman began dipping his net into the water and putting the fish in the boat. The warden then reached back and revealed from his hip pocket the credentials of a game warden! Calmly, the fisherman opened the tackle box again, got out another stick of dynamite, lit the fuse and handed it to the game warden. Then, as the fuse burned down, the fisherman asked, "Are you going to fish or are you just going to sit there?"

Perhaps now is the time to get involved rather than merely being a spectator or a critic.
Dates & Places Used:

152 TOPIC: Commitment

Long-Term Marriage

A young couple preparing to marry assured each other they would work hard to see this marriage last. They would willingly sacrifice for their mutual welfare. They would openly communi-

cate their feelings. After all, seven years is a long time, and there is no reason their marriage couldn't last that long!
Dates & Places Used:

153 TOPIC: Commitment

Turnabout

On a cold, rainy night, the telephone rang in the home of a doctor. The caller identified himself and said that his wife needed urgent medical attention. The doctor was understanding and said that he was willing to come and attend to her needs, but explained that his car was being repaired and asked that the man come and pick him up. The man angrily responded, "What! In this weather?"
Dates & Places Used:

154 TOPIC: Communication

Four-by-Twos

A fellow at the lumber yard asks for some four-by-twos. The clerk says, "You mean two-by-fours?" He says, "Just a moment, I'll check." He goes back to his car where his friends are sitting, they roll down the windows, and he has a short conversation with them. He returns and says, "Yes, I mean two-by-fours." The merchant asks, "How long do you want them?" The fellow says, "Just a minute, I'll check," and he confers with his friends in the car once again. He chats with them for a couple of minutes and comes back and answers, "A long time. We're building a house."
Dates & Places Used:

155 TOPIC: Communication

No Conversation

A woman met with a marriage counselor and abruptly informed him: "I would like to divorce my husband." The counselor replied,

"Do you have any grounds?" She answered, "Why, yes. We have almost an acre." The puzzled counselor asked her, "You don't understand. What I want to know is do you and your husband have a grudge?" The woman answered, "Actually, we don't, but we do have a nice carport." The counselor shook his head and said, "Ma'am, I'm sorry, but I just don't see any reason why you should divorce your husband." The woman answered the counselor, "It's just that the man can't carry on an intelligent conversation."

Dates & Places Used:

156

TOPIC: Communication
Complexity

A cartoon by Mark Pie appeared several years ago in the *New Wine* magazine. It showed a professor beginning a lecture to his class on "Communication" with these words: "Communication is any modus operandi by or through which eventuates the reciprocal transposition of information between or among entities or groups via commonly understood systems of symbols, signs, or behavioral patterns of activity."

Dates & Places Used:

157

TOPIC: CommFunication
Speak Clearly

In marriage one tends to develop sharp communication skills. Sometimes it takes only a glance or a brief clue to communicate with one another. But sometimes the communication shorthand doesn't work exactly as expected. A wife was planning to have duck for dinner so she wrote a reminder to herself and pinned it with a magnet to the refrigerator. It read, cryptically: "Thaw Duck." The next day her husband saw the note and added his comment to it, "Thaw one, too."

Dates & Places Used:

158

TOPIC: Communication

Rights

As precious as the right to speak is the right not to listen.
Dates & Places Used:

159

TOPIC: Companionship

Bad-Luck Wife

A man looked up from his hospital bed and said to his wife, "You've always been with me when I have had trouble. When I lost my shirt in a poor investment, you were there. When I had the car accident, you were with me. I got fired, and you were there. I've come to the conclusion that you're bad luck."
Dates & Places Used:

160

TOPIC: Comparison

Risky Comparison

If you were to stand a truly giant supertanker (the kind that now carries oil around the world) on end next to the World Trade Center, you could stand on the bow and look down on the building—although I would think that would be risky.
Dates & Places Used:

161

TOPIC: Comparison

Relative Wealth

Incredible wealth is any income that is at least $5,000 a year more than what your wife's sister's husband makes.
Dates & Places Used:

162

Life Is Tough, But

·Life itself would be impossible if it weren't for the imperfections of others.

Dates & Places Used:

163

Mental Health

Do you realize that one in every four Americans is unbalanced? Think of your three closest friends. If they seem okay, you're the one! (*Ann Landers*)

Dates & Places Used:

164

A Better Speaker

A pastor was asked to speak for a certain charitable organization. After the meeting the program chairman handed the pastor a check. "Oh, I couldn't take this," the pastor said with some embarrassment. "I appreciate the honor of being asked to speak. You have better uses for this money. You apply it to one of those uses." The program chairman asked, "Well, do you mind if we put it into our Special Fund?" The pastor replied, "Of course not. What is the Special Fund for?" The chairman answered, "It's so we can get a better speaker next year."

Dates & Places Used:

TOPIC: Compassion

Love It In

A mentally impaired youngster seated himself on the floor in a drugstore and began to play with some bottles he had taken from the shelves. The druggist ordered him to stop, then scolded him with an even sharper tone. Just then the boy's sister came up, put her arms around him and whispered something in his ear. Right away, he put the bottles back in place. "You see," his sister explained, "he doesn't understand when you talk to him like that. I just love it into him."

Few of us respond to being scolded, pushed, driven, or harassed. Those six words, "I just love it into him," deserve to be mounted on the walls of every home in America.

Dates & Places Used:

TOPIC: Compassion

Shoot the Wounded

"The church is the only outfit I know that shoots its wounded."
(Chuck Swindoll)
Dates & Places Used:

TOPIC: Compassion

Getting Hugs

Doyal Van Gelder tells about his son, Ronnie, getting ready to go to kindergarten. Ronnie turned to his father and said, "I think I'll be sad today." When asked why, he replied, "Because when you're sad about something, the teachers take turns hugging you."
Dates & Places Used:

TOPIC: Competition

Joyous Imperfection

A nice thing about being imperfect is the joy it brings to others.

Dates & Places Used:

TOPIC: Competition

Keeping Up

A young attorney sat waiting for a red light to change. A boy rode alongside him on a moped. The boy motioned the man to lower his window. As the electric motor lowered the passenger-side window, the boy leaned up and said, "Mister, that's a fine car; what kind is it?" "A Porsche," the annoyed attorney replied. "Does it cost a lot?" the boy asked. "Plenty," the attorney stated. "Is it fast?" asked the boy. Without reply the lawyer quickly accelerated at the change of the light, leaving the youngster behind. As he increased speed, he observed the boy on the moped approaching him! "Zing" as the boy passed the Porsche on the passenger side of the road. "What has that kid got in that thing?" The attorney accelerated, and so did the boy. The boy passed him going very nearly twice as fast. "What is he trying to prove?" the attorney asked aloud. "He won't pass me again." He put the accelerator to the floor. In the rear view mirror he could see the boy accelerating even faster. Just as the moped was about to pass him, the frustrated attorney drove him off the road.

The moped hit a large rock and the youngster landed close to the automobile. The embarrassed lawyer apologized, "I didn't mean to hurt you, son. I just wanted to know how you did that. Is there anything I can do for you?" "Sure Mister, could you unhook my suspenders from your rear-view mirror?"

Dates & Places Used:

170

Success

What a man needs to get ahead is a powerful enemy.
Dates & Places Used:

171

Secure Mediocrity

A boss approached one of his most ambitious men and told him, "I've had my eye on you. You're a hard worker, and you've put in long hours. You're very ambitious."

"Thank you," replied the employee.

But the boss added, "So, consequently, I'm going to fire you. It's men like you who start competing companies."
Dates & Places Used:

172

Mixed Motives

Sometimes our generosity comes from mixed motives. One night some vandals cut down six royal palms along Miami's Flagler Street. Since the palms are very expensive, Dade County authorities weren't sure if they could replace them very soon. But then someone donated six more and even had them put in. The old ones had been about 15 feet tall and provided a nice foreground for a "Fly Delta" billboard. The new palms are 35 feet tall—completely hiding the sign. The new donor was another airline.
Dates & Places Used:

173

TOPIC: Complaints

Belly-Achers

A middle-aged man, famous for constant complaining and a nuisance to everyone who knew him, inherited a lot of money. After observing that it wasn't as much as he thought it should be, he told his wife, a gentle sweet-spirited woman, that he thought he would buy some acreage for them to enjoy in their retirement. "What do you think I should name my spread?" he asked, and she replied, "Why don't you call it 'Belly-Acres'?"

Dates & Places Used:

174

TOPIC: Complaints

Never Satisfied

Among the five thousand who were fed with the two fish and the five loaves of bread were doubtless several who complained about the bones the fish contained.

Dates & Places Used:

175

TOPIC: Complaints

Help You Honk

A man's car stalled in the heavy traffic as the light turned green. All his efforts to start the engine failed, and a chorus of honking behind him made matters worse. He finally got out of his car, walked back to the first driver, and said, "I'm sorry, but I can't seem to get my car started. If you'll go up there and give it a try, I'll stay here and blow your horn for you."

Dates & Places Used:

176

TOPIC: Complaints

Day Eight Complaints

The Lord created the world in six days and rested on the seventh.

On the eighth day, he started to answer complaints.

Dates & Places Used:

177

TOPIC: Complaints

Wrong Egg

A conscientious wife tried hard to please her critical husband, but failed regularly. He was the most cantankerous at breakfast. If she prepared scrambled eggs, he wanted poached; if poached eggs, he wanted scrambled. One morning the wife poached one egg and scrambled the other and placed the plate before him. Anxiously she awaited what surely this time would be his unqualified approval. He peered down at the plate and snorted, "Can't you do anything right, woman? You've scrambled the wrong one!"

Dates & Places Used:

178

TOPIC: Compliments

Can't Say Enough

The problem with giving unexpected compliments is the nagging suspicion that you have not said quite enough.

Dates & Places Used:

179

TOPIC: Compliments

The Forced Truth

A woman and her husband were invited to her rich aunt's home for dinner. The wife insisted that the husband treat the aunt politely. Her dessert was an original recipe. It was terrible. The husband responded, "I must say this is the best cake I have ever tasted."

On the way home his wife told him that she had not meant that he had to lie to her aunt.

The husband replied, "I told the truth; I said, I *must* say this is the best cake I ever tasted."

Dates & Places Used:

180

TOPIC: Compromise

Branded

A city family decided to try life in the wide-open spaces. They bought a Western ranch. Some friends came to visit a month later and asked them what they had named the ranch. The father said, "Well, I wanted to call it the Flying-W and my wife wanted to call it the Suzy-Q, but one of our sons liked the Bar-J and the other preferred the Lazy-Y. So we compromised and called it the Flying-W, Suzy-Q, Bar-J, Lazy-Y Ranch." Their friend asked, "Well, where are your cattle?" The man replied, "None of them survived the branding!"

Dates & Places Used:

181

TOPIC: Compromise

Adjusting to Reality

One bitterly cold winter night a young man plodded through knee-high snow to the home of the girl he had been dating regularly. Tonight was the night. He asked her to marry him. Being very practical, the young woman replied, "When you have several thousand dollars, I will seriously consider it." Six months later, the two strolled hand in hand through a park along the river. He stopped to kiss her and asked, "When are we going to get married?" She inquired, "Well, you remember my condition. Just how much have you saved?" He responded, "Exactly $75." She sighed and smiled, "Oh well, I guess that's close enough!"

Dates & Places Used:

182 TOPIC: Computers

Laws of Computing

1. No matter how much you know about computers, you can find an expert who renders everything incomprehensible.

2. You never run out of disks or printer ribbons during business hours.

3. The price of software is in inverse proportion to the readability of its manual.

4. The size of an error is in direct proportion to the importance of the data lost.

5. For every computer error there are at least two human errors, one of which is blaming it on the computer.

6. No matter how long you delay purchase of a computer product, a faster, cheaper and more powerful version will be introduced within 48 hours.

7. The power never fails at the beginning of a computing session.

8. If you back up your disk, the original will not fail.

9. Printers do not work when first set up. If they do, it is because you didn't follow instructions.

10. You never lose data you don't need.

Dates & Places Used:

183 TOPIC: Computers

Dated by Computers

The big thing today is computer dating.

If you don't know how to run a computer, it really dates you.

Dates & Places Used:

184

Human Thinking

The following story is from the popular book, *In Search of Excellence: Lessons From America's Best-Run Companies* by Thomas J. Peters and Robert H. Waterman, Jr. and published by Harper & Row, New York. The authors attribute this story to Gregory Bateson:

A man wanted to know about mind, not in nature, but in his private large computer. He asked it, "Do you compute that you will ever think like a human being?" The machine then set to work to analyze its own computational habits. Finally, the machine printed its answer on a piece of paper, as such machines do. The man ran to get the answer and found, neatly typed, the words: "That reminds me of a story." Surely the computer was right. This is indeed how people think.

Dates & Places Used:

185

No Real Confession

A man returned to his car in a parking lot and found a note under the windshield wiper. The note read as follows: "I just smashed into your car. The people who witnessed the collision are watching me. They probably think that I am writing down my name and address. I am not. They are wrong." There was nothing more written on the note.

Dates & Places Used:

186

Admitting Mistakes

Nikita Khrushchev and President Kennedy were having a vigorous exchange of strong opinions. Finally, Kennedy asked Khrushchev, "Do you ever admit a mistake?" The Soviet Premier

responded, "Certainly I do. In a speech before the Twentieth Party Congress, I admitted all of Stalin's mistakes."
Dates & Places Used:

187 TOPIC: Confidence

Asserting Leadership

The lion was proud of his mastery of the animal kingdom. One day he decided to make sure all the other animals knew he was the king of the jungle. He was so confident that he bypassed the smaller animals and went straight to the bear. "Who is the king of the jungle?" the lion asked. The bear replied, "Why you are, of course." The lion gave a mighty roar of approval. Next he asked the tiger, "Who is the king of the jungle?" The tiger quickly responded, "Everyone knows that you are, mighty lion." Next on the list was the elephant. The lion faced the elephant and addressed his question: "Who is the king of the jungle?" The elephant immediately grabbed the lion with his trunk, whirled him around in the air five or six times and slammed him into a tree. Then he pounded him onto the ground several times, dunked him under water in a nearby lake, and finally dumped him out on the shore. The lion—beaten, bruised, and battered— struggled to his feet. He looked at the elephant through sad and bloody eyes and said, "Look, just because you don't know the answer is no reason for you to get mean about it!"
Dates & Places Used:

188 TOPIC: Confidence

A Picture of God

A little boy was working hard on a drawing and his daddy asked him what he was doing. The son replied, "Drawing a picture of God." His daddy said, "You can't do that, honey. Nobody knows what God looks like." But the little boy was undeterred

and continued to draw, looked at his picture with satisfaction and said very matter-of-factly, "They will in a few minutes."
Dates & Places Used:

189 TOPIC: Confidence

The Self-Made Mess

A man brought his boss home for dinner for the first time. The boss was very blustery, very arrogant, very dominating! The little boy in the family stared at his father's boss for most of the evening, but did not say anything. Finally, the boss asked the little boy, "Why do you keep looking at me like that, Sonny?" The little boy answered, "My daddy says you are a self-made man." The boss beamed and proudly admitted that indeed he was a self-made man. The little boy said, "Well, if you are a self-made man, why did you make yourself like that?"
Dates & Places Used:

190 TOPIC: Confidence

Second Place

Confidence is entering a sales contest and wondering who's going to come in second.
Dates & Places Used:

191 TOPIC: Confidence

Golfing Tips

The golfer approached the first tee. It was a hazardous hole with a green surrounded by water. The golfer debated if he should use his new golf ball. Deciding that the hole was too treacherous, he pulled out an old ball and placed it on the tee.

86

His new golfing buddy suggested that he use the new ball. He replaced the old ball with the new ball and approached the tee. Before he stepped up to hit the ball, he took a couple of practice swings. Feeling much more confident, the golfer stepped up to the new ball on the tee.

The new golfing buddy who had watched the golfer take his two practice swings interrupted the golfer as he prepared to tee off: "Upon further consideration, I think you ought to use the old ball."

Dates & Places Used:

192

TOPIC: Conflicts

African Proverb

When bull elephants fight, the grass always loses.

Dates & Places Used:

193

TOPIC: Conflicts

True Clout

Three burly fellows on huge motorcycles pulled up to a highway cafe where a truck driver, just a little guy, was perched on a stool quietly eating his lunch. As the three fellows came in, they spotted him, grabbed his food away from him and laughed in his face. The truck driver said nothing. He got up, paid for his food, and walked out.

One of the three cyclists, unhappy that they hadn't succeeded in provoking the little man into a fight, commented to the waitress: "Boy, he sure wasn't much of a man, was he?" The waitress replied, "Well, I guess not." Then, looking out the window, she added, "I guess he's not much of a truck driver, either. He just ran over three motorcycles."

Dates & Places Used:

TOPIC: Conscience

Little Voice Inside

Mark Twain once told the following story in a speech he delivered on "honesty." When I was a boy, I was walking along a street and happened to spy a cart full of watermelons. I was fond of watermelons, so I sneaked quietly up to the cart and snitched one. Then I ran into a nearby alley and sank my teeth into the melon. No sooner had I done so, however, than a strange feeling came over me. Without a moment's hesitation, I made my decision. I walked back to the cart, replaced the melon—and took a ripe one.

Dates & Places Used:

TOPIC: Conscience

Weaker Conscience

A man visited a psychiatrist. He explained, "I've been doing wrong, Doctor, and my conscience is bothering me." The psychiatrist asked, "So you want something that will strengthen your will?" The fellow replied, "Oh, no, I'd rather get something that would weaken my conscience."

Dates & Places Used:

TOPIC: Conscience

Clearing Conscience

It's easy enough to have a clear conscience. All it takes is a fuzzy memory.

Dates & Places Used:

197

TOPIC: Consequence

Events That Reveal

An eager but somewhat unscrupulous salesman was delivering a bid to an engineering firm. While the man waiting on him stepped away from the desk for a few moments, the salesman noticed a competitor's bid on the man's desk, but he couldn't read the amount of the bid, as there was a juice can on top of the part of the bid that showed the total amount. The temptation was just too big and so he reached over to move the can to see what the competition was bidding. As he lifted the can, his heart sank as he watched thousands of BBs pour from the bottomless can and scatter across the floor.

Dates & Places Used:

198

TOPIC: Consequence

Fearful Wisdom

Fear of jail is the beginning of wisdom. *(Nigerian proverb)*

Dates & Places Used:

199

TOPIC: Consequence

Profound Warning

A father was overheard shouting to his son: "If you fall off that rock and break your leg, don't come running to me!"

Dates & Places Used:

200

TOPIC: Consequence

Hung Jury

Years ago my mother lived next door to a dear woman who was very much concerned about her son's actions. The boy had recently been arrested and tried. Seeing the neighbor outside her house, my mother asked what had happened to her son. The woman said, "Well, you know, it was the strangest thing. Not only did they not find my boy guilty, but they hung the jury!"

Dates & Places Used:

201 TOPIC: Consequence

It's in the Bag

One winter day not long ago a man returned to his car from shopping at the local neighborhood mall. He noticed a rather foul odor from under the hood. He checked the engine. In the compartment he discovered a dead cat rather mutilated from being caught in the fan belt. The poor cat had sought shelter from the snow and cold and didn't realize the dangers of resting on the engine block. The man proceeded to scrape, pull, and push the remains of the cat into a plastic bag. He closed the hood and went to wash his hands. As he was returning to take the bag from the hood of the car, he saw a woman walk by, look suspiciously in both directions, grab the bag, and hurry off into the mall. "Well this is too good to be true!" the man thought as he laughed at what the woman had done. He decided to follow her and see what would happen next. She went into a restaurant and surveyed her bounty. She screamed and fainted when she looked into the bag. An ambulance was called and as she was about to be carried away the man couldn't resist. "Hey lady!" he shouted, "don't forget your package!" And with that he gently laid the plastic bag on the woman's chest, just as the ambulance doors were closing!

Dates & Places Used:

202 TOPIC: Consideration

Sporting Golf

Timing Is Everything: It's good sportsmanship to not pick up lost golf balls while they are still rolling. *(Mark Twain)*

Dates & Places Used:

203

TOPIC: Consistency

Consistent Lives

If you resent it, don't do it; if you do it, don't resent it.
Dates & Places Used:

204

TOPIC: Consistency

Ruin It Again

A resident in a seaside hotel breakfast room called over the head waiter one morning and said, "I want two boiled eggs, one of them so undercooked it's runny, and the other so overcooked, it's about as easy to eat as rubber; also grilled bacon that has been left on the plate to get cold; burnt toast that crumbles away as soon as you touch it with a knife; butter straight from the deep-freeze so that it's impossible to spread; and a pot of very weak coffee, lukewarm."

"That's a complicated order, sir," said the bewildered waiter. "It might be a bit difficult."

The guest replied, "Oh, but that's what you gave me yesterday!"
Dates & Places Used:

205

TOPIC: Contentment

Used to Dandelions

A gardener took great pride in caring for his lawn. But one year it grew full of dandelions. He tried every method and product to get rid of them, but nothing worked. Exasperated, he wrote the Department of Agriculture explaining all he had done. "What shall I try next?" he wrote. "Try getting used to them," came the reply.
Dates & Places Used:

206

TOPIC: Conversion

A Cure for Hatred

A woman testified to the transformation in her life that had resulted through her experience in conversion. She declared, "I'm so glad I got religion. I have an uncle I used to hate so much I vowed I'd never go to his funeral. But now, why, I'd be happy to go to it any time."

Dates & Places Used:

207

TOPIC: Conviction

Fighting on the Ice

Senator Russell Long showed great persistence when he once said, "I expect to fight that proposition until hell freezes over. Then I propose to start fighting on the ice!"

Dates & Places Used:

208

TOPIC: Cooking

Kitchen Accidents

The worst thing about accidents in the kitchen is that you usually have to eat them.

Dates & Places Used:

209

TOPIC: Cooking

Deadly Dog Biscuits

Rev. J. Harold Stephens tells of a particular cooking crisis:
There was a young bride, a poor cook, whose husband came home to find her crying. "The dog ate the biscuits," she sobbed. "Never mind, honey," he said. "We'll get us another dog."

Dates & Places Used:

210

Stick Together

A landlubber who could not swim went fishing with a friend and after a while hooked a really big fish. He was so excited about catching this big fish that as he was reeling it in, trying to get it next to the boat, he leaned too far over and fell into the water. He was panic stricken, and began to yell, "Help, save me! Help, save me!"

So his friend just calmly reached out and was going to grab the man by the hair, pull him over a little closer and get him into the boat. But as he pulled, the man's toupee came off and he slipped down under again. He came up again yelling, "Help, save me!" So the friend reached down again, this time catching hold of an arm. As he pulled on it, it came off because it was an artificial limb. The man continued to kick and thrash around, sputter and splash. The friend reached out again, grabbed a leg and as he pulled it, you guessed it, it came off! It was a wooden leg!

As the man continued splashing and calling out and sputtering, his friend turned to him in disgust and said, "How can I help you if you won't stick together?"

Dates & Places Used:

211

Row It or Rock It

A person who rows the boat usually doesn't have time to rock it.

Dates & Places Used:

212

Pedal Together

Two men riding a bicycle built for two came to a long, steep hill. It took a great deal of struggle for the men to complete what proved to be a very stiff climb. When they got to the top, the man in front turned to the other and said, "Boy, that sure was a hard climb." The fellow in back replied, "Yes, and if I hadn't kept the brakes on all the way, we would certainly have rolled down backwards."

Dates & Places Used:

213 TOPIC: Cooperation
People Need People

One of the first episodes in the *Andy Griffith Show* series depicted the following: Following the death of his wife, Sheriff Andy Taylor decided to invite his spinster Aunt Bee to come and live with Opie and him, thinking that she would add the missing feminine touch. Surprisingly, Opie is not too pleased to have Aunt Bee come in and "replace" his mother. Andy tries to help the situation by inviting Aunt Bee to go fishing and frog-catching with them so that Opie can become attached to her. Instead, she fails miserably at fishing and frogging and later at football. Finally, late at night, after Opie is in bed, Aunt Bee talks Andy into taking her to the bus station. Opie hears her crying beneath his bedroom window and guesses that she is leaving. He runs down the stairs and out to the truck, exclaiming, "We can't let her go, Pa, she needs us. She can't even catch frogs, take fish off the hook, or throw a football. We've got to take care of her or she'll never make it."

Dates & Places Used:

214 TOPIC: Cooperation
Our Varied Roles

We are all manufacturers in a way—making good, making trouble, or making excuses. *(H. V. Adolt)*

Dates & Places Used:

215

TOPIC: Courage

Frantic Frog

Have you seen it? It's a great picture: A surprised stork has just begun to swallow a frog, but the frog is not complying. The frog reaches its front legs out of the beak of the unsuspecting stork and grabs the neck of the stork—and squeezes for dear life.

Life is the stork. We are the frantic frog. And we had better grab hold for all we are worth—before we get swallowed. Keep on squeezing!

Dates & Places Used:

216

TOPIC: Courage

Fearless Timing

The prison warden told the condemned man to order whatever he wanted for his last meal, and he offered suggestions: "Lobster, Filet Mignon, Beef Wellington, Caviar or Shrimp?" "No," the prisoner said. "I'll just take a bowl of mushrooms." "Why mushrooms?" the warden asked him. "I've always been afraid to eat 'em."

Dates & Places Used:

217

TOPIC: Courage

An Easy Hug

In the Moscow circus a beautiful woman lion tamer would have a fierce lion come to her meekly, put his paws around her and nuzzle her with affection. The crowd thundered its approval. All except an Armenian who declared, "What's so great about that? Anybody can do that." The ringmaster challenged him, "Would you like to try it?" The Armenian's reply came back: "Yes, but first get that lion out of there."

Dates & Places Used:

218

Motive for Courage

A true story: A young man was almost robbed in New York City. He was walking from the bus depot to his father's apartment in upper Manhattan when he realized he was flanked by two young men. They pulled a gun on him and demanded that he give them his wallet. He said, "No." They repeatedly demanded that he give them his wallet. And each time he said, "No." The robbers finally gave up. When asked why he didn't give them his wallet, he replied, "My learner's permit's in it."

Dates & Places Used:

219

Understandably Brave

Maurice bragged, "I'm not afraid of anything. Once I even cut off a lion's tail with my pen knife." Someone asked, "Why didn't you cut off his head?" Maurice looked a bit sheepish. "Well, to tell the truth, someone had already cut it off."

Dates & Places Used:

220

Wrong Scarecrow

Years ago a boy had a crush on a girl, Laura Mae, in his high school freshman class. Everyone planted gardens in this community and protected them with scarecrows which were as lifelike and original as possible. Riding the school bus one afternoon, they rounded the curve near Laura Mae's house, and her parent's garden came into view. In the middle of the rows, was a figure dressed in an old straw hat, ragged overalls, and a faded checked shirt. A hoe was stuck under his right arm, adding authenticity.

In an effort to gain favor with the girl he loved, this boy said, "Laura Mae, your daddy never has to worry about crows in his garden; anything that ugly will keep everything away." And right at that moment, the scarecrow began hoeing. Laura Mae is married now, but not to that boy.

Dates & Places Used:

221

TOPIC: Creation

Adam Was A Foreigner

A Sunday school teacher asked her class who the first man was. A little boy answered, "George Washington." She then informed him that the first man was Adam. The boy responded "Oh, well, if you are speaking of foreigners, maybe he was."

Dates & Places Used:

222

TOPIC: Credibility

The Cynic in All of Us

The three least credible sentences in the English language:
1. "The check is in the mail."
2. "Of course I'll respect you in the morning."
3. "I'm from the government and I'm here to help you."
(George F. Will)

Dates & Places Used:

223

TOPIC: Critics

Critical Imperfection

A critic is someone who points out how imperfectly other people do what the critic does not do at all.

Dates & Places Used:

224

TOPIC: Critics

A Goalie's Rejection

How would you like a job where, if you made a mistake, a big red light goes on and 18,000 people boo? *(Former hockey goalie, Jacques Plante)*

Dates & Places Used:

225

TOPIC: Critics

Criticizing

Two taxidermists stopped before a window and immediately began to criticize the way an owl had been mounted. Its eyes were not natural; its wings were not in proportion to its head; its feathers were not neatly arranged; and its feet could certainly be improved.

Toward the end of their critique, the old owl turned his head . . . and winked at them!

Dates & Places Used:

226

TOPIC: Customs

Old Expressions

In Muslim countries the weekend is Thursday and Friday. That's where that old expression "Praise Allah, It's Wednesday" comes from.

Dates & Places Used:

227

TOPIC: Cynics

Birth of a Cynic

An optimist is a father who lets his son drive the new car alone.
A pessimist is one who won't.
A cynic is one who did.

Dates & Places Used:

228

TOPIC: Danger

Kids' Candid Responses

The fireman was telling a kindergarten class what to do in case of a fire. He said, "First, go to the door and feel the door to see if it's hot. Then," he said, "fall to your knees. Does anyone know why you ought to fall to your knees?" One of the little tykes said, "Sure, to start praying to ask God to get us out of this mess!"

Dates & Places Used:

229

TOPIC: Dating

Partial Commitment

The owner of a photographic studio tells the story of a college boy who came in with a framed picture of his girlfriend. He wanted the picture duplicated. In removing the photograph from the frame, the studio owner noticed the inscription on the back, written by the girlfriend: "My dearest Tommy: I love you with all my heart. I love you more and more each day. I will love you forever and ever. I am yours for all eternity." It was signed "Dianne" and contained a P.S.: "If we should ever break up, I want this picture back."

Dates & Places Used:

230

TOPIC: Dating

Late Advice

"Momma, do you think I should stick to younger girls? Or should I go out with an older, classier, and more experienced type?"

"Son, you have a way of asking advice that makes it sound like it's too late."

Dates & Places Used:

231

Just Like Family

A secretary was leaving to get married. Her boss gave her a big hug and a kiss saying, "You've been like a daughter to me—insolent, surly, unappreciative."

Dates & Places Used:

232

One for Johnny

In 1926, Johnny Sylvester got kicked in the head by a horse. The wound on his forehead got badly infected. Doctors told his parents the sad news. Johnny would die. "I wish I could see Babe Ruth wallop a homer before I die," Johnny told his parents. So they sent a telegram to the great slugger of the New York Yankees. And Babe Ruth sent an answer. He would hit a homer just for Johnny in the next game.

Johnny Sylvester instantly became one of the most famous boys in baseball history. Did Babe Ruth slug one for Johnny? Yes. In fact, he hit three homers in that game. And to top it all off, he visited Johnny in the hospital.

Were the doctors right? Did Johnny die? Yes they were right. Johnny Sylvester did die. But not until he was 74.

Dates & Places Used:

233

Death From Kids' Views

Death and dying is a subject that is always on the back burners of everyone's mind from preschoolers to the oldest adult. Some nine-year-old children were asked what they thought of death and dying. Jim said, "When you die, they bury you in the ground and your soul goes to heaven, but your body can't go to heaven because

it's too crowded up there already." Judy said, "Only the good people go to heaven. The other people go where it's hot all the time like in Florida." John said, "Maybe I'll die someday, but I hope I don't die on my birthday because it's no fun to celebrate your birthday if you're dead." Marsha commented, "When you die, you don't have to do homework in heaven, unless your teacher is there too."
Dates & Places Used:

TOPIC: Death

Dead or Forgotten

A five-year-old girl, returning home from a funeral of her grand-mother, rode in a car with her other grandmother. "Where did Grandma go?" she asked. "We believe she went to be with God," the other grandmother replied. "How old was she?" "She was eighty years old." "How old are you?" "I am eighty-three." The little girl thought a bit, then said, "I hope God hasn't forgotten you!"
Dates & Places Used:

TOPIC: Death

Simple Immortality

I don't want to achieve immortality through my work. I want to achieve immortality through not dying. *(Woody Allen)*
Dates & Places Used:

TOPIC: Death

Congregational Immunity

A preacher was addressing the people one Sunday, trying to impress upon them the importance of faith. "All you people of

this congregation," he cried from the pulpit, "one day you're going to die. Do you hear me? All you people of this congregation, one day you're going to die." One little man sitting in the front pew started to laugh, so the preacher asked him, "What's so funny?" The man answered, "I don't belong to this congregation."
Dates & Places Used:

237

TOPIC: Death

The Hope of Dying

You may remember the story of a long and rough Atlantic crossing during which the seasick passenger was leaning over the rail of the ocean liner and had turned several shades of bileous green. A steward came along and tried to cheer him up by saying, "Don't be discouraged, sir! You know, no one's ever died of seasickness yet!" The nauseated passenger looked up at the steward with baleful eyes and replied, "Oh, don't say that! It's only the hope of dying that's kept me alive this long!"
Dates & Places Used:

238

TOPIC: Death

Selfish Grief

A visitor at a zoo noticed an attendant crying quietly in a corner. The visitor asked another attendant what the man was crying about and was told that one of the elephants had died. Touched by this, the visitor then asked, "I assume he must have been particularly fond of that elephant?" And the reply came back, "No, it's not that. He's crying because he's the one who has to dig the grave."
Dates & Places Used:

239

TOPIC: Death

Not Really Suitable

An old lady went to a tombstone-cutter's office to order a stone for her husband's grave. After explaining that all she wanted was a small one with no frills, she told him to put the words "To My Husband" in a suitable place. When the stone was delivered, she saw, to her horror, this inscription: "To My Husband—In A Suitable Place."

Dates & Places Used:

240

TOPIC: Death

Historical Perspective

Historian Arnold J. Toynbee at age eighty said, "To be mortal is not any means wholly disadvantageous. When I catch myself resenting not being immortal, I pull myself up short by asking whether I should really like the prospect of having to make out an annual income tax return for an infinite number of years ahead."

Dates & Places Used:

241

TOPIC: Death

Take Out the Bones

Our little girl was fascinated by the pictures of dinosaurs in the encyclopedia. Her little mind just couldn't comprehend how the scientists were able to put all of those bones together to show us what the skeletons of these huge creatures were like. After looking at them for some time, she turned to me and said, "Mom, when we die, are they going to take all of our bones out of us, too?"

Dates & Places Used:

242

TOPIC: Death

The Value of a Marriage

An insurance man was settling up with a woman who had just lost her husband. He had brought a check for $50,000 to present to her. She looked at it and said (with a little catch in her throat), "You know, I miss him so much, I'd give $25,000 of this to have him back."

Dates & Places Used:

243

TOPIC: Death

Learn From the Past

A man's wife had died, and as the mourners were on the way to the cemetery one of the pallbearers tripped over a rock. This shook the casket and revived the woman. She lived another seven years and died again. They were on the way to the cemetery again, and as they approached the same spot the husband shouted out to the pallbearers, "Watch out for that rock!"

Dates & Places Used:

244

TOPIC: Debt

Act Your Wage

The average American family's ambition is to make as much money as they're spending.

The best advice for the average American family: Act your wage!

Dates & Places Used:

245

TOPIC: Debt

Quick Action

To get back on your feet, miss two car payments.
Dates & Places Used:

246

TOPIC: Debt

Deficit Spending

Senator Strom Thurmond explains why Congress doesn't decrease deficit spending: "It's awfully hard to get a hog to butcher itself."
Dates & Places Used:

247

TOPIC: Debt

Forgetful Borrowers

A lot of people are now making money the old fashioned way. They borrow it and then forget from whom.
Dates & Places Used:

248

TOPIC: Debt

The Secret of Progress

All progress is based on a universal innate desire on the part of every organism to live beyond its income. *(Samuel Butler)*
Dates & Places Used:

249

TOPIC: Deception

The Scales of Justice

Numbers 32:23b is clear: "You may be sure that your sin will find you out."

A certain woman, preparing to entertain guests, went to a small grocery store to buy food. She stopped at the meat counter and asked the attendant for a large chicken. He reached down into the cold storage compartment, grabbed the last chicken he had, and placed it on the scale. "This one weighs four pounds, ma'am," he said.

"I'm not sure that will be enough," the woman replied. "Don't you have a bigger one?"

The attendant put the chicken back into the compartment, pretended to search through the melting ice for another one, and then brought out the same bird, discreetly applying some finger pressure to the scale. "Ah," he said with a smile, "this one weighs six pounds."

"I'm just not sure," the woman frowned. "I'll tell you what—wrap them both up for me!"

Dates & Places Used:

250

TOPIC: Deception

The Short Route

A little inaccuracy sometimes saves tons of explanation. *(Saki)*
Dates & Places Used:

251

TOPIC: Deception

Rabbit Resurrection

Here is an original from one of our subscribers:

It was a nice Sunday morning after church in Ramona. My brother and I were playing separately in the back yard. There was a frantic thrashing of bushes that grabbed the attention of us both. Out bounded our dog "Matt," ferociously shaking a black and white lop-eared rabbit.

Matt could not have cared less, but my brother and I knew the rabbit belonged to Mrs. Clausen, the widow next door. There was nothing to do but tell Dad. We knew he had little talent for mending fences, fixing screen doors, or changing spark plugs, but faith and history had taught us that he never encountered a problem that he wasn't up to.

"Everything is simple, don't panic, don't get excited. Take a second look at situations!" he used to say. He never knew disappointment, never experienced despair, and never acknowledged failure (according to the world's interpretation).

We took our rabbit problem to Dad. He studied it in his usual unconcerned manner and told us not to worry. "Just hose the little fellow off real well so he looks nice and clean. Brush him down with this towel, and stick him back in the cage. Mrs. Clausen is still at church. When she comes home and discovers her rabbit, she'll be a little upset but she'll figure he just died a natural death. Oh yes, be sure and tie up the dog."

We did exactly as we were told and then hid in the bushes to get a good vantage point to observe the widow when she noticed her rabbit. Sure enough, just as Dad had promised we saw her come out the back door and head for the rabbit cages. All of a sudden we heard the worst screaming you can imagine. Mrs. Clausen went on and on hollering, shrieking, crying, yelling, and asking God all kinds of questions.

My mom and dad came running out of the house and into her back yard, pleading with her to stop and tell them what had gone wrong. They finally got her to calm down a little and again asked her to explain what had happened. In between sniffs and sobs she finally got it out, "I buried that rabbit three days ago!"

Dates & Places Used:

252 TOPIC: Deception

Mutual Recognition

A man was traveling by train to Nashville to seek employment as a newspaper reporter. When asked for his ticket, he named a prominent paper in Nashville and explained that he was a reporter for that paper and did not need a ticket.

The conductor told him that the editor of the paper was riding in the rear of the train and if he could identify the man, then he would not need to pay. The editor did indeed identify the man as the reporter he had fallaciously claimed to be.

The man later approached the editor and asked him why he had covered for him. The man answered, "I'm not the editor. I'm traveling on his pass and was scared you would give me away."

Dates & Places Used:

253 TOPIC: Deception

The Weasel Word

A junior senator asked a senior senator: "What's a good word for 'No' that sounds like 'Yes'?"

Dates & Places Used:

254 TOPIC: Deception

Priorities

In the comic strip *The Wizard of Id* a poor, bedraggled peasant comes up behind Rodney, points his finger in his back and says, "This is a stick-up! Hand over your money!" Rodney turns around with his hands up and then notices the crook is just using his finger. He comments, "You don't even have a weapon!" The thief agrees and says, "It's the first thing I'm going to buy!"

Dates & Places Used:

255 TOPIC: Decisions

Deferred Decisions

President Reagan tells of shoemaker who was making a pair of shoes for him when he was a lad. The cobbler asked if Ronald

wanted a round or square toe. Ronald was unsure, so the cobbler told him to return in a day or two and let him know. A few days later the cobbler saw young Reagan on the street and asked what he had decided. Reagan was still undecided. The cobbler said the shoes would be ready the next day. When Reagan picked up the shoes, one had a round toe and one had a square toe. Says Reagan, "Looking at those shoes taught me a lesson. If you don't make your own decisions, somebody else makes them for you."
Dates & Places Used:

256

TOPIC: Decisions
_____

How Long Can It Take?

The young town smart alec walked into the blacksmith shop shortly after the blacksmith had thrown a horseshoe on the ground so it could cool. Seeing it there, the young fellow reached down, picked it up, but instantly cast it aside as it burned his fingers. The blacksmith said, "Kind of hot, isn't it, son?" The brash kid said, "No, not too hot. It just doesn't take me long to look at a horseshoe."
Dates & Places Used:

257

TOPIC: Decisions
_____

Quick Sincere Choice

When Bill Hill, a Montana guide, killed a grizzly bear in a protected area, this was his defense: "When I saw that bear come smoking down on me, I didn't have any trouble in deciding who was the endangered species."
Dates & Places Used:

258

TOPIC: Defeat
_____

Perspective

Linus finds Charlie Brown to tell him about the most unbelievable football game ever played. He excitedly tells Charlie about an amazing comeback. With the score 6 to 0 and three seconds to play, the home team had the ball on the one-yard line. The quarterback threw a perfect pass to the left end, who whirled away from four guys and ran all the way for a touchdown! Linus tells about how the fans went wild. The extra point was good. The home team won. Linus describes the excitement and celebration. Linus concludes: "It was fantastic!"

Charlie's only question: "How did the other team feel?" ("Peanuts")

Dates & Places Used:

259

TOPIC: Defeat

Who Beats Whom?

A judge called a young lad into his chambers. He announced to the boy that he had to make a decision as to which parent was to receive custody of him. The judge said, "I believe I shall give you to your mother." "Oh, no!" cried the boy. "Mother beats me." "Then," said the judge, "I shall give your father custody." "Oh, no!" said the boy. "Father beats me." "Then who shall get you?" the judge asked the boy. "Give me to the New York Mets," said the boy. "They never beat anyone!"

Dates & Places Used:

260

TOPIC: Delays

Rapid Transit

An old train on a secluded railroad was chugging slowly through the countryside when it suddenly came to a dead stop. There was only one passenger in the car, a salesman riding the line for the first time. He asked the conductor why they had stopped the train. The conductor said, "There's nothing to worry about, sir. There's a cow on the track."

In about ten minutes the train got under way again, but after chugging along for a few more miles, it again came to a halt. "There's a temporary delay," the conductor said. "We'll continue shortly." The frustrated salesman asked, "What's the probem now? Did we catch up to that cow again?"

Dates & Places Used:

261

TOPIC: Delegation

Don't Learn to Do

Never learn to do anything. If you don't learn, you will always find someone else to do it for you. *(Mark Twain)*

Dates & Places Used:

262

TOPIC: Denial

One Man's Logic

Today, 1,600 people belong to the International Flat Earth Research Society of America. Their president, Charles K. Johnson, says, "I've been a flat-earther all my life. When I saw the globe in grade school, I didn't accept it. To me, it was illogical."

Dates & Places Used:

263

TOPIC: Denominations

Colson's Change

In July of 1984 Charles Colson was speaking at a Baptist gathering. He told of his change from being an Episcopalian to becoming a Baptist. He had considered a change dictated by his study of Scripture and his developing personal convictions. But he did not want his change to be offensive to his dear friends who remained Episcopalian. Not knowing how to approach the issue, he found himself avoiding his friends. Then one day his fears were put to rest. He encountered one of his Episcopalian cronies who assured him there was no problem with his change, but only benefit. His encouragement to Chuck was, "When you left the Episcopalian Church and joined the Baptist Church, you raised the intellectual level of both groups!"

Dates & Places Used:

264

TOPIC: Denominations

Three Cheers!

Three Lutheran pastors were invited by a Catholic priest to attend Mass one Sunday at his church. They arrived a bit late. All the pews were filled, and they had to stand in the back of the church. The priest noticed them as he began the Mass and he whispered to one of the altar boys, "Get three chairs for our Lutheran friends." The altar boy didn't hear, so the priest spoke a bit louder, motioning to the rear of the congregation: "Three chairs for the Lutherans." Dutifully, the boy arose, stepped to the altar rail and loudly proclaimed to the congregation, "Three cheers for the Lutherans!"

Dates & Places Used:

265

TOPIC: Denominations

Catholic Baths

The two members of the Hell's Angels brought their motorcycles to a stop at a crosswalk. A nun with her arm in a sling crossed in front of them. One of the bikers called out to her, "Hey, what happened to you?" The nun explained that she had slipped in the bathtub and broken her arm. As they rode on, one Hell's Angel asked the other, "What's a bathtub?" The other replied, "How should I know? I'm not a Catholic."

Dates & Places Used:

266

TOPIC: Denominations

Now I See!

A Baptist preacher tells the story on himself about receiving a call from a woman who was quite upset over the death of her pet cat, Homer. She wanted the preacher to conduct the funeral service for Homer! The Baptist preacher explained that this was a little out of his line, and he referred her to a friend, a Presbyterian pastor at a church down the street. Later, the preacher learned that his Presbyterian friend had referred her to a Methodist minister, who had referred her to someone else. About an hour later, she called the Baptist preacher back and she was still upset. The woman said she was at her wit's end. She couldn't find a preacher to conduct Homer's services and didn't know what to do. She said she planned to give $1,000 to the church of the minister who performed this service for Homer. The Baptist preacher said it took him only a moment to mull this over and then say to her, "Well, why didn't you tell me Homer was a Baptist cat in the first place?!"

Dates & Places Used:

267

TOPIC: Denominations

Episcopal Lethargy

Two little boys in the neighborhood were talking. One said to the other, "You've been trying out all the churches in town. Which one did your family choose to attend?"

The other boy said, "My mother likes the Episcopal lethargy best."

Dates & Places Used:

268

Beyond Satisfied

A little boy went to see his favorite aunt. When he arrived, his aunt asked him what he wanted to do. He answered, "I love your pancakes, and when we have pancakes at home, I only get to eat three. While I'm here at your house, I want to eat as many pancakes I want."

The next morning, the boy's aunt began to pile the pancakes on his plate. The little guy just kept eating and eating the pancakes as fast as he could. By the time he had eaten his tenth pancake, his pace had slowed considerably. In the middle of eating his eleventh pancake, the boy came to an abrupt stop. His aunt asked, "Are you ready for some more pancakes?" With a pained expression on his face, the boy looked up at his aunt and said, "Oh no, I don't want any more. In fact, I don't even want the pancakes I've already eaten."

Dates & Places Used:

269

Where's the Paint Can?

One man landed a job painting the yellow line down the center of the highway. This he had to do by hand. After three days the foreman complained. "Your first day out, you did great," he exclaimed. "You painted that line for three miles. Your second day wasn't bad. You painted two miles. But today you painted only one mile, so it looks as though I'll have to fire you."

On his way out of the office the employee looked back and said, "It's not my fault. Every day I got farther from the paint can."

Dates & Places Used:

270

Do As You're Told

The blacksmith was instructing a novice in the way to treat a horseshoe. "I'll bring the shoe from the fire and lay it on the anvil. When I nod my head you hit it with this hammer." The apprentice did exactly as he was told, but he'll never hit a black-smith again!

Dates & Places Used:

271 TOPIC: Details
A Cold Test

British Railways was looking for a way to test locomotive windshields when they heard about an unusual test cannon at British Airways. Airways used the cannon to fire birds at great force into the windshields of passenger jets to insure designs and materials were up to par. They gladly let the railway borrow it. Just before the test run, British Railways sent someone out to buy a dead chicken for ammunition. The cannon was then loaded, aimed, and fired at the windshield. The bird smashed through the windshield, broke the engineer's chair, and made a large dent in the rear wall. Railways was furious. They called Airways demanding an explanation. Airways checked it out. "No problem," they reported. "Next time you buy a chicken, make sure it isn't frozen."

Dates & Places Used:

272 TOPIC: Details
First Priority

A young ensign, after nearly completing his first overseas cruise, was given an opportunity to display his capabilities at getting the ship under way. With a stream of commands, he had the decks buzzing with men, and soon the ship was steaming out the channel en route to the States. His efficiency established a new record for getting a destroyer under way, and he was not surprised when a seaman approached him with a message from the captain. He was a bit surprised, though, to find it a radio message and even more surprised to read: "My personal congratulations

upon completing your underway preparation exercise according to the book and with amazing speed. In your haste, however, you have overlooked one of the unwritten rules. Make sure the captain is aboard before getting under way."
Dates & Places Used:

273 TOPIC: Details

Back Seat Driver

A man was desperately late for an important appointment as he drove into the basement parking garage of the large office building. He jumped out of his four-door sedan, then opened the back door to get his briefcase.

Just then an attendant came up and explained to him that this was a self-park garage and he would have to park it himself.

Since he was in such a hurry he quickly jumped back into the car, rolled down the window and said, "OK, OK, which way do I go?" The attendant leaned in the window and said, "Up the ramp to your right, sir, but first you'll have to get into the front seat."
Dates & Places Used:

274 TOPIC: Devil

Devil Dad

Two young boys were walking home from Sunday school and sharing their reflections on the lesson. They had been studying the temptation of Christ in the wilderness.

Little Peter said to his friend John, "Do you believe that stuff about the devil? Do you think there really is a devil?" John looked at him and said, "Naah—it's just like Santa Claus—it's your dad."
Dates & Places Used:

275

TOPIC: Diets

Only Take What You Can Eat

A man went into a pizza parlor and ordered a medium sized pizza. When it was ready, the cook asked him if he wanted it cut into four pieces or six. The man thought a moment, then said, "Better make it four pieces. I don't think I can eat six pieces."
Dates & Places Used:

276

TOPIC: Diets

Hold the Twinkies

A generously overweight man stepped onto the scales, turned to his friend, and exclaimed, "I don't believe it! I began this diet yesterday, but the scales say I'm heavier. Here, Norm, hold my jacket. Oh, no! It still says I'm heavier. Here, hold my Twinkies."
Dates & Places Used:

277

TOPIC: Diets

More Careful Thought

At a Weight Watchers meeting a new member was disappointed because she had lost only a few pounds during her first week. She complained, "A friend of mine who was also on Weight Watchers said she'd lost ten pounds her first week. She said I'd do the same."

The leader, stressing the idea that slow weight loss is permanent weight loss, asked, "Who is she to say? Is she a doctor?" The woman answered, "No." "Is she a nurse?" She thought about it and replied, "No." "Well, is she a nutritionist, a Weight Watchers leader? Anything?"

The new member thought for a moment, then replied, "I think she's a liar."
Dates & Places Used:

TOPIC: Diets

An Acceptable Diet

We live in one of the most diet-conscious societies that has ever existed. Some of them are more realistic than others. Here's one that has been called The Stress Diet:

Breakfast: 1/2 grapefruit, 1 slice whole wheat toast, 8 oz. skim milk.

Lunch: 4 oz. lean boiled chicken breast, 1 cup steamed zucchini, 1 Oreo cookie, herb tea.

Mid-Afternoon Snack: rest of the package of Oreos, 1 quart Rocky Road ice cream, 1 jar hot fudge.

Dinner: 2 loaves garlic bread, large cheese and mushroom pizza, large pitcher of beer, 3 Milky Way candy bars, entire Sara Lee cheesecake eaten directly from the refrigerator.

And here are some helpful diet tips that go with the regimen:

1. If no one sees you eat it, it has no calories.

2. If you drink a sugar-free can of pop along with a candy bar, they cancel each other out.

3. When eating with someone else, calories don't count if you both eat the same amount.

4. Food used for medicinal purposes NEVER counts, such as hot chocolate, brandy, toast, and Sara Lee cheesecake.

5. If you fatten up everyone else around you, you look thinner.

6. Movie-related foods don't count because they are simply part of the entire entertainment experience and not a part of one's personal fuel, such as Milk Duds, popcorn with butter, and candy-coated almonds.

Enjoy your diet!

Dates & Places Used:

TOPIC: Diets

The Ungrateful Child

A fourth-grade Sunday school boy was experiencing his first summer at a church camp. Soon he sent his mother a brief but pointed letter: "Dear Mom, please send me lots of food. All we get here is breakfast, lunch, and dinner."

Dates & Places Used:

280

TOPIC: Diets

Stretchin' It a Little

Joe Cannon of *West Lane News* suggests these ways to know when you need to lose weight: When tourists say to you, "I didn't know the Pillsbury Dough Boy lived here." When you rent a canoe and they put large weights at the opposite end of the thing to balance it. When you take a trip to the zoo and the children start throwing peanuts your way. When five people trying to get a tan ask you to move because you're blocking out the sun. When a child asks if he can use the life preserver around your waist and you're not wearing one.

Dates & Places Used:

281

TOPIC: Diets

Weight Loss

When a matron was signing up for exercise classes, the instructor told her to be sure to wear loose clothing to class. She responded, "Listen, if I had any loose clothing, I wouldn't need this class."

Dates & Places Used:

282

TOPIC: Diplomacy

Whitewashing Sheep

The children in a prominent family decided to give their father a book of the family's history for a birthday present. They commissioned a professional biographer to do the work, carefully warning him of the family's "black sheep" problem: Uncle George had been executed in the electric chair for murder. The biographer assured the children, "I can handle that situation so that there will be no embarrassment. I'll merely say that Uncle George occupied a chair of applied electronics at an important

government institution. He was attached to his position by the strongest of ties and his death came as a real shock."
Dates & Places Used:

283 ▸ TOPIC: Diplomacy

Not Too Subtle Signs

The federal government in Brazil has ordered the state of Cerna to replace many of its road safety signs. The current signs, in the government's view, are "detrimental to the public's education." An example of their current approach that the government doesn't feel is too helpful: "Don't Drive Plastered, Not Everyone Wants To Go To Hell."
Dates & Places Used:

284 ▸ TOPIC: Direction

Take the Truck

A woman called the fire department in agitation one day. "Come as quickly as you can," she cried. "My house is on fire." "OK, lady," said the dispatcher, calmly, "tell us how to get there." "Oh," she paused for a moment, "don't you have your little red truck anymore?"
Dates & Places Used:

285 ▸ TOPIC: Direction

Awareness Is the Key

When he was eighty-eight years old, the late Supreme Court Justice Oliver Wendell Holmes once found himself on a train. When the conductor came by, Justice Holmes couldn't find his ticket, and he seemed terribly upset. He searched all of his pockets and fumbled through his wallet without success. The conductor was sympathetic. He said, "Don't worry, Mr. Holmes, the Pennsylvania Railroad will be happy to trust you. After you reach your destination you'll probably find the ticket and you can just mail it to us." But the conductor's kindness failed to put Mr. Holmes at ease. Still very much upset, he said, "My dear man, my problem is not 'Where is my ticket?' The problem is, 'Where am I going?'"

Dates & Places Used:

286

TOPIC: Direction

Lost Cause

A tourist who was visiting New York City lost all sense of direction one evening and stopped at a newsstand to get directions. The tourist asked the newsstand vendor which direction was north.

"Look, buddy," he replied in a loud and annoyed voice. "We got uptown, we got downtown, and we got crosstown. We don't got north."

Dates & Places Used:

287

TOPIC: Disappointment

False Hopes

Probably nothing in the world arouses more false hopes than one good watermelon at the beginning of the season.

Dates & Places Used:

288

TOPIC: Discretion

Face the Facts Boldly

An Englishman went abroad, leaving his much-loved dog and servant home. While away, the man received a cablegram from the servant with the message saying, "Your dog died." The man was most distraught both at the news and the abrupt manner it was sent. Upon returning home, he upbraided the servant for not breaking the news to him more gently. Confused, the servant asked his master how such news could have been delivered more gently. The man said he could have sent a first cable saying, "Your dog is stuck on the roof." This could be followed the next day with the message, "Your dog fell from the roof and is doing poorly." Later a third message could have said, "Your beloved dog has gone to his eternal reward." Some time afterwards, the man went abroad again. While there, he received a cable from his servant saying, "Your mother is stuck on the roof."

Dates & Places Used:

289 TOPIC: Discretion

Sin Will Find a Way Out

When her daughters were very small girls, Mrs. Dwight Morrow gave a high tea at which one of the guests was to be the senior J. P. Morgan. The girls were to be brought in, introduced, and ushered out. Mrs. Morrow's great fear was the possibility that Anne, the most outspoken of them, might comment audibly upon Mr. Morgan's celebrated and conspicuous nose. She therefore took pains beforehand to explain to Anne that personal observations were impolite and cautioned her especially against making any comment about Mr. Morgan's nose, no matter what she might think of it. When the moment came and the children were brought in, Mrs. Morrow held her breath as she saw Anne's gaze fix upon the banker's most prominent facial feature and remain there. Nonetheless, the introduction was made without incident. The little girls curtsied politely and were sent on their way. With a sigh of relief, Mrs. Morrow turned back to her duties as hostess and inquired of her guest, "And now, Mr. Morgan, will you have cream or lemon in your nose?"

Dates & Places Used:

290

TOPIC: Disobedience

Insincere Warning

If you know what a wine brick is, you were drinking during prohibition. When wine was outlawed, bootleggers began to press grape concentrate into the form of bricks, which wasn't against the law. On the label this warning was printed: "Do not let this brick sit in a gallon of water for 21 days. It will ferment and become illegal wine."

Dates & Places Used:

291

TOPIC: Divorce

Mixed Motives

Arnold Schwarzenegger is quoted as saying: "I read where one wife plans to divorce her husband as soon as she can find a way to do so without making him happy."

Dates & Places Used:

292

TOPIC: Doctors

The High Cost of Love

The rancher's daughter had just broken off her engagement with a young doctor. "Do you mean to tell me," exclaimed her girl friend, "that he actually asked you to return all his presents?"

The ranch gal nodded. "Not only that," she replied, "he also sent me a bill for forty-four house calls!"

Dates & Places Used:

293

TOPIC: Doctors

Plan B

I have a very fine doctor. If you can't afford the operation, he touches up the X-rays. *(Henny Youngman)*
Dates & Places Used:

294

TOPIC: Doctors

Foot Doctor

I went to visit the doctor with my sore foot. He said, "I'll have you walking in an hour." He did. He stole my car. *(Henny Youngman)*
Dates & Places Used:

295

TOPIC: Doctors

Confidence in Experts

Surgeon to patient: "I had to remove one of your livers, but you'll be up and around in no time, or I don't know my medicine."
Dates & Places Used:

296

TOPIC: Donations

Perennial Pledges

Nothing lasts forever—with the possible exception of public broadcasting pledge weeks.
Dates & Places Used:

297

A Hard Winter

The winter had been especially difficult in the mountains of North Carolina. Heavy snowfall and cold temperatures had allowed the snow to accumulate to several feet at the higher elevations. The people who lived in the small mountain village located in a valley became concerned about an older couple who lived in an isolated cabin up on the mountainside. No one had seen either the husband or the wife for several weeks. Realizing that they were snowed in, the villagers would watch for smoke coming from the cabin chimney. One day when smoke was no longer apparent, the people of the village decided to call in the Red Cross. A helicopter flew over the cabin but no sign of life could be seen. Two Red Cross workers equipped with medical supplies and food parachuted into a clearing some distance from the cabin. The two young men made their way through the deep snow, clearing a path to the door of the cabin. One of them knocked. Momentarily an old man appeared at the door. The young rescuer replied, "We are from the Red Cross." The old man looked at him and said, "Well, you know it has been a right hard winter up here and I just don't hardly see how we can give anything this year."

Dates & Places Used:

298

New Sources of Funds

For a number of years, Andrew Carnegie, whose wife loved classical music, made up the annual deficit of the New York Philharmonic Society. Then one year, at a meeting of the directors, he made the suggestion that the responsibility should not be his alone. He told them, "From now on, I think the burden should be shared. You raise half the deficit from other donors, and I will give you the remaining half." A few days later the directors informed the philanthropist that his condition had been met. He was pleased by the news. He said, "I told you the money could be

easily raised. Where did you get it?" They replied, "We got it from Mrs. Carnegie."
Dates & Places Used:

299

TOPIC: Doubt

Persisting Unbelief

A man and his dog are walking along the beach when they come upon another visitor to the beach. The owner of the dog is proud of his dog's newly mastered feat—so he says to the visitor, "Watch this!" He tosses a piece of driftwood far out into the sea and the dog immediately runs on top of the ocean and fetches the wood and runs back. The visitor just shakes his head in disbelief. Whereupon the owner repeats the procedure twice. Finally he asks the visitor, "Did you notice anything unusual?"

The visitor responds, "Your dog can't swim, can he?"
Dates & Places Used:

300

TOPIC: Drivers

Watch Out

While driving down the road, a woman hit a man crossing the street. She yelled, "Watch out!"

"Why?" asked the man, "Are you coming back?"
Dates & Places Used:

301

TOPIC: Drivers

Part-Time Idiots

One day as a young mother and her kindergarten-aged son were driving down the street, the inquisitive little boy asked a revealing question. He asked, "Mommy, why do the idiots only come out when Daddy drives?"
Dates & Places Used:

302

TOPIC: Drivers

Don't Give Up

A hesitant driver, waiting for traffic to clear, came to a complete stop on a freeway ramp. The traffic thinned, but the intimidated driver still waited. Finally, an infuriated voice yelled from behind, "The sign says to yield, not to give up."
Dates & Places Used:

303

Topic: Drunkenness

Better Than Lame

In *Man of the House: The Life and Political Memoirs of Speaker Tip O'Neill*, Mr. O'Neill tells an old Irish story something like this: It's about Uncle Denny, who is walking down the street and meets the pastor. He says, "Good morning, Father." The pastor replies, "Good morning yourself. Denny, you ought to be ashamed of yourself. Three weeks ago you came in and took the pledge and vowed that you'd never take another drink as long as you live. And now look at you—you're drunk!" Uncle Denny says, "I'm not drunk, Father. What makes you say a thing like that? I'm not drunk at all." The pastor replies, "Well, if you're not drunk, then why were you walking along with one foot on the curbstone and one foot in the gutter?" Denny says, "I was?" "Indeed you were." And Uncle Denny replies, "Well, thanks be to the Good Lord, I thought I was lame."
Dates & Places Used:

304

TOPIC: Easter

Get the Story Straight

The teacher was extremely enthusiastic. She looked at the class of four-year-olds and asked this question: "Does anyone know what today is?" A little girl held up her finger and said,

"Yes, today is Palm Sunday." The teacher exclaimed, "That's fantastic. That's wonderful. Now does anyone know what next Sunday is?" The same little girl held up her finger. She said, "Yes, next Sunday is Easter Sunday." Once again the teacher said "That's fantastic. Now, does anyone know what makes next Sunday Easter?" The same little girl responded and said, "Yes, next Sunday is Easter because Jesus rose from the grave." Before the teacher could congratulate her, she kept on talking and said, "But if he sees his shadow, he has to go back in for seven weeks."
Dates & Places Used:

305

TOPIC: Easter

Happy Ending

Young Jonathan, who had been promised a new puppy for his tenth birthday, had a tough time choosing one from the dozen likely candidates at the neighborhood pet shop. Finally he decided on one nondescript shaggy pup who was wagging his tail furiously. Explained Jonathan, "I want the one with the happy ending." In the resurrection of Jesus Christ, God offers us a "happy ending."
Dates & Places Used:

306

TOPIC: Easter

An Easter Rose

The youngster came home from Sunday school on Easter Sunday and told his mother he could understand about Christ but not about the roses. So he asked his mom, "Why was Christ a rose?"
Dates & Places Used:

307

TOPIC: Economics

Change the Answers

A university alumnus, shown a list of examination questions by his old economics professor, exclaimed, "Why, those are the same questions you asked when I was in school twenty years ago!" "Yes," said the professor, "we ask the same questions every year." The alumnus said, "But surely you know that students pass along the questions from one year to the next." "Of course," said the professor, "but in economics, we change the answers."

Dates & Places Used:

308

TOPIC: Economics

Christmas Corsage

On January 1 a certain man's New Year's resolution was to become a nonconformist. For instance, he resolved never again to take part in the overcommercialization of Christmas. He would become a shopping-mall dropout. "To think," he said angrily, "that I paid fifteen dollars for a Christmas tree, and on Christmas Day my wife wore it as a corsage!"

Dates & Places Used:

309

TOPIC: Economists

Economic Clarity

Alan Greenspan, Federal Reserve Chairman, at age 62 before speaking on the economy to the 323rd meeting of the Economic Club of New York: "I guess I should warn you, if I turn out to be particularly clear, you've probably misunderstood what I've said."

Dates & Places Used:

310

TOPIC: Economists

Seeing the Future

Isn't it strange? The same people who laugh at gypsy fortune-tellers take economists seriously.

Dates & Places Used:

311

TOPIC: Education

Character Crisis

Six-year-old Mark was thumbing through a Japanese cookbook and asked about the squiggly symbols. His father explained that they were Japanese words, and that he couldn't read them.

Mark paused and said, "Well, sound them out!"

Dates & Places Used:

312

TOPIC: Education

Unspoiled Motivation

Avis Hewett's second-grade Sunday school class had been emphasizing the memorization of Scripture. One little seven-year-old was beginning to get into the program. And it seems he was working on his memory work at home.

His dad was inquiring into the whole procedure and asked him what prize or reward he would get if he learned all those verses.

His son eyed him with that simple childlike look and said, "We get to learn more!"

Dates & Places Used:

313

TOPIC: Education

You, Me, and We

John Berger, the principal, encountered a ninth-grade boy walking out of room 209 with a dour expression on his face. The concerned principal asked the boy, "And how are we today?"

The boy replied, "Awful. I don't understand all that stuff the math teacher wants us to learn—all those logarithms and postulates and stuff."

The principal said smoothly and comfortingly, "Well, I'm sure we can't find it all that bad, can we?"

The boy huffed back, "Well, sure we can say that! Because the you half of we doesn't have to learn that stuff all over again with the me half of we."

Dates & Places Used:

314

TOPIC: Education

Much Responsibility

A college professor gave his class a chance to evaluate his course. One of his students wrote, "I think this is an excellent class, but I am concerned that the professor puts too much responsibility for learning on the students."

Dates & Places Used:

315

TOPIC: Effort

Attempting Failure

If you have tried to do something and failed, you are vastly better off than if you had tried to do nothing and succeeded.

Dates & Places Used:

TOPIC: Emergencies

Going to Get Help

Once, when some people were riding in a four-engine propeller airplane over Kansas, three of the engines conked out. Immediately the cabin door opened, and the pilot appeared with a parachute on his back. "Keep calm, folks, and don't panic!" he ordered. "I'm going for help!"

Dates & Places Used:

TOPIC: Emergencies

That's More Like It

A frontier couple, Zeb and Martha, built a cabin, a barn, and a corral for their livestock. Zeb hung a big bell in a tree and explained, "There are renegades around here, Martha. If you need me, ring the bell—but only in an emergency." Days later, as Zeb was cutting wood in the fields, he heard the bell ring. He headed home at full gallop. "What's wrong?" "I just thought maybe you'd like some fresh coffee," Martha said. "Tarnation, woman, the bell is for emergencies. Half the day is gone, and I still have chores to do." Once more he rode out. Just as he picked up the ax, he heard the bell. Again he raced home. "The washtub's leaking," reported Martha. "That ain't no blasted emergency! I've gotta cut the wood." Two hours later Zeb was chopping down a tree and the bell rang. He charged home to find the cabin in flames, the barn burned to the ground, and his cattle stampeding away. Martha was near the bell, with an arrow in her shoulder. "Now, Martha," Zeb exclaimed, "this is more like it!"

Dates & Places Used:

318

TOPIC: Emotions

Emotive Friends

Dr. Steven Brown gave the following account: "Jimmy Durante once said, I couldn't warm up to that guy if we were cremated together." Steve Brown added, "True, but if you were crucified together you might have a shot at it."
Dates & Places Used:

319

TOPIC: Empathy

Both Drunk

Father O'Reilly reprimanded one of his parishioners who was staggering out of a bar. "Drunk again!" "Me too," admitted the man.
Dates & Places Used:

320

TOPIC: Empathy

Movie Cue

A small boy went to the movies with his still smaller brother and, after they'd seated themselves, asked, "Can you see, Willie?" "Nope," was the reply. "Well," said the older brother, "just laugh when I laugh."
Dates & Places Used:

321

TOPIC: Empathy

Limp Understanding

A surgeon was discussing a case with medical students: "The muscle in the patient's right leg has contracted until it is shorter

than the left. Therefore, he limps. What would you do in such a circumstance?" A student raised his hand and said, "I'd limp too."
Dates & Places Used:

322
TOPIC: Empathy
Talkers and Walkers

An old Spanish proverb observes: "Two great talkers will not travel far together."
Dates & Places Used:

323
TOPIC: Employee
Model Motivation

On an employee bulletin board: "In case of fire, flee the building with the same reckless abandon that occurs each day at quitting time."
Dates & Places Used:

324
TOPIC: Encouragement
Share Troubles

The cynic says: "Don't bother telling people your troubles. Half of them don't care, and the other half figure you probably had it coming."
Dates & Places Used:

325

TOPIC: Encouragement

New Blessings

One discouraged salesman said to another: "What I need is a blessing that *isn't* in disguise."
Dates & Places Used:

326

TOPIC: Enemies

Enemies Accumulate

"Friends come and go, but enemies accumulate." *(Chuck Swindoll)*
Dates & Places Used:

327

TOPIC: Energy

Temporal Generation Gap

It's hard to know just where one generation ends and the next one begins, but it's somewhere around 9 P.M.
Dates & Places Used:

328

TOPIC: Eternity

Eternal Epitaph

I am told that an Indiana cemetery has a tombstone over one hundred years old that bears the following epitaph: "Pause Stranger, when you pass me by. As you are now, so once was I. As I am now, so you will be. So prepare for death and follow me." An unknown passerby read those words and underneath scratched this reply: "To follow you I'm not content, Until I know which way you went." *(J.M. Kennedy)*
Dates & Places Used:

329

TOPIC: Evangelism

Generation of Mules

The church today is raising a whole generation of mules. They know how to sweat and to work hard but they don't know how to reproduce themselves.
Dates & Places Used:

330

TOPIC: Evangelism

Evangelism Methods

A woman criticized D. L. Moody for his methods of evangelism in attempting to win people to the Lord. Moody replied, "I agree with you. I don't like the way I do it either. Tell me, how do you do it?" The woman replied, "I don't do it." Moody retorted, "Then I like my way of doing it better than your way of not doing it."
Dates & Places Used:

331

TOPIC: Evangelism

Limited Atonement

A while ago my friends were amazed to hear their five-year-old daughter, Lindsay, telling her little friend about Jesus. The children were sitting on the front steps of the house, and the parents tiptoed up to the window to see and hear better.

Lindsay told her friend that if she believed in Jesus and prayed, he would forgive her sins and she would go to heaven. The little girl was convinced, and prayed.

When she was done praying, she looked up at my friend's daughter and asked, "Will my mommy be in heaven too?"

Lindsay thought for a moment and replied, "Yeah, if she believes in Jesus. But if you don't want her there, don't tell her about Jesus!"
Dates & Places Used:

332

TOPIC: Evangelism

A Better Way

One evening, after a particularly grueling rehearsal of a locally produced Passion play, one of the cast members—who had a particularly bad time remembering his lines—was heard to say, "I've finally figured out why God wants me in this play. He's trying to teach me how easy street evangelism is!"

Dates & Places Used:

333

TOPIC: Excuses

Best Alibi

When the Police League of Indiana sponsored a Best Speeding Alibi contest, one honorable mention award went to an exasperated father who was stopped with a load of fighting, squalling children in his backseat.

He told the officer, "I was trying to get away from all the noise behind me."

Dates & Places Used:

334

TOPIC: Excuses

Worst Alibi

This story comes from the *Pittsburgh Press:* "George Shamblin insisted to police that he was trying to save his wife from drowning when he threw rocks at her as she struggled in the Kanawha River. 'I was trying to drive her back to shore,' he said."

Dates & Places Used:

335

TOPIC: Excuses

Accidents

Some people who had automobile accidents were asked to summarize on their insurance forms exactly what happened. The following quotes were taken from these forms and published in the *Toronto Sun* on July 20, 1977:

Coming home, I drove into the wrong house and collided with a tree I don't have. I collided with a stationary truck coming the other way. The guy was all over the road; I had to swerve a number of times before I hit him. I had been driving my car for 40 years when I fell asleep at the wheel and had an accident. My car was legally parked as it backed into the other vehicle. An invisible car came out of nowhere, struck my vehicle and vanished. I told the police that I was not injured, but on removing my hat, I found that I had a skull fracture. The pedestrian had no idea of which way to go, so I ran over him. The indirect cause of this accident was a little guy in a small car with a big mouth. The telephone pole was approaching fast; I was attempting to swerve out of its path when it struck me.

Dates & Places Used:

336

TOPIC: Excuses

Number Seven Rejection

Some girls in a college dorm had the problem of what to do when they wanted to turn down a date with someone they didn't want to go out with. To solve the problem one of them wrote a list of ten handy excuses and tacked them up next to the phone in the hall. It worked pretty well except for the time one girl got flustered and said to the earnest caller, "I'd love to go out with you, Tom, but I can't—because of Number Seven."

Dates & Places Used:

337

TOPIC: Excuses

Flight Patterns

It's tough to soar with eagles when you work with turkeys.
Dates & Places Used:

338

TOPIC: Excuses

Making Something

We are all manufacturers. Some make good, others make trouble, and still others make excuses.
Dates & Places Used:

339

TOPIC: Excuses

Notable Excuses

The *Associated Press* ran a story recently about some excuses that were sent into Leesville High School in Louisiana. They were compiled by the Assistant Principal Richard Carter. Some were probably made up by the students; others might well have been written by the parents in this rural northwest Louisiana parish. When they were printed, the students kept their anonymity by being given the names of Mary or Fred.

"My son is under the doctor's care and should not take Physical Education today," one parent wrote. "Please execute him." "Please excuse Mary for being absent. She was sick and I had her shot." "Mary was absent from school yesterday as she was having a gangover," wrote one parent who apparently expected the school to be tolerant of social follies. "Mary could not come to school today because she was bothered by very close veins."

"Fred has an acre in his side." And lastly, the most generic excuse of all: "Please excuse Fred for being. It was his father's fault."
Dates & Places Used:

340

A Ready Excuse

Frank Robinson, the local sci-fi writer, was browsing through a used-book store and found a copy of his novel, *The Gold Crew*, autographed warmly to his friend, Burleigh Sutton.

A mutual friend, Tom Youngblood, was there when the book was discovered in the bookstore and couldn't wait to warn his friend, Burleigh, "You've been found out!"

But the next time Burleigh ran into Robinson, the author, at a party, his first words were: "Frank! Did you hear about my burglary?"

Dates & Places Used:

341

Alibi

A husband and wife were sitting in a movie theater, engrossed in a suspenseful Hollywood "whodunit" in which there were at least a dozen possible murder suspects. "I bet Paul Newman is the killer," whispered the wife to her spouse. "Don't be dumb," came the reply. "Paul Newman isn't even in this picture." "That's what I mean!" exclaimed the wife. "What an alibi!"

Dates & Places Used:

342

Man Needs a Wife

Every man needs a wife, because there are many things that go wrong that he can't blame on the government.

Dates & Places Used:

343

TOPIC: Exercise

Entertaining Exercise

One way to get more exercise is to put your TV at one end of your house and the refrigerator at the other.
Dates & Places Used:

344

TOPIC: Expectations

All Goes Wrong

A young paratrooper was learning to jump. He was given the following instructions: First, jump when you are told, second, count ten and pull the ripcord, third, in the very unlikely event that it doesn't open, pull the second chute open, and fourth, when you get down, a truck will take you back to the base. The plane ascended up to the proper height, the men started peeling out, and the young paratrooper jumped when told. He counted to ten and pulled the cord, but the chute failed to open. He proceeded to the back-up plan: he pulled the cord of the second chute. It, too, failed to open. "And I suppose," he complained to himself, "the truck won't be there either when I get down."
Dates & Places Used:

345

TOPIC: Expectations

I'll Alter Him

A nervous young bride was counseled by her pastor: "When you enter the church tomorrow, you will once again walk down the aisle you've walked down so many times before. Concentrate on that. And when you get halfway down the aisle, concentrate on the altar, where you and your family have worshiped for so many years. Concentrate on that. And as you reach the end of the aisle, your groom will be waiting for you. Concentrate on him."

It worked to perfection, and on her wedding day the nervous bride boldly completed her processional. But people in the audience were a bit taken aback to hear her chanting, all the way down the aisle, what they understood as "I'll–alter–him."

Dates & Places Used:

346

TOPIC: Expectations

Very Pious Thinking

The pastor asked his children, "What's gray, has a bushy tail, and gathers nuts in the fall?" One child hesitantly answered, "I know the answer should be Jesus," he began, "but it sure sounds like a squirrel to me."

Dates & Places Used:

347

TOPIC: Expectations

The Previous Pastor

The new pastor wasn't at all like the former pastor. He didn't care to do the repairs and mowing around the church and parsonage. He hired someone to do these chores. The additional cost concerned the church elders. One of them approached the new pastor and addressed this issue, "Our previous pastor mowed the lawn himself. Have you considered this approach?" The new pastor responded, "Yes, I'm aware of this. And I asked him. But he doesn't want to do it anymore!"

Dates & Places Used:

348

TOPIC: Expenses

Poise

Poise is the ability to keep talking while the other person picks up the check.

Dates & Places Used:

349

TOPIC: Experience

Experience Mistakes

Experience is a wonderful thing. It enables you to recognize a mistake when you make it again.

Dates & Places Used:

350

TOPIC: Experience

Help from Experience

Two hunters flew deep into the remote backwoods of Canada to hunt elk. They bagged six elk. The pilot told them the plane could carry only four of the elk out. "But the plane that carried us out last year was exactly like this one," the hunters protested. "The horsepower was the same, the weather was similar, and we had six elk then." Hearing this, the pilot reluctantly agreed to try. They loaded up and took off, but sure enough, there was insufficient power to climb out of the valley with all that weight, and they crashed. As they stumbled from the wreckage, one hunter asked the other if he knew where they were. "Well, I'm not sure," replied the second, "but I think we are about two miles from where we crashed last year."

Dates & Places Used:

351

Price of Experience

When a person with experience meets a person with money, the person with experience will get the money. And the person with the money will get experience. *(Leonard Lauder)*
Dates & Places Used:

352

TOPIC: Experience

Profit from Failure

A young man of thirty-two had been newly appointed president of the bank. He approached the venerable Chairman of the Board and asked for advice. The old man came back with just two words: "Right decisions!" The young man responded, "That's really helpful, and I appreciate it, but can you be more specific? How do I make right decisions?" The wise old man simply responded, "Experience." The young man said, "Well, that's just the point of my being here. I don't have the kind of experience I need. How do I get it?" Came the terse reply, "Wrong decisions!"
Dates & Places Used:

353

TOPIC: Experience

Careful Tracking

A cowboy was riding across the prairie and he came across another, who was lying on the ground with his ear to a wagon track. The following conversation then took place:
Second cowboy: "Wagon, two horses—one white, one black. Man is driving, smoking pipe. Woman has blue dress, wears a bonnet."
First cowboy: "You mean you can tell all that by listening to the ground?"
Second cowboy: "No! It ran over me, half an hour ago."
Dates & Places Used:

354

Bad Timing

Experience is the comb we receive after we've lost our hair.
Dates & Places Used:

355

A Quick Count

A census taker knocked on the door of a backwoods shack. A fellow came to the door. "The president has sent us across the country to find out how many people live in the United States." The man replied. "I'm sorry you came all the way out here to ask me, 'cause I ain't got the faintest idea."
Dates & Places Used:

356

Plans

During World War II, General MacArthur called in one of his Army engineers and asked, "How long will it take to throw a bridge across this river?" The man immediately responded: "Three days." MacArthur snapped back, "Good. Have your draftsmen make drawings right away."

Three days later MacArthur sent for the engineer and asked how the bridge was coming along. The engineer reported, "It's all ready. You can send your troops across right now if you don't have to wait for the plans. They aren't done yet."
Dates & Places Used:

357

Authoritative Advice

While enjoying a transatlantic cruise, Billie Burke, the famous actress, noticed that a gentleman was suffering from a bad cold. She asked him sympathetically, "Are you uncomfortable?" The man nodded. She said, "I'll tell you just what to do for it. Go back to your stateroom and drink lots of orange juice. Take two aspirins. Cover yourself with all the blankets you can find. Sweat the cold out. I know just what I'm talking about. I'm Billie Burke from Hollywood." The man smiled warmly and introduced himself in return. He said, "Thanks. I'm Dr. Mayo of the Mayo Clinic."

Dates & Places Used:

358

Explanations

Just before a presidential election, a lowly Democratic party candidate was worried about the outcome. He was concerned that voters did not know about the election. He appealed to the committee to get a big sign and music to rally the people. The committee finally agreed to give him $100 to rent a truck. Off rushed the man, and on Saturday afternoon, as Iowans shopped, the truck rumbled by, music blaring, placards urging a vote for the Democratic party. On Tuesday Democrats across the nation swept into office, winning the presidency, fifteen U. S. Senate seats, ten governorships, including Iowa's, the local Congressional district as well as control of the U. S. House of Representatives, the city manager race, and three out of five ward alderman races. At local headquarters, amid all the joy, the victorious candidate approached the committeeman and jubilantly exclaimed, "What did I tell you? It was the truck!"

Dates & Places Used:

359

TOPIC: Failure

Deadly Experience

If at first you don't succeed, so much for sky-diving.
Dates & Places Used:

360

TOPIC: Failure

Win or Lose

It doesn't make any difference whether you win or lose—until you lose. ("Peanuts")
Dates & Places Used:

361

TOPIC: Failure

Who's Blamed?

A professional football coach was hired to manage the team. They had been experiencing a bad season. As with all football teams, if they don't win, the coach is replaced. To succeed in football you must win. The new coach was given two sealed envelopes when he accepted the coaching position. He was told that when he got into difficulty the next season, he should open the first sealed envelope. It was a note of encouragement from the former coach telling him that he should blame everything on him. He released the information that the present failures of the team were because of the former coach.

If the disappointment of the season persisted, he was to open the second sealed letter. This he did. The terse note merely read: "Prepare two envelopes!"
Dates & Places Used:

362

TOPIC: Failure

Wrong Horse Won

Two Kentucky farmers who owned racing stables had developed a keen rivalry. One spring, each of them entered a horse in a local steeplechase. Thinking that a professional rider might help him outdo his friend, one of the farmers engaged a crack jockey. The two horses were leading the race at the last fence, but it proved too tough for them. Both horses fell, unseating their riders. But this calamity did not stop the professional jockey. He quickly remounted and won the race.

Returning triumphant to the paddock, the jockey found the farmer who had hired him fuming with rage. "What's the matter?" the jockey asked. "I won, didn't I?" "Oh, yes," roared the farmer. "You won all right, but you still don't know, do you?" "Know what?" asked the jockey. "You won the race on the wrong horse."

Dates & Places Used:

363

TOPIC: Faith

Believe It to See It

Some things must be believed before they can be seen.

Dates & Places Used:

364

TOPIC: Faithfulness

Preacher's Prayer

The old Nazarene evangelist Bud Robinson is reported to have prayed the following prayer each day: "O Lord, give me a backbone as big as a saw log and ribs like the sleepers under the church floor. Put iron shoes on my feet and galvanized breeches on my body. Give me a rhinoceros hide for skin and hang up a wagon-load of determination in the gable-end of my soul. Help me to sign the contract to fight the devil as long as I've got a tooth—and then gum him until I die."

Dates & Places Used:

TOPIC: Fame

Stained-Glass Fame

A young boy, away at boarding school, wrote home after his first visit to the school's chapel: "It has lovely stained-glass windows with pictures of people who were famous in God's time."

Dates & Places Used:

TOPIC: Family

The Growing Family

A bride brought her new husband up to meet Granny at the family picnic. The old woman looked the young fellow over carefully and then said to him, "Young man, do you desire to have children?" He was a bit startled by her candid approach but finally came out with, "Well, yes, as a matter of fact, I do." She looked at him scornfully and then surveyed the very large clan of children gathered around half a dozen picnic tables and said, "Well, try to control it!"

Dates & Places Used:

367

TOPIC: Farmers

Subsidized Farming

Two farmers each won a million dollars in the state lottery. The first farmer said he was going to use his money to retire, move to Florida, and live the good life." When the second farmer was asked what he planned to do, he replied, "I don't know, I think I'll just keep on farming until it's all used up."
Dates & Places Used:

368

TOPIC: Fashion

Nerd Dad

You know it's going to be a bad day when your teen-ager asks to wear your clothes to school on Nerd Day.
Dates & Places Used:

369

TOPIC: Fashion

Law of Clothes Life

A bad-fitting suit never wears out.
Dates & Places Used:

370

TOPIC: Fathers

Collect Calls

Illinois Bell Telephone reports that the volume of long-distance calls on Father's Day is growing faster than the number on Mother's Day. The delay in compiling the statistics was attributed to the extra billing of calls: most of them were collect.
Dates & Places Used:

371

Getting Rid of Daddy

A family talked Mother into getting a hamster as long as they took care of the creature. Two months later, when Mother was caring for Danny the hamster, she made some phone calls and found a new home for him. She broke the news to the children, and they took it quite well; but they did offer some comments. One of the children remarked, "He's been around here a long time—we'll miss him." Mom agreed, saying, "Yes, but he's too much work for one person, and since I'm that one person, I say he goes." Another child offered, "Well, maybe if he wouldn't eat so much and wouldn't be so messy, we could keep him." But Mom was firm. "It's time to take Danny to his new home now," she insisted. "Go and get his cage." With one voice and in tearful outrage the children shouted, "Danny? We thought you said 'Daddy'!"

Dates & Places Used:

372

Kidding Aside

A five-year-old boy had a very precocious interest in motorcycles. Whenever he saw one, he would let out a howl of joy, accompanied by animated remarks like, "Look at that! Look at that! I'm going to get a motorcycle someday." His father's answer was always the same, "Not so long as I'm alive, you won't." One day, while the boy was talking to his friend, a brand new stylish bike zoomed by. He excitedly pointed it out to the boy and exclaimed, "Look at that! Look at that! I'm getting one of those—as soon as my dad dies."

Dates & Places Used:

373

Fear of Zeal

As a child Theodore Roosevelt was called "Teedie." His mother Mittie had found he was so afraid of the Madison Square Church that he refused to set foot inside if he was alone. So she pressed him to tell her why. He was terrified, she discovered, of something called the "zeal." He had heard the minister read about it from the Bible. Using a concordance, she read him those particular passages containing the word "zeal" until suddenly, very excited, he told her to stop. The line was from John 2:17 (KJV): "And his disciples remembered that it was written, The zeal of thine house hath eaten me up."

Dates & Places Used:

374

Equal Time

A little boy and girl had just been introduced and were trying to decide what game to play, and the little boy said, "I have an idea! Let's play baseball!" But the little girl said, "Oh, no, I wouldn't want to do that; baseball is a boy's game. It's not feminine to run around on a dusty vacant lot. No, I wouldn't want to play baseball." So the boy replied, "Okay, then, let's play football." She answered, "Oh, no, I wouldn't play football. That's even less feminine. I might fall and get dirty. No, that's not a girl's game." He said, "Okay, I've got an idea. I'll race you to the corner." She replied, "No, girls play quiet games; we don't run and get all sweaty. Girls should never race with boys." The boy then scratched his head, trying to think of what she might want to do, and finally he said, "Okay, then, let's play house." She said, "Good! I'll be the daddy!"

Dates & Places Used:

375

The Modern Woman

Woman to her date: "Tell me, Donald, do you think I'm too aggressive? I want a straight answer, and I want it now."
Dates & Places Used:

376

TOPIC: Feminism

Revealed Secrets

I'm furious about the Women's Liberationists. They keep getting on soapboxes and proclaiming that women are brighter than men. That's true, but it should be kept very quiet or it ruins the whole racket.
Dates & Places Used:

377

TOPIC: Fishing

Costly Catch

Two men from Minnesota went fishing up in Canada. They caught only one fish. When they got back, one of them said, "I figured out that fish cost us $400." "Well," said the other one, "at that price it's a good thing we didn't catch any more than one!"
Dates & Places Used:

378

TOPIC: Fishing

Liquid Courage

Two fellows were bass fishing out on a lake, side by side in a boat. But the one fellow was getting all the fish. The other had nary a nibble. After watching his buddy pull in all the fish, he finally got exasperated and said, "I just don't understand this at all. Here we are, sitting in the same boat, on the same lake, using the same kind of pole, the same kind of bait, and yet you're getting all the fish. I just don't get it." The other fellow smiled and said, "Well, my bait has a PLUS FACTOR." So the first fellow looked in his buddy's bait pail and did notice that his minnows were swimming around with a great deal more enthusiasm than were his own. He investigated more closely and then realized that his friend had poured some brandy into his bait bucket. So, he reached over to the brandy bottle and gave his minnows a good dose of spirits too. He then tied a fresh minnow on his line and threw it in. Immediately he had a strike. Wow! It was a five-pound fish. And that poor bass didn't have a chance. The minnow had a death grip around his throat!

Dates & Places Used:

379

TOPIC: Fishing

Just in Case

Seen on a bumper sticker: "Work is for those who don't know how to fish!"

Dates & Places Used:

380

TOPIC: Flexibility

Credit for Long Life

A reporter asked a man on his ninety-fifth birthday, "To what do you credit your long life?" The old-timer responded, "Well, I'm not sure yet. My lawyer's negotiating with two breakfast-cereal companies."

Dates & Places Used:

381

TOPIC: Flexibility

Flexible Building

A farmer was seen erecting a new building. When asked what he was building, he replied, "Well, that depends; if I can rent it, then it's a rustic cottage. If I can't, then it's a cow shed."
Dates & Places Used:

382

TOPIC: Flexibility

It's Relative!

Manager: "I'm sorry I can't hire you. There just isn't enough work to keep you busy."

Applicant: "You'd be surprised how little it takes."
Dates & Places Used:

383

TOPIC: Focus

The One Who Is Seen

There are two types of people in the world: Those who come into a room and say, "Here I am!" and those who say, "Ah, there you are!"
Dates & Places Used:

384

TOPIC: Foolishness

Intellectual Limits

Genius has limits; stupidity does not.
Dates & Places Used:

385

TOPIC: Forgiveness

Partial Forgiveness

Two little brothers, Harry and James, had finished supper and were playing until bedtime. Somehow, Harry hit James with a stick, and tears and bitter words followed. Charges and accusations were still being exchanged as mother prepared them for bed.

The mother instructed, "Now, James, before you go to bed you're going to have to forgive your brother." James was thoughtful for a few moments, and then he replied, "Well OK, I'll forgive him tonight, but if I don't die before I wake up, he'd better look out in the morning."

Dates & Places Used:

386

TOPIC: Forgiveness

Deserves to Forgive

Martin Luther's colleague, Philip Melanchthon, vexed his more ebullient friend by his quiet and virtuous ways. "For goodness' sake, why don't you go and sin a little?" cried Luther in exasperation. "Doesn't God deserve to have something to forgive you for?"

Dates & Places Used:

387

TOPIC: Friends

Acquaintance

An acquaintance is a person whom we know well enough to borrow from, but not well enough to lend to. *(Ambrose Bierce)*
Dates & Places Used:

388

Fit to Kill

During World War II pianist and wit Oscar Levant appeared before the draft-board examiner. The official asked him, "Do you think you can kill?"

Levant answered, "I don't know about strangers, but friends, yes."

Dates & Places Used:

389

A Friend

A true friend is one who dislikes the same people you dislike.

Dates & Places Used:

390

Brilliant Conversation

A gossip talks about others, a bore talks about himself, and a brilliant conversationalist talks about you.

Dates & Places Used:

391

Who Rubs Off on Whom?

Sid Guillen tells that his mother had an interesting way of describing the importance of keeping good company. She used to say, "You don't work in the garden with white gloves. The gloves will become dirty, the dirt will not become glovey."

Dates & Places Used:

TOPIC: Friends

Friends

Good old friends are worth keeping whether you like them or not. *(Andy Rooney)*
Dates & Places Used:

TOPIC: Friends

Endearment

When you have a lot of rough edges, you're easy to get hold of but hard to embrace.
Dates & Places Used:

TOPIC: Friends

394

Don't Explain

Never explain your actions; your friends do not need it, and your enemies will not believe it anyway.
Dates & Places Used:

TOPIC: Frugality

395

Looking Out for Mom

A penny-pinching miser defended himself against criticism aimed at his parsimonious ways. He said in his own defense, "Why, I couldn't stand for my mother to go on year after year, working every night, scrubbing and cleaning office floors, so I just bought out the office building." The listener asked, "Well, what did you do

for your dear mother then?" The man smiled proudly and said, "Well, she was immediately moved to the day shift."
Dates & Places Used:

396

TOPIC: Frustration

Fruit of Hard Work

A management consultant makes the following observation: "Be the first in the office every morning, be the last to leave every night, never take a day off, slave through the lunch hour, and the inevitable day will come when the boss will summon you to his office and say, 'I've been watching your work very carefully, Jackson. Just what are you up to, anyhow?'"
Dates & Places Used:

397

TOPIC: Function

Worn-Out Water

The guide at the Grand Coulee Dam in Washington State was asked by a tourist: "What is the water good for once they take the electricity out of it?"
Dates & Places Used:

398

TOPIC: Funeral

The Right Man

They were burying a rather unsavory character who had never been near a place of worship in his life. The services were being conducted by a minister who had never heard of him. Carried away by the occasion, he poured on praise for the departed man. After ten minutes of describing the late lamented as an excep-

tional father, husband, and boss, the widow, whose expression had grown more and more puzzled, nudged her son and whispered: "Go up there and make sure it's Papa."
Dates & Places Used:

399 TOPIC: Gambling
Lost Last Two

A young married couple were spending a week at a casino. On the sixth day all they had left was two dollars and an admission ticket to the local race track. They agreed that the young man would take the two dollars to the track and take one last chance. He picked long shots until he had won $10,000. On the way back to the hotel he stopped off at a gambling casino to try once more. Within an hour he had run his bankroll up to a neat $40,000 at roulette. As he was leaving he had a new hunch, and bet their entire $40,000 on the black. The ball bounced, rolled and settled. The croupier called out "Red!" The young man made his way back to the hotel room. His wife asked, "How did you make out?" He replied nonchalantly, "I lost the two dollars!"
Dates & Places Used:

400 TOPIC: Gambling
Raffle Baffle

"We're having a raffle for a poor widow. Would you like to buy a ticket?"

"I'm afraid not. Even if I won, my wife wouldn't let me keep her."
Dates & Places Used:

401 TOPIC: Gambling
A Good Bet

The minister felt sorry for the old man he saw every morning in the park through which he walked to his office. It seemed the world had been hard for him. One morning he handed him an envelope with $10 inside and a note that read, "Never Despair." The next day the man handed him $60. "What is this for?" the astonished minister asked. "Never Despair was in the money paying 6 to 1 odds in the second race," the man answered.

Dates & Places Used:

402

TOPIC: Generations

A Tradition Ended

There is a story about a family who had a treasure. It had been handed down through several generations. It was a genuine antique vase. It was kept on the mantel in the living room as a special object of enjoyment. One day when the lady of the house came home, she was greeted by her daughter. The daughter said, "Mamma, you know that vase you told us has been passed down from generation to generation?" Her mother acknowledged that she did in fact know the vase and her daughter then said, "Mamma, this generation just dropped it."

Our generation has been dropping many things—many of the values, standards, and attitudes about the public good.

Dates & Places Used:

403

TOPIC: Generosity

A Painless Way to Give

Having a little trouble getting enough money in the offering at your church? You may want to try a new approach. There was a minister who told everyone to stand during the offertory at which time he instructed everyone to reach forward to the person standing in front of him and get his pocketbook. Then he added, "Now open the pocketbook and give as you always wanted to, but felt you couldn't afford."

Dates & Places Used:

404

TOPIC: Generosity

Painful Choices

In one particular *Peanuts* comic strip, Linus is watching TV and Lucy comes up behind him with a pad and pencil and says, "Which would you rather have, a stomachache or a headache?"

Linus says, "I don't know . . . a headache, I guess."

As Lucy walks away writing on her pad she says, "Good! I'll put you down for a headache."

Linus turns to the TV and says, "It's nice having someone in charge who's so considerate." ("Peanuts")

Dates & Places Used:

405

TOPIC: Gifts

Practical Gift for Dad

Dad suggested that the family get him a gift that the whole family could get something out of.

So they did. They bought Dad a new wallet.

Dates & Places Used:

406

TOPIC: Gifts

Christmas Shopping Hint

The wisest choice for the man who has everything is a burglar alarm.

Dates & Places Used:

407

TOPIC: Gifts

The Unexpected Gift

My wife still hasn't spoken to me since last Christmas. I asked her what she wanted for Christmas, and she said, "Oh, just surprise me." So, at three o'clock Christmas morning, I leaned over and went, "BOO!"

Dates & Places Used:

408

TOPIC: Gifts

The Gift You Don't Need

Did you hear about the pastor who gave each of his parishioners a gift certificate worth four hours of free advice?

Dates & Places Used:

409

TOPIC: Gifts

Gift Exchange with Jesus

It was the day after Christmas at a church in San Francisco. The pastor of the church was looking over the creche when he noticed that the baby Jesus was missing from among the figures. He hurried outside and saw a little boy with a red wagon, and in the wagon was the figure of the little infant Jesus. So he walked up to the boy and said, "Well, where did you get your passenger, my fine friend?"

The little boy replied, "I got him from the church."

"And why did you take him?"

The boy said, "Well, about a week before Christmas I prayed to the little Lord Jesus and I told him if he would bring me a red wagon for Christmas I would give him a ride around the block in it."

Dates & Places Used:

410

TOPIC: Goals

Life Goals

If you don't have goals in your life, you will never be able to tell if you're a failure.

Dates & Places Used:

411

TOPIC: Goals

Short-Term Goals

Charlie Brown is at bat. STRIKE THREE! He has struck out again and slumps over to the bench. "Rats! I'll never be a big-league player. I just don't have it! All my life I've dreamed of playing in the big leagues, but I know I'll never make it."

Lucy turns to console him. "Charlie Brown, you're thinking too far ahead. What you need to do is set yourself more immediate goals."

He looks up. "Immediate goals?"

Lucy says, "Yes. Start with this next inning when you go out to pitch. See if you can walk out to the mound without falling down!" ("Peanuts")

Dates & Places Used:

412

TOPIC: God's Presence

Omniproblem

A young lad was accompanying his mother to church. They stopped for a quick sandwich along the way. The child ran out of time before he ran out of sandwich. His mother insisted that they had to leave or they would be late. He stuck the sandwich in his pocket to be finished later.

That evening the preacher spoke about the ability of God to be present in all places at each and every given moment. The boy bowed his head during the sermon and prayed, "God, if you are in my pocket, please don't eat my sandwich!"

Dates & Places Used:

413

TOPIC: God's Presence

Let Jesus Get It

A little boy was afraid of the dark. One night his mother told him to go out to the back porch and bring her the broom. The little boy turned to his mother and said, "Mamma, I don't want to go out there. It's dark." The mother smiled reassuringly at her son. "You don't have to be afraid of the dark," she explained. "Jesus is out there. He'll look after you and protect you." The little boy looked at his mother real hard and asked, "Are you sure he's out there?" "Yes, I'm sure. He is everywhere, and he is always ready to help you when you need him," she said. The little boy thought about that for a minute, then went to the back door and cracked it a little. Peering out into the darkness, he called, "Jesus? If you're out there, would you please hand me that broom?"

Dates & Places Used:

414

TOPIC: God's Presence

Low Presence

A pastor boarded an airplane to take the first flight he had ever flown. As they were about to take off, the flight attendant noticed his clerical garb and also his panicky look and his white knuckles as he gripped the seat in semi-terror. She walked over to the pastor and said, "Sir, I'm surprised at you. You are obviously a man of faith—you shouldn't be so nervous about flying. Don't you have any faith in God?" The cleric looked at her and said, "Look, young lady, the promise in Scripture is, 'Lo, I am with you always.' It doesn't say anything about 'High.'"

Dates & Places Used:

415

Missing God

After attending church with his father one Sunday morning and before getting into bed that evening, a little boy knelt at his bedside and prayed, "Dear God, we had a good time at church today, but I wish you had been there."

Dates & Places Used:

416

Your Way or God's Way

Two ministers resolved their doctrinal conflict when one told the other, "Look, what are we fighting over? We're both striving to do the Lord's work. You do it your way and I'll do it his way!"

Dates & Places Used:

417

Guidance on Dieting

An overweight man always stopped by the bakery on his way to work to pick up goodies for the staff coffee break. This practice was scrapped when the man went on a diet, and the staff understood. One day he had to drive by the bakery on a work-related errand. As he approached the old bakery, he said to himself, "Maybe God wants me to stop by the bakery this morning and pick up some goodies for the office." So he told the Lord he would only stop if God made a parking spot available right in front of the bakery. And, sure enough, there it was, a parking spot, right in front of the bakery—on his eighth trip around the block.

Dates & Places Used:

TOPIC: Golf

Golfer's Timing

It seems that Arnold Palmer was invited to come to a convention of blind golfers. The golfers told how they were able to know what direction to hit the ball. One blind golfer explained that the caddy went out ahead of him with a little bell, which he would ring as he stood near the hole. The blind golfer would then hit the ball toward the sound of the bell. Arnold asked how well it worked, and the blind golfer said that it worked so well he was willing to take on Arnold Palmer for a round of golf; and just to make it interesting, was willing to bet Palmer $10,000 he could beat him. Palmer said, "OK. What time do we tee off?" And the blind man said, "10:30 tonight!"

Dates & Places Used:

TOPIC: Golf

Sportsmanlike Conduct

Two men were golfing together near a cemetery. While the one man was preparing to putt, a hearse turned into the cemetery. He immediately looked up, dropped his putter, removed his cap and bowed his head. After a couple of minutes he returned his attention to golf. When the two men returned to the clubhouse, his partner told the man that he was deeply moved by the respect shown toward the deceased. The man acknowledged him by saying, "I really feel it was the least I could do after being married to her for the last thirty-four years."

Dates & Places Used:

TOPIC: Golf

One Last Fling

A friend of mine was with a group of golfers watching a fellow who was having some difficulty on this particular course. The frustration became too much by the 13th hole, as this poor guy placed shot after shot into the pond. Finally, in complete exasperation he picked up his golf bag, spun around like a discus thrower, and heaved the whole thing into the middle of the lake, and stormed off the course, apparently forever.

Moments later, however, he returned. As he waded into the pond my friends smiled as they recognized his embarrassment. He had "come to his senses." He fished out the dripping bag, unzipped a pocket on the side, took out his car keys, and flung the bag once again, this time even further than before. Then he went home.

Dates & Places Used:

421

TOPIC: Golf

Golf Clubs with Pools

A woman stockbroker who had made millions of dollars for an Arabian oil sheik was offered all kinds of valuable gifts. She refused them all. But the sheik insisted. "Well," the woman said, "I've recently taken up golf. A set of golf clubs would be a fine gift." Weeks went by. One morning the stockbroker received a letter from him. "So far I have bought you three golf clubs," it said, "but I hope you will not be disappointed, because only two of them have swimming pools."

Dates & Places Used:

422

TOPIC: Gossip

Talents

A hot-headed woman told John Wesley, "My talent is to speak my mind." Replied Mr. Wesley, "Woman, God wouldn't care a bit if you would bury that talent."

Dates & Places Used:

423

Kept Secrets

Some secrets are worth keeping. Others are too good to keep.
Dates & Places Used:

424

TOPIC: Gossip

A Shorter Story

Nothing makes a long story short like the arrival of the person you happen to be talking about.
Dates & Places Used:

425

TOPIC: Gossip

Moving Dirt

R. G. LeTourneau, owner of a large earth-moving equipment company, told this story. "We used to have a scraper known as the model 'G.' Somebody asked one of our salesmen one day what the 'G' stood for. The salesman, after thinking a few seconds, replied, "Well, I guess the 'G' stands for gossip, because like gossip, this machine moves a lot of dirt and moves it fast."
Dates & Places Used:

426

TOPIC: Grace

Abundant Entreaties

We are told that the Reuben Donnelly Company of Chicago is the nation's largest printer of magazines. They have a huge machine that sends out notices to people whose subscriptions have expired. One day a tiny spring in the machine broke and a rancher in Powder Bluff, Colorado, received 9,734 notices that his subscription to *National Geographic* had expired. He rode the ten miles to the post office, sent his money, and wrote, "Send me the magazine. I give up!"

That's how God brings many a person to salvation. He hits them with the message so many times that they finally give up. Also, that's how God's blessings and love are toward us. He piles them on so much that we must surrender to him.

Dates & Places Used:

427 TOPIC: Grace
Conversational Grace

An attractive woman was taken to dinner one night by William E. Gladstone, the distinguished British statesman. The next evening she attended a dinner where she sat next to Benjamin Disraeli, his equally distinguished opponent.

Asked her opinion of the two men, she replied thoughtfully: "When I left the dining room after sitting with Mr. Gladstone, I thought he was the cleverest man in England. But after sitting next to Mr. Disraeli, I thought I was the cleverest woman in England."

Dates & Places Used:

428 TOPIC: Grades
Near Miss

Six-year-old Angie came home from school with a blue ribbon she said she had won for knowing an answer in natural history: "I said a giraffe had three legs."

Her mother responded, "But a giraffe has four legs."

Angie agreed, "I suppose so, but I was the closest of anybody in the class."

Dates & Places Used:

170

429

TOPIC: Grades

A Silver Lining

A youngster brought home his report card heavy with poor grades. His mother asked, "What have you to say about this?"

The boy replied, "One thing is for sure—you know I ain't cheating!"

Dates & Places Used:

430

TOPIC: Grades

Good and Original

A student confronted the professor after class and asked for an explanation of the notations on his examination paper. The student inquired, "How come I only got a D on a paper you marked 'good and original'?"

The professor said that the explanation was simple: "The part that was good wasn't original, and the part that was original wasn't good."

Dates & Places Used:

431

TOPIC: Grades

Preparing Perspective

The following is a letter that was sent home by a daughter who was away at college:

Dear Mom and Dad: I'm sorry to be so long in writing again, but all my writing paper was lost the night the dormitory was burned down by demonstrators. I'm out of the hospital now, and the doctor says my eyesight should be back to normal sooner or later. The wonderful boy, Bill, who rescued me from the fire kindly offered to share his little apartment with me until the dorm is rebuilt. He comes from a good family, so you won't be too surprised when I tell you we are going to get married. In fact, you always wanted a grandchild, so you will be glad to know that you will be grandparents next month. Please disregard the above practice in English composition. There was no fire, I haven't been in the hospital, I'm not blind. I'm not pregnant, and I don't even have a boyfriend. But I did get a "D" in French and an "F" in Chemistry, and I wanted to be sure you received this news in proper perspective. Love, Mary.

Dates & Places Used:

432 TOPIC: Greed

Always a Little More

A reporter once asked the elder Rockefeller, "How much money does it take to satisfy a person?"

The billionaire snapped back, "Always a little more!"

Dates & Places Used:

433 TOPIC: Greed

A Profitable Venture

A woman asked at the bank to open a joint account. When asked if the account would be with her husband, she replied, "Oh no, couldn't I have one with someone who has a lot of money?"

Dates & Places Used:

434 TOPIC: Growing Up

Become Possible

The teacher asked her class what each wanted to become when they grew up. "President," "a fireman," "a teacher." One by one, they answered until it was Billy's turn. The teacher asked,

"Billy, what do you want to be when you grow up?" "Possible," Billy responded. "Possible?" asked the teacher. "Yes," Billy said, "my mom is always telling me I'm impossible. When I grow up I want to become *possible*."
Dates & Places Used:

435

TOPIC: Growing Up

Tough to Be a Saint

Young Brian, age five, had heard the story of the "pillar-monk," Symeon the Stylite, in Sunday school. Captivated by this approach to seeking God's approval, the boy decided to imitate him. Mother interrupted his holy pilgrimage by explaining, "Brian, get down off that stool on the table before you break your neck." Brian complied, but went storming from the room announcing, "You can't even become a saint in your own home!"
Dates & Places Used:

436

TOPIC: Habits

The Guilty Party Exposed

Dad was brushing his teeth when his seven-year-old daughter barged into the bathroom. "Aha," she rebuked, "so you're the one who keeps putting the cap back on the toothpaste!"
Dates & Places Used:

437

TOPIC: Habits

Don't Go Too Far!

Two men were adrift on a raft in the open sea, and it looked bad for them. Finally one of them, frightened, began to pray:

"O Lord, I've broken most of the commandments. I've got some pretty bad habits—I drink, I curse, I steal, I treat people like dirt. But if my life is spared now, I promise you that I'll change, that I'll never again curse, that I . . ." Suddenly his friend cried out to him: "Wait, Jack. Don't go too far. I think I see another ship."

Dates & Places Used:

438 TOPIC: Habits

Partial Repentance

A man with a nagging secret was unable to keep it any longer. He went to confessional and admitted that for years he had been stealing building supplies from the lumberyard where he worked.

"How much lumber did you take?" the priest asked.

"I took enough to build my home and enough for my son's house. Then I took enough to build houses for my two daughters. Oh, and our cottage at the lake."

"This is a very serious offense," the priest said. " I'll have to think of a far-reaching penance. Have you ever considered doing a retreat?"

"No, Father, I never have," the man replied. "But if you can get the plans, I can get the lumber."

Dates & Places Used:

439 TOPIC: Habits

The Cat's Habit

Bill and Ted were neighbors. Bill always brought his dog that loved to chase cats. Ted had a cat that hated dogs. Whenever Bill came to visit Ted, his dog would come along. The dog would chase the cat up a certain maple tree in Ted's yard. This same scene would take place every time Bill came to visit Ted. After a couple of years Ted cut down the tree. A couple of days later Bill and his dog came to visit. Out around the house ran the cat with the dog right on his tail. Suddenly, about thirty feet in the air, the cat realized something was different.

Dates & Places Used:

440

TOPIC: Happiness

Get the Smile Over

W. C. Fields: "Smile first thing in the morning and get it over with."
Dates & Places Used:

441

TOPIC: Haste

Inside and Out

A tourist on a rush tour of Europe screeched to a stop in front of Chartres Cathedral, jumped out, and called to his wife, "You take the inside, I'll do the outside. Meet you here in five minutes."
Dates & Places Used:

442

TOPIC: Health

Limits to Life

A man had just had his annual physical exam and was waiting for the doctor's initial report. The doctor came in with his charts in his hand and said: "There's no reason why you can't live a completely normal life as long as you don't try to enjoy it."
Dates & Places Used:

443

TOPIC: Health

Young Enough to Make It

It was Aunt Sarah's birthday. Aunt Sarah was ninety-nine years old, the oldest resident in a small town. Among the guests at her birthday party was her thirty-nine-year-old pastor. As the pastor was preparing to leave, he said, "Now, Aunt Sarah, I hope that one year from this very day, I will be able to come and celebrate your one-hundredth birthday with you." Aunt Sarah looked at him for a moment, then said, "I don't see why not! You look fairly healthy to me!"

Dates & Places Used:

444 TOPIC: Hearing

Aging

Great-aunt Lucy was losing her hearing. A specialist suggested an operation to improve her hearing. But she promptly vetoed the idea, saying: "I'm ninety-four years old, and I've heard enough."

Dates & Places Used:

445 TOPIC: Heaven

Not Long Ago

When Fred arrived at the Pearly Gates, he was met by an official-looking angelic being who began to process his entry data. Fred was asked for some purely unselfish, kindly deed he had done on earth. Well, Fred thought about it for a minute and then said, "Oh, yes. I think I have something you might be interested in. One day I was walking along and I came upon a little old lady who was being mercilessly beaten up by a huge motorcycle-gang type of fellow. He was smacking her back and forth. Well, I just stepped right up and first I pushed over his motorcycle just to distract his attention. And then I kicked him real hard in the shins and told the old lady to run for help. And then I hauled off and gave the guy a great shot right to the gut with my fist."

The angel looked at Fred with a great deal of interest and said, "Wow, that's quite a story. I'm very impressed." Then taking his clipboard in hand he said, "Could you tell me just when this happened?"

Fred looked at his watch and said, "Oh, about two or three minutes ago."

Dates & Places Used:

446

Entry Requirement

Lutherans believe you cannot get into heaven unless you bring a covered dish.

Dates & Places Used:

447

TOPIC: Heaven

United Kingdom

An executive who had recently hired an English secretary had to go on a business trip to London. While he was away, a salesman who had never spoken to the new secretary made one of his periodic telephone calls to the executive's office. The secretary responded to the call by saying, "Mr. Allen is in the United Kingdom." The salesman was shocked and replied, "I'm terribly sorry. Is it too late to send flowers?"

Dates & Places Used:

448

TOPIC: Heaven

Getting into Heaven

Little Billy, caught in mischief, was asked by his mother, "How do you expect to get into heaven?"

He thought for a moment and then said, "Well, I'll just run in and out and keep slamming the door until they say, 'For heaven's sake, either come in or stay out.' Then I'll go in."

Dates & Places Used:

TOPIC: **Heaven**

Make Your Eternity

The following story has been told in a variety of ways from a variety of sources. Here is a compiled version:

There is much speculation concerning what heaven and hell will be like. One contrast of heaven and hell tells of a man who had a dream that he was allowed to see both places. He was first taken to hell. He was taken into a room in the middle of which there was a large pot of stew. The stew smelled delicious. But all around this pot there were people who were starving and in desperation. They all held spoons in their hands that had unusually long handles which reached all the way to the pot, but because the spoon handles were longer than their arms, they were unable to return the spoons filled with stew to their mouths. Their suffering was terrible and continuous.

The man was then taken to heaven. Heaven was identical to hell; the rooms were identical, the pot of stew in the middle of the room was the same, and the spoons were the same. But the people in this room were well-fed and joyous. The man was perplexed when he first walked into the room. But as he watched the people in this room, he learned the difference. The people had spoons that would not allow them to feed themselves, so they fed each other.

Dates & Places Used:

450

TOPIC: **Hell**

A Friend to the End

A priest was preaching to his congregation concerning heaven and hell. To emphasize the difference between the two, he asked that all who wanted to go to heaven stand up with him. All the congregation rose. He then asked that all who wanted to go to hell stand up with him. No one rose.

For full dramatic impact he waited for several seconds before continuing. The silence was broken by a small boy who slowly rose to his feet. The astonished priest spoke to the boy, "Surely son, a fine young man like yourself does not want to go to hell."

The boy answered, "Maybe not sir, but I just couldn't stand the sight of you standing there all alone."
Dates & Places Used:

451

TOPIC: Help

Partial Commitment

A man was overheard as he was leaving his companion at the entrance to the Internal Revenue Service office:

"As your tax consultant, I said in case of an audit I would accompany you to the IRS. I never said anything about going in with you."
Dates & Places Used:

452

TOPIC: Helpfulness

Happy Formula

You should do something every day to make other people happy, even if it's only to leave them alone.
Dates & Places Used:

453

TOPIC: Heroes

A Hero Not Braver

A hero is no braver than anyone else, but he *is* brave five minutes longer.
Dates & Places Used:

454

TOPIC: Hesitation

Cold Feet

Psychiatrists say that in the process of thinking, blood is drawn from the feet to the brain, suggesting that this may explain why, when we think very long about doing something, we get cold feet.
Dates & Places Used:

455

TOPIC: History

Most Neglected Men

The most neglected men in history are Whistler's father and Lord Godiva.
Dates & Places Used:

456

TOPIC: History

Cynical View of History

History is an account, mostly false, of events, mostly unimportant, which are brought about by rulers, mostly knaves, and soldiers, mostly fools. *(Ambrose Bierce)*
Dates & Places Used:

457

TOPIC: History

A Decisive Moment

Former Secretary of Labor Raymond Donavan tells about a personal experience on board Air Force One. He was in the back compartment of the jet while President Reagan was in the front in his compartment. The phone rang in the back compartment and the voice said, "Mr. Donavan, the president would like for you to join him for lunch." Secretary Donavan straightened his tie and thought to himself how important he was to have the president ask him to join him for lunch. Just as Secretary Donavan walked through the doorway into the president's compartment, the Red Phone rang, the presidential hotline, next to the president. Wow—what a moment to be present. The president picked up the phone and said, "Yes—uh huh—yes. What are my options?" Donavan's heart almost stopped. His mind raced. Then the president continued, "OK. I'll have the iced tea!" and hung up. So much for ego.

Dates & Places Used:

458 TOPIC: History

How So Stories

Traveling west by covered wagon, a group got caught in a blizzard in the mountains. One man told his best friend, "I ain't gonna make it, Joe." "Sure you are, Al." "No, Joe, I ain't. So I want you to promise me something." "Anything, Al." "Promise me that when you and Little Joe get there, you'll name a town after me." "Sure, Al." At this Al turned to Little Joe and said, "Little Joe, will you remind your pa to name a town after me?" And Little Joe replied, "I promise, Mr. Buquerque."

Dates & Places Used:

459 TOPIC: Holidays

Explain Thanksgiving

In a *Dennis the Menace* cartoon, Dennis is speaking to one of his little friends as they peer into a department store window decorated for Christmas: "Last month was our giving thanks holiday, an' Christmas is God's 'You're Welcome.'"

Dates & Places Used:

460

TOPIC: Home

Equal Time

Toward the end of the calendar year a young pastor was sharing his aspirations with his congregation. His somewhat ambitious goal had been to visit every family in the congregation before the year ended. Apologizing for failing to reach his lofty goal, the pastor asked any family who desired such a visit before the end of the year to please raise their hands. One lone person raised her hand—the pastor's wife!

Dates & Places Used:

461

TOPIC: Home

Summer Scene

When a little boy returned home from camp, his parents asked him, "Didn't you get homesick while you were at camp?" He shrugged his shoulders and answered, "Not me, but some of the kids who have dogs did."

Dates & Places Used:

462

TOPIC: Home

Independent Teen

A mother is overheard talking about her teen-age daughter: "Oh, she's very independent. She lives alone at our house."

Dates & Places Used:

463

TOPIC: Honesty

When It Happens Twice

An employee looked at his paycheck and found that he had been overpaid, but he failed to report the error. The next week, the accountant, correcting the error, deducted the same amount from the employee's pay. The employee noticed the error again, but this time complained. When asked by the accountant why he had not complained last week, the employee responded, "I can overlook one error, but when it happens two times in a row, it's time to complain!"

Dates & Places Used:

464

TOPIC: Honesty

A Child's Candor

There was an elderly lady who said to a little girl, "How do you do, my dear?" The girl replied, "Quite well, thank you." After a long pause the woman asked, "Why don't you ask me how I am?" The child paused and said calmly, "Because I'm not interested."

Dates & Places Used:

465

TOPIC: Honesty

Honesty Pays

One of two women who were riding on a bus suddenly realized she hadn't paid her fare. "I'll go right up and pay it," she said.

"Why bother?" her companion replied. "You got away with it. So what?"

"I've found that honesty always pays," the other said virtuously, and went up to pay the driver.

"See, I told you honesty pays!" she said upon her return. "I handed the driver a quarter, and he gave me fifty cents change."

Dates & Places Used:

466

TOPIC: Honeymoons

Clever Disguise

The bride was a bit self-conscious about being a new bride and wanted to disguise the fact that they were honeymooning, so she asked her new husband while they were on the plane if there was any way they could make it appear that they had been married a long time. The husband said, "Sure, you carry the suitcases."

Dates & Places Used:

467

TOPIC: Honor

A Right Nice Tribute

Then there's the story of the uninformed Protestant who happened to be visiting Rome on a day when the pope was holding an audience at the Vatican. Throngs of people were cheering him as he appeared out on the balcony. The Protestant looked up and saw all the adulation and said to his guide, "Who's that they're cheering for?" The guide said, "That's the pope. He lives here. He's in charge." The people kept cheering the pope. The Protestant said, "That's mighty nice. How did he get all of this?" The guide said, "The cardinals voted him in." The Protestant said, "I'm impressed. You know, the Giants should've done something like this for Willy Mays."

Dates & Places Used:

468

TOPIC: Hope

Second Time Around

A gentleman who had been very unhappy in marriage married a second time, immediately after his first wife died. Samuel Johnson said of him: "His conduct was the triumph of hope over experience."

Dates & Places Used:

469

Not What They Seem

The pastor went to call on one of the elderly widows of the church. While visiting with her, he noticed a bowl of shelled peanuts on the coffee table. During the conversation he began nibbling on them and soon the bowl was empty. He then apologized to the woman for eating all of her peanuts.

She replied, "That's OK, Reverend. It's no bother. You see, three weeks ago I had all my teeth pulled. Since that time, I've just been sucking the chocolate off the peanuts and putting them in that bowl."

Dates & Places Used:

470

TOPIC: Hospitality

Feeling at Home

Tact is making your friends feel at home, even when you wish they were.

Dates & Places Used:

471

TOPIC: Humility

Famous Humble Doctor

Of course, one of the greatest sources of modern illustration is the delightful comic strip *Peanuts* by Charles Schultz. One of my favorites shows Linus and Charlie Brown sitting and talking about their plans when they grow up.

Linus says, "When I get big I'm going to be a humble little country doctor. I'll live in the city, see, and every morning I'll get up, climb into my sports car and zoom into the country! Then I'll start healing people. I'll heal everybody for miles around!" And he concludes this speech with "I'll be a world-famous humble little country doctor."

Dates & Places Used:

472

TOPIC: Humility

Dilemma for the Humble

Two men died and waited at the Pearly Gates for admission into heaven. "We've got room for only one more," Saint Peter declared. "Which one of you is more humble?"

Dates & Places Used:

473

TOPIC: Humility

The Power Crowd

Fuller Seminary recently celebrated its fortieth anniversary with the inauguration of the President's Lectureship in early November. The four speakers included such heavy hitters as Carl F. H. Henry, theologian; Samuel Hugh Moffett, professor emeritus of ecumenism and mission at Princeton; Mary Steward Van Leeuwen, professor of interdisciplinary studies at Calvin College; and Cary Wisiger III, retired pastor.

In his opening address, Wisiger displayed characteristic humility in the company of such academic luminaries: I have been a pastor, by the grace of God. If I could do it all over again, I would be a pastor. I have never, frankly, regarded myself as a scholar. I have tried to be studious, and I want to thank Dr. David Hubbard for including me in this program today. A farmer once put his mule in a horse race and his friends said to him, "Silly, that mule can't run with those thoroughbreds." The farmer said, "I know it, but you have no idea how good it makes him feel to be with all those horses!"

Dates & Places Used:

474

TOPIC: Humor

Humor, Etc.

Jokes are no laughing matter to the brain. They are a type of release valve that enables us to think the unthinkable, accept the unacceptable, discover new relationships, adjust better, and maintain our mental health. They are also funny. Without them we probably would be a dull, dim-witted society, trapped in a harsh world too serious to bear.

Dates & Places Used:

475

TOPIC: Humor

Self-Perspective

As long as you laugh at your troubles, you may be sure you will never run out of something to laugh at.

Dates & Places Used:

476

TOPIC: Hunting

Autumn Rituals

The start of the deer-hunting season in Vermont is an event of special significance. Each year, on opening day, a substantial portion of the male population retires to outlying cabins and lodges where they eat, drink, and play cards. Any deer foolish enough to bust in the door or poke his head through the window is shot on the spot.

Dates & Places Used:

477

TOPIC: Husbands

Advice on Marriage

I was calling on one of our senior church members the other night, Lillian Davenport. A delightful woman from Georgia, she told me about her early life in the South. Then she told me about her uncle, Rev. James P. McMillan, D. D., and she showed me a letter he wrote to her in 1921. I asked her if I could share it with you. It went this way:

Dear Lillian, I approve of your caution in not hastening your marriage. I don't see the necessity of your marrying at all. You already have a good home where you are useful. You have a dog to growl for you, a little trained parrot easily kept could be trained to curse, even a trained monkey could smoke for you; and almost any old cat could stay out at nights. Thus you have all the traits found in some husbands and at so much less cost than a husband. So I am glad that you are not trying to catch up with a husband. Your Uncle James.

Dates & Places Used:

478

TOPIC: Hypocrisy

Sinners and Saints

There is the story of the man who came down from the Carolina mountains one day. He was all dressed up and carrying his Bible. A friend saw him and asked, "Elias, what's happening? Where are you going all dressed up like that?"

Elias said, "I've been hearing about New Orleans. I hear that there is a lot of free-runnin' liquor and a lot of gamblin' and a lot of real good, naughty shows."

The friend looked him over and said, "But Elias, why are you carrying your Bible under your arm?"

Elias answered, "Well, if it's as good as they say it is, I might stay over until Sunday."

Dates & Places Used:

479

TOPIC: Hypocrisy

The First Confessional

A noted Washington monsignor was to be the guest of honor at a Washington banquet. A prominent politician was to serve as chairman but had been unavoidably detained. The toastmaster proceeded without him. Honor after honor was heaped upon the deserving churchman, and then he arose to accept their tributes.

"The seal of the confessional," he said, "can never be broken, and therefore I can only hint of my impressions when I came to Washington some twenty-five years ago. Oh, I thought I had wandered into a terrible place. The first man who entered the confessional told me a hair-raising tale of his graft and corruption, but as the days went on I knew I'd entered a fine community of lovely people and it has indeed been an honor to have been among you for all these fine years."

As he spoke, the chairman arrived and rushed to the front. The politician spoke next: "I'll never forget the first day our honored guest arrived at this parish. In fact, I have the honor of being the first to go to his confessional."

Dates & Places Used:

480

TOPIC: Hypocrisy

Something of Nothing

A religious leader and his associate were rehearsing a service. To make his point dramatic the minister fell to his knees, beat his breast and said, "I am nothing. I am nothing!" Then his associate fell to his knees, beat upon his breast, and repeated, "I am nothing. I am nothing!" The janitor witnessed this scene. Moved by what he saw and heard, the janitor fell to his knees and cried, "I am nothing. I am nothing!" When the minister and associate heard the janitor, the minister turned to the associate and said, "So look who has the gall to think he is nothing."

Dates & Places Used:

481

TOPIC: Idealism

The Desire for Peace

Ramsey MacDonald, one-time prime minister of England, was discussing with another government official the possibility of

lasting peace. The latter, an expert on foreign affairs, was unimpressed by the prime minister's idealistic viewpoint. He remarked cynically, "The desire for peace does not necessarily ensure it." This, MacDonald admitted, saying, "Quite true. But neither does the desire for food satisfy your hunger, but at least it gets you started toward a restaurant."
Dates & Places Used:

482 TOPIC: Ideas

Exhilarating Pause

Exhilaration is that feeling you get just after a great idea hits you and before you realize what's wrong with it.
Dates & Places Used:

483 TOPIC: Impact

The Offense of Life

Any church that is alive will always be living on the edge of heresy.
Dates & Places Used:

484 TOPIC: Incarnation

Personal Directions

Pastor Clifford S. Stewart of Louisville, Kentucky, sent his parents a microwave oven one Christmas. Here's how he recalls the experience:

"They were excited that now they, too, could be a part of the instant generation. When Dad unpacked the microwave and plugged it in, literally within seconds, the microwave transformed two smiles into frowns! Even after reading the directions, they couldn't make it work."

"Two days later, my mother was playing bridge with a friend and confessed her inability to get that microwave oven even to boil water. 'To get this thing to work,' she exclaimed, 'I really don't need better directions; I just need my son to come along with the gift!'"

When God gave the gift of salvation, he didn't send a booklet of complicated instructions for us to figure out; he sent his Son.
Dates & Places Used:

485 TOPIC: Inertia

Ignorance and Apathy

The pastor was rather disappointed that things were not "happening" in his church, and so he asked one of the leading deacons, "What is wrong with our church? Is it ignorance or apathy?" The deacon responded, "I don't know, and I don't care."
Dates & Places Used:

486 TOPIC: Inflation

What Money Can't Buy

Among the things that money can't buy is what it used to.
Dates & Places Used:

487 TOPIC: Inflation

Inflated Water

Sign on a water cooler at Hughes Aircraft in Torrance: "Due to the inflation and other rising costs, the water in this cooler is now twice as free as it used to be."
Dates & Places Used:

488

TOPIC: Inflation

The Cost of Giving

A man had posted himself in front of an office building with a tray of shoelaces. One executive made it a daily habit to give the unfortunate man a dime, but he never took the laces. One day the peddler, on receiving the dime, tapped his departing benefactor on the back: "I don't like to impose, sir, but the laces are now fifteen cents."

Dates & Places Used:

489

TOPIC: Inheritance

Our Inheritance

I'm not sure how excited you get about what I call tortured alliterations in sermons, but here's a set I used on the inheritance described in 1 Peter 1:3–4. Our inheritance is Galvanized (imperishable), Germ-Proofed (undefiled), Grecian-Formulated (unfading, admittedly that's a pretty awful example), and Guaranteed (reserved in heaven).

Dates & Places Used:

490

TOPIC: Inheritance

A Miser's Money

A miser isn't any fun to live with, but he makes a wonderful ancestor.

Dates & Places Used:

491

TOPIC: In-Laws

Recognized Her Laugh

"Officer," the guy yelled, "my mother-in-law knocked me down with her car!" "Are you sure that it was your mother-in-

law?" asked the officer. "Absolutely," the man said. "I'd recognize that laugh anywhere."
Dates & Places Used:

492

TOPIC: In-Laws

Formidable Dilemma

A man, his wife, and his mother-in-law went on a safari in Africa. They hired a guide and set out into the jungle. One morning the married couple awoke to find the mother missing. After a lengthy search, they found the woman in a clearing, face-to-face with a huge lion. The terrified wife cried out to her husband, "Dear, what should we do?" The husband replied, "Not a thing. The lion got himself into this mess; let him get himself out of it."
Dates & Places Used:

493

TOPIC: In-Laws

Genetic Miracle

One of the great mysteries of life is how the idiot that your daughter married can be the father of the smartest grandchildren in the whole wide world.
Dates & Places Used:

494

TOPIC: In-laws

Honest Outlaws

One big difference between outlaws and inlaws is that outlaws don't promise to pay it back.
Dates & Places Used:

495

TOPIC: Insults

A Reason to Die

During the second World War, a woman of the "upper crust" of English society was overheard upbraiding, chiding, and criticizing Sir Winston Churchill at a social gathering. She concluded her chastisement by looking Sir Winston square in the face and saying, "Sir, if I were your wife, I'd put poison in your tea."

Sir Winston's prompt reply was, "Lady, if you were my wife, I'd drink it!"

Dates & Places Used:

496

TOPIC: Insurance

A Bad Day When

You know it's going to be a bad day when you wake up in a hospital all trussed up and your insurance agent tells you that your accident policy covers falling off the roof but not hitting the ground.

Dates & Places Used:

497

TOPIC: Intelligence

Break Retraining

I don't want to say he's stupid, but his boss won't give him a coffee break because it takes too long to retrain him!

Dates & Places Used:

498

TOPIC: Intelligence

Fill the Void

A young child came to her mother complaining that her stomach hurt. "Oh, honey, your stomach is empty," the mother responded. "You just need to get something in it and you'll be fine."

About a week later, the pastor was speaking with her mother and he happened to mention that he had a headache. "Oh pastor, my mommy says that your head is empty," the girl responded. "You just need to get something in it and you'll be fine."
Dates & Places Used:

499

TOPIC: Intelligence

Brain Weight

The average human body contains sixty-six pounds of muscle, forty-two pounds of bone, and only three and a half pounds of brain, which probably explains a lot of things.
Dates & Places Used:

500

TOPIC: Intelligence

Know the Letters

"It's not the most intellectual job in the world, but I do have to know the letters." *(Vanna White)*
Dates & Places Used:

501

TOPIC: Intentions

Up or Down

"You must be brave to come down in a one-hundred-mile-per-hour gale like this in a parachute," the farmer said to the young soldier.

"I didn't come down in a chute," said the soldier. "I went up in a tent."
Dates & Places Used:

502

TOPIC: Interpretation

Tale of Two Virgins

A teacher's aide at an elementary school tells this story.
A first-grader named Jacob approached her and said, "Mrs.
Phillips, did you know that the Bible is divided into two halves?
There's the old virgin and the new virgin!"

Dates & Places Used:

503

TOPIC: Interpretation

Communication

After telling the story of Jonah and the whale to her Sunday
school class, the teacher decided to quiz them. She asked,
"Timmy, what is the moral of the story?" Timmy thought for a
minute, then said, "People make whales throw up!"

Dates & Places Used:

504

TOPIC: Interpretation

Interpretive Bias

Whenever we interpret Scripture, we tend to lean towards our
own bias. We need to recognize the reality of such biases that we
all have. I like the story I read in *Sunday Sermons* about the driver of a tour bus in Nashville, Tennessee. The driver was point-
ing out the sights of the Civil War Battle of Nashville. He said,
"Right over here a small group of Confederate soldiers held off a
whole Yankee brigade." A little farther along he said, "Over there
a young Confederate boy, all by himself, fought off a Yankee platoon." This went on and on until finally, a member of the tour
group asked, "Didn't the Yankees win anything in the battle of
Nashville?" The bus driver replied, "Not while I'm the driver of
this bus, they didn't."

Dates & Places Used:

505

TOPIC: Interpretation

Asking Her Age

A young mother had been too busy to visit her elderly neighbor, who was ill. She said to her small son, "Johnny, run over and see how 'old Mrs. Smith' is." Within a few minutes, the boy was back. "She says it's none of your business how old she is."

Dates & Places Used:

506

TOPIC: Interpretation

To the Essence

A visiting American textile-buyer told a long but amusing anecdote at a luncheon in Seoul, Korea. The translator repeated it to the group in just a few words, and the audience laughed and applauded. Later, the textile-buyer commented to the translator, "I think it was wonderful the way they appreciated my joke. It's amazing how you were able to shorten it in Korean." The interpreter replied, "Not at all. I merely said, 'Man with big checkbook has told funny story. Do what you think is appropriate.'"

Dates & Places Used:

507

TOPIC: Interpretation

Timing Problem

A little girl came home from school and said to her mother, "I wish you would let me take my bath in the morning before I go to school, instead of at night before I go to bed."

"What difference does it make?" her mother asked.

"Every day at school," the little girl said, "Miss Taylor tells everybody to stand up who had a bath today. And I haven't been able to stand up one time since school started three months ago."

Dates & Places Used:

508

Some Baby

The pastor of a small town church sent one of his parishioners to the big city to order a Christmas sign to be hung outside on the door of the church. The parishioner lost the note which the pastor gave him which gave the dimension of the sign and the inscription that was to be printed on it. So he wired the pastor: "Rush copy of motto and dimensions."

A new clerk in the Western Union office got the reply and almost fainted. It read: "Unto us a child is born. Eight feet long, three feet wide."

Dates & Places Used:

509

Obedience

When I read the Bible, the parts that trouble me the most are not the ones I don't understand, but the ones I do understand. (*Mark Twain*)

Dates & Places Used:

510

Drink for a Dime

An enterprising young boy placed a sign over his new lemonade stand that read, "ALL YOU CAN DRINK FOR A DIME."

His first customer was a businessman who enjoyed his product so much he asked the young fellow for another glass. The boy asked for another dime. The man protested and referred to the sign.

The boy explained, "That, sir, *is* all you can drink for a dime!"

Dates & Places Used:

511

TOPIC: Intimacy

You're in a Small Town

You know you're in a small town when:

The airport runway is terraced.

Third Street is on the edge of town.

Every sport is played on dirt.

You don't use your turn signal because everyone knows where you're going.

You dial a wrong number and talk for fifteen minutes anyway.

You drive into the ditch five miles out of town and the word gets back into town before you do.

You write a check on the wrong bank and it covers it for you.

The pickups on Main Street outnumber the cars three to one.

You miss a Sunday at church and receive a get-well card.

Someone asks you how you feel and then listens to what you say.

Dates & Places Used:

512

TOPIC: Intimacy

Go First

Let us live! Let us love! Let us share the deepest secrets of our souls! You go first!

Dates & Places Used:

513

TOPIC: Jews

Jewish Advantage

After the Six-Day War, Egypt's president, Gamal Abdel Nasser, said the war was unfair because Israel had two million Jews and he didn't have any.

Dates & Places Used:

514

TOPIC: Jews

Change the Light

Synagogues have an Eternal Light in front of the altar. One youngster was wriggling and wiggling through the service and then asked his mother, "When the light turns green, can we go?" *(Rabbi Silver)*
Dates & Places Used:

515

TOPIC: Jobs

Rubbed Wrong Way

Did you hear the one about the fellow who was fired from his job in the massage parlor because he rubbed people the wrong way?
Dates & Places Used:

516

TOPIC: Justice

Cries for Mercy

Many of those who cry so loudly for justice would soon beg for mercy if justice were done to them. *(Richard J. Needham)*
Dates & Places Used:

517

TOPIC: Justice

In Need of Police

Here's a true story told by Anthony Evans: One of our Sunday school teachers was telling her preschoolers about Jesus' arrest, trial, and crucifixion and had their undivided attention. Even Michael was listening. When she finished the lesson and asked for questions, Michael's hand shot into the air; the teacher was

thrilled. "I just want to know one thing," he said. "Where were the State Police when all this was going on?!?!"
Dates & Places Used:

518   TOPIC: Knowledge
Using Your Head

God gave us two ends, one to think with and one to sit on. Heads you win; tails you lose.
Dates & Places Used:

519   TOPIC: Language
Chip off the Profane Block

The boy's mother was furious. "Young man, where did you learn to talk that way?"

The boy hesitated, looked toward his father, and asked, "Well, Dad, should I tell her?"
Dates & Places Used:

520   TOPIC: Laughter
Laugh Cure

Dr. Fry calls laughter a stationary jogging. He says, "There is hardly a system in the body a hearty laugh doesn't stimulate." A few years ago, Norman Cousins, famous editor of *Saturday Review*, actually cured himself of a deadly form of spinal arthritis using massive doses of vitamin C and a tremendous amount of laughter every day. More than sixty years ago, the world-famous physical culturist, Bernard MacFadden, wrote about laughter as

a form of exercise. He and his followers derived so much benefit from laughter as an exercise that he called it his Laugh Cure.
Dates & Places Used:

TOPIC: Lawyers

521

Caught

A new lawyer watches the very first person enter his office. He decides he should look busy, so he picks up the phone and starts talking: "Look, Harry, about that amalgamation deal. I think I better run down to the factory and handle it personally. Yes. No. I don't think three million will swing it. We better have Rogers from Seattle meet us there. OK. Call you back later." He looks up at the visitor and says, "Good morning, how may I help you?" And the prospective client says, "You can't help me at all. I'm just here to hook up your phone."
Dates & Places Used:

TOPIC: Lawyers

522

Lawyers and Rabbits

Question: What is the difference between a car accident involving a rabbit and one involving a lawyer?
Answer: There are skid marks leading up to the rabbit.
Dates & Places Used:

TOPIC: Lawyers

523

A Lawyer's Brief

A lawyer is someone who writes a thirty-page document and calls it a brief. (*Alfred E. Neuman*)
Dates & Places Used:

524

TOPIC: Lawyers

What You Want It to Be

Stanford Research Institute was studying the differences in vocational perceptions. They devised a short but succinct test. The first to be tested was an engineer. The researchers asked him: "What does two plus two make?" The engineer simply said, "In absolute terms: four." The researchers made their notes and dismissed him. They called in an architect. They asked him the same question, and he said, "Well, there are several possibilities: two and two make four, but so do three and one—or two and one-half and one and one-half—they also make four. So, it is all a matter of choosing the right option." The researchers thanked him and made their notes. The last of the three to come in was an attorney. They said to him, "What does two and two make?" The attorney looked around furtively, asked if he could close the door for privacy and then came over close, leaned toward them and said, "Well, tell me, what would you like it to be?"

Dates & Places Used:

525

TOPIC: Lawyers

To Die Like Jesus

As an aged man lay dying in the hospital he summoned his nurse. "Would you call to me my lawyer and my doctor, right away?" he requested.

Within a half hour both the man's doctor and his attorney were at his side. The man's breathing was labored by this time but he remained silent.

The attorney spoke "What did you need us for?"

The reply came momentarily, "Nothing," he said. "I have heard Jesus died between two thieves," he continued. "I wanted to know what it felt like."

Dates & Places Used:

526

TOPIC: Law

Adjusting to the Realities

A factory manager found that production was being hampered by the tardiness of his people returning from the lunch hour. When the whistle blew, few were at their machines. He posted a sign by the suggestion box offering a cash award for the best answer to this question: "What should we do to insure that every man will be inside the factory when the whistle blows?" Many suggestions were submitted and one was selected that solved the problem. But the manager, a man with a sense of humor, liked this one best, though he could not use it: "Let the last man in blow the whistle."

Dates & Places Used:

527

TOPIC: Laws

The Cost of Short Sight

A man crashed his plane in the desert. Stranded without water, the unfortunate man trudged through the desert for hours until he could no longer stay on his feet. Then, as he began crawling across the burning sands, he encountered a necktie salesman. "Can I interest you in a nice new tie?" the salesman asked. "Are you crazy?" the man gasped. "I'm dying of thirst and you want to sell me a necktie?" The salesman shrugged his shoulders and moved on, and the dying man resumed his crawling.

Finally, he came upon an unbelievable sight. There, before his eyes, in the middle of the desert, was a magnificent restaurant with neon lights blazing and a parking lot filled with cars. The desperate man crawled to the front door. With his voice growing weaker and weaker, he said to the doorman, "Please, help me in, I must have something to drink."

To which the doorman replied, "Sorry sir, gentlemen are not admitted without a tie."

Dates & Places Used:

528

TOPIC: Laws

Frugal Rules

Papa lay dying, and his sons and daughters were gathered about him in his bedroom. The eldest son moved forward and respectfully asked, "Papa, is there anything you want?" The old man whispered, "Yes, one last wish. I smell something familiar and delicious. It smells like your mother's apple strudel. Bring me a piece of your mother's strudel. There is none better." The son was gone to the kitchen longer than expected. When he returned empty handed, the dying father asked, "What took you so long? And why no apple strudel?" The son looked with a sad face and said, "Papa, you know how Mama is. Always so practical, and so strict. She says the strudel is for after the funeral."
Dates & Places Used:

529

TOPIC: Laziness

Right Track

Even when you are on the right track, you'll get run over if you just sit there.
Dates & Places Used:

530

TOPIC: Laziness

Wait for an Earthquake

Mere longing for a better world can be a lazy person's way to face life. There is an old story of a farmer who said lightning struck an old shed and thus saved him the trouble of tearing it down, and rain washed off his car and saved him that chore too. When asked what he was doing now, he replied, "Waiting for an earthquake to shake the potatoes out of the ground."
Dates & Places Used:

531

TOPIC: Leadership

Remove the Pressure

Two disillusioned college presidents were discussing what they'd do if they had their lives to live over. One said, "I'd like to run an orphanage with no parents to contend with." The other said, "I'd rather run a penitentiary with no alumni pressure groups."
Dates & Places Used:

532

TOPIC: Leadership

Blow First

A farmer owned a mule that was very important to him because it was a good plowing animal. The mule got sick one day, and the farmer called in the veterinarian. The vet looked the mule over, and then gave the farmer some extremely large pills. "Give the mule one of these pills three times a day, and he'll recover," the vet said. The pills were so huge the farmer asked how he was supposed to get them down the mule's throat. "Easy," replied the vet. "Find a piece of pipe wide enough to fit the pill into. Then, put one end of the pipe into the mule's mouth, and put the pill into the pipe, and then blow into the other end. Before the mule knows what is happening, he'll swallow the pill."

It sounded easy enough, but just a few hours later the farmer walked into the veterinarian's office looking terribly sick himself. "You look just awful! What happened?" the vet asked. The farmer replied, "THE MULE BLEW FIRST!!"
Dates & Places Used:

533

TOPIC: Lectures

Parting Shot

A Frenchman, a Japanese and an American faced a firing squad. Offered a last wish, the Frenchman asked to hear the Marseillaise.

The Japanese asked to give one more lecture on Japanese management. The American asked to be shot first. He explained, "I can't stand another lecture on Japanese management."
Dates & Places Used:

534

TOPIC: Lies

Ego Time

A Hollywood producer calls his friend, another Hollywood producer, on the telephone. "Hello?" answers his friend.

"Hi, Bernie," says the first producer, "this is Harold! How are you doing?"

"Great!" says the friend, "I just signed a multimillion dollar deal with a major studio; I just sold a screenplay for over a million dollars to a hot new director; I have a new TV series that's coming on the air next month, and everyone says it's going to be a big hit. I'm doing great! How are you?"

"Fine," says the first producer. "Listen, Bernie, I'll call you back when you're alone."
Dates & Places Used:

535

TOPIC: Lies

To Tell a Lie

In Boston a minister noticed a group of boys standing around a small stray dog. "What are you doing, boys?" "Telling lies," said one of the boys. "The one who tells the biggest lie gets the dog."

"Why, when I was your age," the shocked minister said, "I never ever thought of telling a lie."

The boys looked at one another, a little crestfallen. Finally one of them shrugged and said, "I guess he wins the dog."
Dates & Places Used:

536

Persistent Liar

A little girl had developed a bad habit. She was always lying. Once when she was given a St. Bernard dog for her birthday, she went out and told all the neighbors that she had been given a lion. The mother took her aside and said, "I told you not to lie. You go upstairs and tell God you are sorry. Promise God you will not lie again." The little girl went upstairs, said her prayers, then came down again. Her mother asked, "Did you tell God you are sorry?" The little girl replied, "Yes, I did. And God said sometimes he finds it hard to tell my dog from a lion too."

Dates & Places Used:

537

On Second Thought

Four-year-old Billy had grown tired of blowing soap bubbles, so he asked his mother to read him the Bible story about the golden streets. "Very well, dear," she said, "but have you taken the soap out of the water?" "I'm pretty sure I have," said Billy.

When his mother read the words, "And there shall in no wise enter into it any that maketh a lie," Billy slid out of his chair and said, "I think I'll go see about that soap."

Dates & Places Used:

538

Shut Out the Truth

One time a friend drove me to see some people who lived about fifty miles away. We had a nice visit, but when it was time to leave, we discovered that the keys were locked in the car. None of us knew what to do, so my friend had to call her husband, who had a spare key. Understandably he was quite annoyed.

A few minutes later, I decided to try the back doors of the car. Sure enough, one was unlocked. My friend rushed back into the house, hoping to reach her husband before he left, but it was too late.

"Wait till he sees this!" I said, "He'll be more than upset. What are you going to do?"

"What any red-blooded American wife would do," she replied, grinning. Then she walked out to the car, opened the back door, pushed down the lock button, and slammed the door shut!

Dates & Places Used:

539

TOPIC: Lies

My Father Speaking

A school principal received a phone call. The voice said, "Thomas Bradley won't be in school today." The principal was a bit suspicious of the voice. He asked, "Who is speaking?" The voice came back, "My father."

Dates & Places Used:

540

TOPIC: Lies

Tiring Test

The locus classicus on the flushing out of the deceitful heart of man is the oft-quoted story about the four boys who cut class one morning in a Chicago suburb and didn't get to class until noon. Their explanation was that they had had a flat tire.

The teacher said, "That's OK, boys. You did miss a test, but you can make it up right now on your lunch time." Whereupon she seated them in the four corners of the room and then gave them the one question on the test: "Which tire was flat?"

Dates & Places Used:

541

When Life Begins

A Roman Catholic priest was discussing on the radio the important theological topic of "When Does Life Begin?"

He pointed out that some feel it begins at the moment of conception, while others are convinced it starts when the baby takes the first breath. But, he pointed out, there is an increasing number who feel that life doesn't really begin until the last kid leaves home and the dog dies.

Dates & Places Used:

542

Mule-Team Scenery

Kathryn Jensen tells us, "Life is like being on a mule team. Unless you're the lead mule, all the scenery looks about the same."

Dates & Places Used:

543

Light to Light

Back when electricity was first being introduced to a little Scottish village, almost everybody in a particular church switched from the propane lanterns to electricity just as soon as it could be hooked up. However, the oldest couple in the congregation couldn't get their electricity because they were waiting for the poles to go up and the wire to be strung. So they continued to use their propane lanterns.

The day finally came when the electricity was brought into their home. Everyone came for the festive event. The old man waited for it to get extra dark; then he told his wife to go turn on the switch. When she did, the light filled the room, and everyone rejoiced. The old man grinned from ear to ear, picked up a propane lamp and said, "It sure makes lighting my lamps easier." And with that he lit a lamp, and his wife turned off the electricity.

Sometimes we're just like that. We can't see the light for need to hang on to the darkness of our past. As one person put it, we have "eyes that grope in a fog that never lifted."

Dates & Places Used:

544

TOPIC: Listening

Talking to Oneself

One man said to his friend one day, "My wife talks to herself a lot." His friend answered, "Mine does too, but she doesn't know it. She thinks I'm listening."

Dates & Places Used:

545

TOPIC: Listening

Strategy of Listening

The only way to entertain some folks is to listen to them.

Dates & Places Used:

546

TOPIC: Listening

Reason to Listen

It's impossible for a worthwhile thought to enter your mind through an open mouth.

Dates & Places Used:

So Many Answers

I was once asked to arbitrate for an instructor colleague and his student. They both agreed to accept the verdict of my impartial arbitration. I read the examination question. "Show how it is possible to determine the height of a tall building with the aid of a barometer." The student had answered: "Take the barometer to the top of the building. Attach a long rope to it. Lower the barometer to the street—then bring it up, measuring the length of the rope. [Pause] The length of the rope is the height of the building." I suggested that the student had a strong base for full credit since he had answered the question completely and correctly, but the answer did not reflect a knowledge of physics.

I suggested that the student have another try at answering the question. They both agreed. The student was given six minutes to answer the same question reflecting an understanding of physics. After five minutes he had written nothing. I asked if he wished to give up. He said he had so many answers to the problem, he was trying to think of the best one! I excused myself for interrupting him and asked him to go on. In the next minute he dashed off his answer, which read: "Take the barometer to the top of the building and lean over the edge of the roof—drop the barometer, timing its fall with a stopwatch—then using the formula S=1/2 at the power of 2, calculate the height of the building." My frustrated colleague conceded and gave the student almost full credit.

Before leaving I asked the student what the other possibilities were. He listed them: "There are many ways of getting the height of a tall building with the aid of a barometer—for example, you could take the barometer out on a sunny day and measure the height of the barometer—the length of its shadow and the length of the shadow of the building and by the use of simple proportion determine the height of the building." "Fine," I said. "And others?" "Well, there is a very basic measuring, if you'd like. You take the barometer and begin to walk up the stairs. As you climb the stairs, you mark off the length of the barometer along the wall—then you count the number of marks and this gives you the height of the building in barometer units—this is a very direct method. Of course, the best method is to take the barometer to the basement and knock on the superintendent's door. When he answers, you say

to him, "Mr. Superintendent, here I have a fine barometer. If you'll tell me how tall this building is, I'll give it to you."
Dates & Places Used:

548 TOPIC: Logic

That's the Only Problem

A young man had finished his first semester in college, and was spending the weekend at home. Somewhat bored with the old place, he was regaling his father with the wonders of his campus and the enlightened people there. After getting up a head of steam and warming up to his subject he said, "Why, Dad, in our chemistry lab at college we have made an acid that will dissolve any known substance." The father turned and looked at him and slowly said, "That's mighty fine. What do they keep it in, son?"
Dates & Places Used:

549 TOPIC: Logic

Reduce the Steps

A survey showed that ninety percent of accidents on staircases involved either the top or the bottom stair. This information was fed into a computer to find out how stairway accidents could be reduced. The computer's answer: "Remove the top and bottom stairs."
Dates & Places Used:

550 TOPIC: Lostness

Futile Shots

Two inexperienced hunters went hunting in the woods. The game warden had warned them that they might get lost. He told them that if they did get lost to shoot three shots in rapid succession. In due course, they did get lost. One of them said to the other, "You'd better fire three shots." So he fired three shots. Nothing happened. After a while, the first hunter said, "You had better fire another three shots." So three more shots were fired. They waited another hour or so, and still nothing happened. Again, the first hunter turned to the second and said, in great distress, "I guess you had better fire three more shots." His friend said, "I can't. I've run out of arrows."

Dates & Places Used:

551 TOPIC: Lostness

Confused

After his presidential defeat, Thomas Dewey gave an analogy of how he felt: A mourner passed out from too much drinking at a wake and was laid in a spare coffin in the funeral parlor, to sleep it off. When he came to and realized where he was lying, he asked himself, "If I'm alive, why am I in this coffin? And if I'm dead, why do I have to go to the bathroom?"

Dates & Places Used:

552 TOPIC: Love

Never Changed His Mind

Ole and Olga lived on a farm in Iowa. Olga was living on a starvation diet of affection. Ole never gave her any signs of love, and Olga's need to be appreciated went unfulfilled. At her wit's end, Olga blurted out, "Ole, why don't you ever tell me that you love me?" Ole stoically responded, "Olga, when we were married I told you that I loved you, and if I ever change my mind, I'll let you know."

Dates & Places Used:

553

TOPIC: Love

Can't Talk About Love

Lucy says to Charlie Brown: "You know what I don't understand? I don't understand love!" He says, "Who does?" She says, "Explain love to me, Charlie Brown." He says, "You can't explain love. I can recommend a book or a poem or a painting, but I can't explain love." She says, "Well, try, Charlie Brown, try." Charlie says, "Well, let's say I see this beautiful, cute little girl walk by." Lucy interrupts: "Why does she have to be cute? Huh? Why can't someone fall in love with someone with freckles and a big nose? Explain that!" Charlie: "Well, maybe you are right. Let's just say I see this girl walk by with this great big nose." Lucy: "I didn't say GREAT BIG NOSE." Charlie: "You not only can't explain love, you can't even talk about it." ("Peanuts")
Dates & Places Used:

554

TOPIC: Loyalty

Loyalty to the End

A wealthy old man was very enthusiastic about his lovely young bride but sometimes wondered whether she might have just married him for his money, so he asked, "If I lost all my money, would you still love me?"

She retorted, "Of course I would still love you. Don't be silly. But I would miss you!"
Dates & Places Used:

555

TOPIC: Loyalty

Immutable Presbyterian

A grandmother was told by her her grandson that in Sunday school the teacher said Jesus was Jewish. The Presbyterian

grandmother said, "Well, that may be, but I assure you, God is still a Presbyterian."
Dates & Places Used:

556 TOPIC: Luck
It's All in How You View It

David, a second-grader, was bumped while getting on the school bus and suffered a two-inch cut on his cheek. At recess he collided with another boy and lost two teeth. At noon, while sliding on ice, he fell and broke his wrist. Later at the hospital, his father noticed David was clutching a quarter in his good hand. David said, "I found it on the ground when I fell. This is the first quarter I ever found. This sure is my lucky day."
Dates & Places Used:

557 TOPIC: Luck
Getty's Success

J. Paul Getty's Formula for Success: "Rise early, work late, and strike oil!"
Dates & Places Used:

558 TOPIC: Luck
What's in a Name?

A newspaper ad read: "Lost—One Dog. Brown hair with several bald spots. Right leg broken due to auto accident. Rear left hip hurt. Right eye missing. Left ear bitten off in a dog fight. Answers to the name 'Lucky.'"
Dates & Places Used:

559

TOPIC: Luck

Really Lucky

A certain man decided to make a living by gambling in the lottery, and indeed, he was lucky. He won millions. When asked how he did it, he replied, "I was smart and I was lucky. I like the number 7. I figured two 7s would be luckier than one, so I multiplied 7 times 7 and put all my money down on number 48 and I won!" The friend said, "But 7 times 7 is 49, not 48!" The man replied, "I know, that's the lucky part."

Dates & Places Used:

560

TOPIC: Lust

Disgusting

A minister and his family were walking down a street in Daytona Beach, Florida. Two women, wearing skimpy bikinis passed by. The minister remarked, "How disgusting!" His wife retorted, "If it is so disgusting, why do you look?" The twelve-year-old son spoke up and said, "I think Dad likes to be disgusted."

Dates & Places Used:

561

TOPIC: Lust

Old Temptations

Middle age is when you have two temptations, and you choose the one that will get you home by nine. *(President Ronald Reagan)*

Dates & Places Used:

562

TOPIC: Manipulation

Say the Magic Word

One woman is overheard saying to her friend: "I have a marvelous meatloaf recipe. All I do is mention it to my husband and he says, 'Let's eat out.'"

Dates & Places Used:

563

TOPIC: Manipulation

Child Manipulator

When my daughter Shannon was five years old, she came into the kitchen minutes before supper asking, "May I have a Twinkie please?" I replied, "No! Supper will be served in just a few minutes." Shannon began to moan and dance around, demanding a Twinkie since she was starving! Again, I said no. I said no several times more. Shannon began to pout.

While she pouted, I picked her up and asked, "You are still going to be my sweet precious love and the joy of my life and my dearest darling daughter, aren't you?"

With a sour face and lips poked out, Shannon whined, "I ain't gonna be your nothin' if you don't give me a Twinkie."

Dates & Places Used:

564

TOPIC: Manipulation

Thieves Don't Give

A minister in a small town was having trouble with his collections. So one Sunday he announced from the pulpit: "Before we pass the collection plate, I would like to request that the person who stole the chickens from Brother Harvey's henhouse please refrain from giving any money to the Lord. The Lord doesn't want money from a thief."

The collection plate was passed around, and for the first time in many months, everybody gave.
Dates & Places Used:

565

TOPIC: Manipulation

The Right Song

Before the service the preacher told the organist to play the appropriate music after he asked those who were willing to contribute four hundred dollars toward the church's mortgage to stand up. The accompanist asked what was the appropriate music. The preacher answered, "Play 'The Star Spangled Banner.'"
Dates & Places Used:

566

TOPIC: Manners

Secured Position

Customer: "Why do you have your thumb on my steak?"
Waitress: "So I won't drop it again."
Dates & Places Used:

567

TOPIC: Marriage

The Trick to Marriage

Marriage is like twirling a baton, turning handsprings, or eating with chopsticks. It looks easy until you try it.
Dates & Places Used:

568

TOPIC: Marriage

Unlucky Marriages

He's been unlucky in both his marriages. His first wife left him and his second wife won't.
Dates & Places Used:

569

TOPIC: Marriage

Seeds of Marriage

The difference between courtship and marriage is the difference between the pictures in the seed catalog and what comes up.
Dates & Places Used:

570

TOPIC: Marriage

Happiness

I didn't know what happiness was until I got married, but then it was too late. *(Michael Meaney)*
Dates & Places Used:

571

TOPIC: Marriage

Reasons for Marriage

Husband to Wife: How can someone so beautiful be so stupid?
Wife to Husband: God made me beautiful so you would marry me; he made me stupid so I would marry you!
Dates & Places Used:

572

TOPIC: Materialism

Catching Monkeys

During a three-week stay in Africa, we spent one afternoon in a game park near Nairobi. There we heard how monkeys are captured for zoos in the United States.

A shining metallic object is placed in a long-necked jar tied to a tree. As monkeys swing through the trees, their eyes catch the reflection of the sun on the shining object. Reaching into the jar poses no problem to them, but when they try to bring their closed fists through the narrow openings, they can't make it. To gain freedom, all the monkeys need to do is to let go of the worthless object. Instead, the monkeys sit by the jar holding onto the object until their captors come to take them away.

Perhaps there is something in your hand that is keeping you from freedom. Perhaps it is time to let it go (See Romans 12:1–2).

Dates & Places Used:

573

TOPIC: Materialism

Yuppies' Prayer

Now I lay me down to sleep,
I pray my Cuisinart to keep,
I pray my stocks are on the rise,
And that my analyst is wise,
That all the wine I sip is white,
And that my hot tub's watertight.
That racquetball won't get too tough,
That all my sushi's fresh enough.
I pray my cordless phone still works,
That my career won't lose its perks.
My microwave won't radiate,
My condo won't depreciate.
I pray my health club doesn't close,
And that my money market grows.
If I go broke before I wake,
I pray my Volvo they won't take.

Dates & Places Used:

574

TOPIC: **Materialism**

Christian Shoppers

Onward Christian soldiers, marching as to war,
Stopping at each shop, to buy a little more.
Christ, the Royal Master, leads against the foe,
But with so much baggage, we're moving kind of slow.

Dates & Places Used:

575

TOPIC: **Maturity**

Teenagers' Demise

It seldom occurs to teenagers that someday they will know as little as their parents.

Dates & Places Used:

576

TOPIC: **Maturity**

Opportunity of a Lifetime

We can only be young once, but we can be immature indefinitely.

Dates & Places Used:

577

TOPIC: **Maturity**

Be Specific

A little boy heard the phone ring. He ran to the phone, picked it up and answered it. The caller was a telemarketer, and the following conversation ensued: "Is your mother home?" "Nope." "Then is your father home?" "Nope." "Is there anyone else there I can speak to?" "Yep, my sister's here." "May I speak with her please?" "OK."

The telemarketer waited for a long time. Finally, the boy returned: "I'm back." "Where's your sister?" "I can't lift her out of the playpen."

Dates & Places Used:

578 TOPIC: Meals
Mother the Cook

The most remarkable thing about my mother is that for thirty years she served the family nothing but leftovers. The original meal has never been found. *(Calvin Trillin)*

Dates & Places Used:

579 TOPIC: Meetings
Words and Actions

A poster is displayed in all the conference rooms at IMI (computers and disc-drives manufacturer). It shows two or three large, ponderous hippopotami standing around with their gigantic mouths wide open. The words on the poster read, "When all is said and done, more is said than done."

Dates & Places Used:

580 TOPIC: Memory
Forgetful Middle Years

Here's a story submitted by Donald E. Worch:
Dear Cousin:
Just a line to say I'm living, that I'm not among the dead.
Though I'm getting more forgetful and mixed up in the head.

For sometimes I can't remember when I stand at foot of stairs,
If I must go up for something or I've just come down from there.
And before the "fridge" so often my poor mind is filled with doubt,
Have I just put food in there or have I come to take some out?
There are times when it's dark out with my nightcap on my head,
I don't know if I'm retiring or just getting out of bed.
If it's not my turn to write you there's no need of getting sore.
I may think that I have written and don't want to be a bore.
So remember I do love you and wish that you were here,
But now it's nearly mail time so I must say goodbye, my dear.
P.S. There I stood beside the mail box with my face so very red.
Instead of mailing you the letter, I had opened it instead.

Dates & Places Used:

581 TOPIC: Memory

Aspects of Aging

One of the most disturbing aspects of aging is the growing
inability to recall vitally important information—such as the
gross national product of Liberia, the Greek alphabet, and where
you put your slippers. This affliction becomes particularly pronounced when you go upstairs to get something. Half-way up,
you realize that you have no inkling of what you were going
upstairs to fetch. Then—you have to decide whether to go back
downstairs and try to remember what you needed, or continue
on up and look for something that needs bringing down. Unable
to decide, you resort to sitting on the landing and sulking, only to
discover that you have completely forgotten whether you were
originally upstairs, going down, or downstairs, going up!

Dates & Places Used:

582 TOPIC: Mercy

How's That Again?

Psychologist James Dobson reports seeing a sign on a convent
in Southern California reading: "Absolutely No Trespassing—

Violators Will Be Prosecuted to the Full Extent of the Law."
Signed, "The Sisters of Mercy."
Dates & Places Used:

583 TOPIC: Messes

We're Gonna Be in a Big Mess

A little boy's prayer: "Dear God, please take care of my daddy and my mommy and my sister and my brother and my doggy and me. Oh, and please take care of yourself, God. If anything happens to you, we're gonna be in a big mess."
Dates & Places Used:

584 TOPIC: Military

Say Something Funny

In the days before World War II, television comedy writer and producer Frank Galen reported for his Army physical when his draft notice came. When he finally reached the front of the line, the sergeant read his papers and said, "So you're a comedy writer, huh? Say something funny." The young man thought for a moment, turned to face the long line of recruits standing behind him in their underwear and yelled, "The rest of you men can go home now. The position has been filled."
Dates & Places Used:

585 TOPIC: Miracles

When God Answers

During the minister's prayer, there was a loud whistle from the congregation. Gary's mother was horrified. Later she asked, "Gary, whatever made you do that?" Gary answered soberly, "I asked God to teach me to whistle, and just then he did!"
Dates & Places Used:

586

TOPIC: Miracles

A Wife Is Born

A five-year-old excitedly reported to his parents about what he had learned in Sunday school. He told the story of Adam and Eve and how Eve was created from one of Adam's ribs. A few days later he told his mother: "My side hurts. I think I'm having a wife."

Dates & Places Used:

587

TOPIC: Miracles

Another Miracle

A traveler was found by a U.S. Customs official to be carrying a half-gallon bottle in from Mexico. The official asked the man what it contained. The traveler replied, "It's just holy water. I took it from the shrine I visited." The inspector was suspicious and opened the bottle and took a sniff. He shouted, "This isn't holy water, it's tequila!" The traveler lifted his eyes to the sky and cried out, "Good heavens! Yet another miracle."

Dates & Places Used:

588

TOPIC: Miracles

The Nun and the Bedpan

A little nun was on a much desired mission assignment to the Apache Indians. She was so excited that she drove past the last gas station without noticing that she needed gas. She ran out of gas about a mile down the road, and had to walk back to the station. The attendant told her that he would like to help her, but he had no container to hold the gas.

Sympathetic to her plight, he agreed to search through an old shed in the back for something that might suffice. The only container that would hold fuel was an old bedpan. The grateful nun told him that the bedpan would work just fine. She carried the gasoline back to her car, taking care not to drop an ounce. When she got to her car, she carefully poured the contents of the bed pan into the tank.

A truck driver pulled alongside the car as the nun was emptying the container into the tank. He rolled down his window and yelled to her, "I wish I had your faith, Sister!"

Dates & Places Used:

589
TOPIC: Mistakes
Keep Your Pants On

It was one of Mother's hectic days. Her small son, who had been playing outside, came in with his pants torn. "You go right in, remove those pants, and start mending them yourself," she ordered.

Some time later she went in to see how he was getting along. The torn pants were lying across the chair, and the door to the cellar, usually kept closed, was open. She called down the stairs, loudly and sternly: "Are you running around down there without your pants on?"

"No ma'am," was the deep-voiced reply. "I'm just down here reading your gas meter."

Dates & Places Used:

590
TOPIC: Mistakes
Simple Solutions

For every problem, there is a solution that is simple, neat, and wrong. *(H. L. Mencken)*

Dates & Places Used:

591
TOPIC: Mistakes
A Futile Call for Unity

Misspellers of the world—UNTIE!

Dates & Places Used:

592

Carpet Cleanout

Poor Mrs. Dora Wilson! On February 18, 1981, this English homemaker looked out her window in Harlow, Essex, and saw a group of men loading her neighbors' priceless collection of Persian carpets into a moving van. Knowing that her neighbors were on vacation, Mrs. Wilson called out, "What are you doing?"

"We're taking them to be cleaned, madam," the men replied.

Quick as a flash Mrs. Wilson decided to take advantage of the service they offered. "Will you please take mine, too?" she asked.

The men obliged. You guessed it; they were burglars.

Dates & Places Used:

593

Ennies or Nuns

Our three-year-old daughter Pam was playing with the two children next door. They were of the Catholic faith and had obviously been talking about their priest. Their mother came up on them just in time to hear Pam ask, "Just who do you keep calling 'Father' all the time?" The mother clarified, "You see, Pam, we call our preacher, Father." Not to be outdone, Pam simply replied, "Huh, that's nothin', so do we!"

On another occasion, we were riding along, with this same woman and her children and Pam in the back seat. I had previously lectured Pam on proper English, explaining that she was never to say, "I don't have none," but rather, "I don't have any."

We had gone no more than five blocks from the house when Pam pointed out two Catholic nuns and clearly shouted, "Oh, Daddy, look at the 'ennies.'" Totally embarrassed and wondering what our neighbor lady must be thinking, I quickly replied, "They're not 'ennies,' Pam. They're nuns." She curtly answered, "Well, Daddy, make up your mind."

Dates & Places Used:

594

TOPIC: Morality

A Careful Choice

We don't become more moral as we grow older, we just choose our sins more carefully.
Dates & Places Used:

595

TOPIC: Mothers

My Name Is

A teacher had just given her second-grade class a lesson on magnets. She reviewed: "My name starts with an 'M' and I pick up things. What am I?" A boy replied instantly, "A mother?"
Dates & Places Used:

596

TOPIC: Mothers

Mother's Day Break

After dinner one Mother's Day a mother was washing the dishes when her teen-age daughter walked into the kitchen. Horrified to see her mother at the sink, she exclaimed, "Oh, mother, you shouldn't have to do dishes on Mother's Day." The mother was touched by this seeming thoughtfulness and was about to take off her apron and give it to her daughter when the daughter added, "They'll keep till tomorrow."
Dates & Places Used:

597

TOPIC: Mothers

Practical Present

A little boy was talking to the girl next door: "I wonder what my mother would like for Mother's Day." The girl answered: "Well, you could promise to keep your room clean and orderly; you could go to bed as soon as she tells you; you could go to her as soon as she calls you; you could brush your teeth after eating; you could quit fighting with your brothers and sisters." The boy looked at her and said, "No, I mean something practical."

Dates & Places Used:

598

TOPIC: Mothers

The New Baby

A young mother held her almost four-year-old son on her lap and told him he was going to have a new baby brother soon. She explained that he could hold the baby's bottle, bring a clean diaper when needed, and push the baby carriage.

He finally got off her lap, stood in front of her and very seriously said, "And what are *you* going to be doing while *I* do all the work?"

Dates & Places Used:

599

TOPIC: Money

Greedy Giving

"God, you can have anything you can pry out of my hands!"

Dates & Places Used:

600

TOPIC: Money

Check Your Wallet, Sir?

Pat Williams, Orlando Magic general manager, on NBA commissioner David Stern's new five-year, $27.5 million contract: "All

I know is that on airplane trips, David's wallet will be considered carry-on baggage."
Dates & Places Used:

601

TOPIC: Morals

Dogs Welcome

A man seeking a hotel room for himself and his dog received the following reply from an innkeeper in Kingston, Jamaica: "I've been in the hotel business for forty years and never had to eject a disorderly dog. Never has a dog set fire to a bed. Never has he sneaked a girl into his room. Never has a dog stolen a towel or blanket or gotten drunk. Your dog is very welcome. If he will vouch for you, you can come along as well."
Dates & Places Used:

602

TOPIC: Mothers

Masked Mom

A mother put her two young children to bed and then got ready for bed herself. She put on some old clothes. She washed her hair and wrapped a towel around her head to dry her hair. She applied cold cream on her face to remove her makeup. Just as she was about to wipe off the cream, she heard the noise of her children playing in their room.

She stormed into the room sent the kids back into bed, turned out the light, and slammed the door. As she left the room, one of the children asked the other, "Who was THAT?"
Dates & Places Used:

603

TOPIC: Mothers

Measure of a Mom

Spanish proverb: An ounce of mother is worth a pound of clergy.
Dates & Places Used:

604

Recipe for Mothers

Here is a recipe for mothers: Preheat oven, but first check for rubber balls or plastic "He-Men" that might be lurking inside. Clear counter of wooden blocks and "Key-Cars." Grease pan. Crack nuts. Measure flour. . . . Remove Johnny's hands from flour. Re-measure flour. Crack more nuts to replace those Johnny ate. Sift flour, baking powder, and salt. Get broom and dustpan. Sweep up pieces of bowl Johnny knocked on floor. Find a second bowl. Answer doorbell. Return to kitchen. Remove Johnny's hands from bowl. Wash Johnny. Answer telephone. Return. Remove half inch of salt from greased pan. Call for Johnny. Look for Johnny. Give up search. Grease another pan. Answer phone. Return to kitchen. Find Johnny. Remove Johnny's hands from bowl. Remove layer of nut shells from greased pan. Sternly turn to Johnny . . . who knocks second bowl off counter while running away from you. Wash kitchen floor and counter and dishes . . . and walls. Final scene: Call bakery. Place order. Take two aspirins. Lie down.

Dates & Places Used:

605

Just Can't Catch Up

As our church observed the annual ritual of presenting flowers on Mother's Day, we first gave a carnation to the newest mother. Next we gave a flower to the mother with the most children present. Last, we gave a carnation to the oldest mother.

When the final three mothers in the last category told their ages, one sat dejectedly next to my wife who was in the choir and whispered seriously, "She was older than me last year, too."

Dates & Places Used:

606

TOPIC: Mothers

Free Roses

Mother's Day gas station ad: "Free rose for Mother with gas."
Dates & Places Used:

607

TOPIC: Mothers

Pit-Stop Momma

The cartoon strip *Momma* has the son running up and saying, "Hi, Momma! Can you sew on this button, in a hurry? And iron these slacks? And give me a cold glass of water? Thanks, Momma. Got to run." Momma looks at him leaving and sighs, "In the 'Indy 500' of life, mothers are the pit stops."
Dates & Places Used:

608

TOPIC: Mothers

Mom Is the Light

A little girl was reciting memory work in front of the entire church. In front of such a crowd her mind went blank. In the front row, her mother was almost as frantic as the little girl.

The mother gestured, moved her lips, trying to form the words for the girl, but it did no good. Finally, the mother, in desperation, whispered the opening phrase of the memorized Scripture: "I am the light of the world." Immediately the child's face lit up and relaxed and a smile appeared on it as she said with supreme confidence: "My mother is the light of the world!" Of course, everybody smiled and some laughed out loud.

Upon further reflection, the little girl, in many ways, was right. For the mother is the light of the child's world.
Dates & Places Used:

233

609

Thanks for the Help

Friends of a young mother with three young children were surprised when they received the following thank you note: "Many thanks for the play pen. It is being used every day. From 2 to 3 P.M. I get in it to read, and the children can't get near me."
Dates & Places Used:

610

Mother's Day Sound

The sounds of Mother's Day: A mixer whirs, out of control, then stops abruptly as a voice cries, "I'm telling." A dog barks and another voice says, "Get his paws out of there. Mom has to eat that!" Minutes pass and finally, "Dad! Where's the chili sauce?" Then, "Don't you dare bleed on Mom's breakfast!"

The breakfast is fairly standard: a water tumbler of juice, five pieces of black bacon that snap in half when you breathe on them, a mound of eggs that would feed a Marine division, and four pieces of cold toast. The kids line up by the bed to watch you eat and from time to time ask why you're not drinking your Kool-Aid or touching the cantaloupe with black olives on top spelling M-O-M. Later in the day, after you have decided it's easier to move to a new house than clean the kitchen, you return to your bed where, if you're wise, you'll reflect on this day. For the first time, your children have given instead of received. They have offered up to you the sincerest form of flattery: trying to emulate what you do for them.
Dates & Places Used:

611

Gift of Motivation

There was a young man who took a shortcut home late one night through the cemetery. And he fell into an open grave. He called, and he tried to climb out. To no avail. There was no one around to hear his cries or lend a hand. So he settled down for the night in a corner of the darkened grave to await morning. A little while later another person came the same route through the cemetery, taking the same shortcut home and fell into the same grave, and started clawing and shouting and trying to get out just as the first had done.

Suddenly, the second fellow heard a voice out of the dark corner of the grave saying, "You can't get out of here." But he did!
Dates & Places Used:

612   TOPIC: Motivation

Great Title

A seminarian turned in his typed-up sermon to his homiletics professor for grading, and when he met with him for a conference, the professor started out very positively. He said to the young man, "I like your exegesis. You have presented the meaning of the text in a helpful and clear fashion. Your three points make sense, they show balance and progression. Your introduction and your conclusion both show a great deal of thought. The illustrations you used seemed most appropriate. However, I am going to give you a D on the sermon." The seminarian was taken aback and said, "Why a D if it's all that good?" The professor said, "Well, frankly, it's because of your sermon title. It is one of the worst I've ever seen. Nobody will want to come to hear a sermon entitled: 'The Pericopes of Jesus in Relationship to the Eschatology of the Apostle Paul.' I tell you what I'll do. You see if you can come up with a better sermon title and I'll reconsider the grade. What you want is a title that will reach out and grab people by the heart, a title that will compel them to come and hear what you have to say. Imagine that title out on the sign in front of a church with such impact that if a bus stopped in front of the church and the people on the bus saw the sign, it would be so powerful it would motivate them to immediately get off the bus and run into the church." The young man said he would give it his best shot. So he went home and he wrestled with this task all night long, sweating bullets. The next morning he showed up at his professor's office and handed him his new sermon title, which read: "Your Bus Has a Bomb on It!"

Dates & Places Used:

613 TOPIC: Motivation

Sudden Skills

Nothing improves a person's driving skills like the sudden discovery that his license has expired.

Dates & Places Used:

614 TOPIC: Motivation

Puppy Punishment

A certain announcement appeared in the bulletin of a church in Sarasota, Florida: "The Magic of Lassie, a film for the whole family, will be shown Sunday at 5 P.M. in the church hall. Free puppies will be given to all children not accompanied by parents."

Dates & Places Used:

615 TOPIC: Motivation

Agree for Jobs

The minister of music rushed in to the new senior pastor's office. He began to complain about the minister of education. The string of complaints was long, but the new pastor called for a halt until the minister of education could be summoned. Once he was in the office, the pastor bade the minister of music to continue his diatribe. He refused. "All right," said the pastor, "you two step into the hallway and thresh this out. If you can't reach an agreement

in fifteen minutes, I'll have to let one of you go." In five minutes they were back. Both were smiling.
Dates & Places Used:

616 TOPIC: Motivation

Good Manners

Even folks with bad manners know how to be polite to those who can do something for them.
Dates & Places Used:

617 TOPIC: Motivation

Effective Strategy

As a mother said goodbye to her son who was returning to school after spring vacation, she reminded him to write often. Another woman standing nearby heard the plea and gave this advice: "The surest way to get your son to write home is to send him a letter saying, 'Here's 50 dollars. Spend it any way you like.'" "And that will make my son write home?" "Yes indeed. You forget to enclose the money."
Dates & Places Used:

618 TOPIC: Murphy's Laws

Law of Parenting

The later you stay up, the earlier your child will wake up.
For a child to become clean, something else must become dirty.
Toys multiply to fill any space available.
The longer it takes to make a meal, the less your child will like it.
Dates & Places Used:

619

Prayer Principles

1. People forget to pray for others in direct proportion to the frequency with which they say, "I'll pray about that."

2. In any prayer group at any given moment, 95 percent of the people will not be paying attention to your prayer. 55 percent will be daydreaming, 20 percent will be thinking about what they're going to say, 14 percent will be wishing you wouldn't blab so long, 5 percent will have their eyes open, and 1 percent will be wondering why you have your shirt on inside out.

Dates & Places Used:

620

Murphy's Shoes

Any shoe salesman can tell you: "If the shoe fits, it's the wrong color."

Dates & Places Used:

621

Modern Music

The trouble with a lot of songs you hear nowadays is that somebody forgot to put them to music.

Dates & Places Used:

622

The Golden Bargains

"One of the nice parts about heading toward middle age," notes Ken Floyd, "is that you can find all your favorite music in the bargain bin."

Dates & Places Used:

623

TOPIC: Music

Another Opinion

Swans sing before they die; 'twere no bad thing
Should certain persons die before they sing.

Dates & Places Used:

624

TOPIC: Music

Music Lover

Oscar Wilde was asked to buy a subscription to the opera. However, he found the opera boring and refused. It was pointed out to him that his friend had bought a subscription and his friend was even deaf.

Wilde replied, "If I were deaf, I would buy one too."

Dates & Places Used:

625

TOPIC: Music

A Reason to Sing

This story is from an old out-of-print book entitled *English Hymns:*

There was once a difficulty in Rev. Dr. Samuel West's congregation in the old New England times. The choir had declined to proceed with the music. So the shrewd clergyman introduced the services with the hymn "Come, We Who Love the Lord" and asked the congregation to begin with the second verse: "Let Those Refuse to Sing Who Never Knew Our God."

Dates & Places Used:

626

A Musical Clock

A certain trumpet player never hesitates to hock his watch or clock. He explains, "I live in an apartment house, and when I want to know what time it is during the night, all I have to do is start rolling the scales on my trumpet, and it ain't long before someone will holler: 'What's the idea, playing that thing at three-thirty in the morning?'"

Dates & Places Used:

627

TOPIC: Music

Wrong Verse

A pastor in the Chicago area started a church with just a few attenders. This group became a large, vibrant fellowship. In its early days, however, everyone was needed. His junior-high son was in the early stages of learning the piano but was quickly recruited to play for the Sunday evening service in their home. The son survived the first verse of the first song. Then his father confidently continued, "Now let's sing the second verse."

The pastor's son panicked, "But Dad, I only know how to play the first verse!"

Dates & Places Used:

628

TOPIC: Needs

Four Men Needed

A woman needs four men in her life: a banker, an actor, a minister, and a mortician. One for the money, two for the show, three to get ready, and four to go!

Dates & Places Used:

240

629

TOPIC: Negotiation

A Fair Price

In Harrieta, Michigan, a thirty-year-old man entered a Methodist church on a Sunday morning and held the congregation hostage with a rifle.

While police were en route, one parishioner asked how much the gun cost; he said $500. Another offered him $500 for it, and he accepted. The hostages took up a collection for the $500, he handed the rifle over, and the police arrested him.

Dates & Places Used:

630

TOPIC: Noise

Noise Tolerance

The amount of noise that anyone can bear stands in inverse proportion to his mental capacity. *(Arthur Schopenhauer)*

Dates & Places Used:

631

TOPIC: Noise

Croaking Frogs

A farmer asked the owner of a restaurant if he would be able to use a million frog legs. The proprietor asked where he could find so many frogs. "There's a pond at home just full of them," the farmer replied. "They drive me crazy night and day."

After they made an agreement for several hundred frogs, the farmer returned home. He came back a week later with two scrawny frogs and a foolish look on his face. "I guess I was wrong," he stammered. "There were just two frogs in the pond, but they sure were making a lot of noise!"

Next time you hear a lot of noise, remember, it may just be a couple of croakers.

Dates & Places Used:

632

TOPIC: Noise

Volume of Maturity

The first sign of maturity is that the volume knob turns to the left.
Dates & Places Used:

633

TOPIC: Nudity

A Loose Leaf

The pastor was so proud of his new "loose-leaf" Bible and decided to use it as he began preaching a series from Genesis. The second week of his series he was on the story of the fall of man and as he was reading his text he read, "And Adam said to Eve . . ." Then he turned the page to complete the verse but looked puzzled for a few seconds.

Finally realizing what had happened, he looked up rather embarrassed and said, ". . . it looks like a leaf is missing!"
Dates & Places Used:

634

TOPIC: Obedience

Scat Cat

I was recently reminded of the old story of the man who had nine cats. One day his friend was visiting him and noticed that he had nine separate little kitty doors cut into the wall. He was puzzled by this and asked why the cats couldn't all use the same door.

The man replied "When I say 'scat' I mean 'scat'!"
Dates & Places Used:

635

TOPIC: Obedience

Requirements to Drive

On his sixteenth birthday the son approached his father and said, "Dad, I'm sixteen now. When I get my license, can I drive the family car?" His dad looked at him and said, "Son, driving the car takes maturity, and first, you must prove you are responsible enough. And one way you must do that is to bring up your grades. They are not acceptable. Second, you must read the Bible every day. And finally, I want you to get that hair cut; it looks outrageous." The son began the task of fulfilling his father's requirements, knowing that the last might be impossible.

When his grades came out he came to his dad with a big smile. "Look, Dad, all A's and B's on my report card. Now can I drive the family car?" "Very good, son. You are one-third of the way there, but have you been reading the Bible?" the father replied. "Yes, Dad, every day," said the son. "Very good, Son. You are two-thirds of the way there. Now when are you going to get that hair cut?" The son, thinking he could outsmart his dad, responded, "Well, I don't see why I should get my hair cut to drive the car. Jesus had long hair, didn't he?" The father looked at his boy and said, "That's right, son, and Jesus walked everywhere he went."

Dates & Places Used:

636 TOPIC: Obedience

Backward Obedience

One of the first things one notices about any backward country is that the children obey their parents.

Dates & Places Used:

637 TOPIC: Offerings

Pay or Get Off

A conductor on the Santa Fe was converted and united with the church. After he had been faithful in his religious duties for some weeks, he was asked one Sunday morning to help take the offering.

He started down the aisle, and all went well until he came to a richly dressed woman. She allowed the plate to go past her, whereupon the conductor unconsciously reached up for the bell

rope to stop the train, and said, "Madam, if you don't pay, you'll have to get off."
Dates & Places Used:

638 TOPIC: Offerings

Crowd Control

A young policeman was asked during an oral exam what he would do to break up a crowd. His answer revealed a genuine knowledge of human nature. His answer: "I'd just take up a collection."
Dates & Places Used:

639 TOPIC: Opinions

Opinions or Thoughts

A great many people do not have a right to their own opinions because they don't know what they are talking about. (*Andy Rooney*)
Dates & Places Used:

640 TOPIC: Opportunity

Good from Bad

Hauling clay for a landfill, a truck driver backed his dump truck too far over the grade. The weight of the load lifted the front end of the truck several feet off the ground.

"Now what do we do?" asked his helper as the driver jumped from the truck. The driver looked at the truck, grabbed some things out of the cab, slid under the truck and said, "I guess I'll grease her. I'll never have a better chance."
Dates & Places Used:

TOPIC: Opportunity

Blown Opportunity

Late one Christmas Day a resident of the posh community of Hillsborough, California, accompanied by his wife and children, set out to sing carols for the neighbors. As they were tuning up outside their first stop, the woman of the house came to the door, looking distraught. "Look fella," she said, "I'm just too busy. The plumbing's on the blink, I can't get anybody to fix it, and there's a mob coming for dinner. If you really feel like singing carols, come back about nine o'clock, okay?" "Yes, ma'am," replied Bing Crosby respectfully, as he herded his troupe elsewhere.

Dates & Places Used:

TOPIC: Opportunity

If Shoe Fits, Sell It

There were once two shoe salesmen who went to Africa to open new sales territories. Three days after they arrived, the first salesman faxed a message: "I will be returning on next plane. I can't sell shoes here. Everyone goes barefoot all the time."

There was no report from the second salesman for about two weeks. Then came a fat airmail envelope with this message for the home office. "Fifty orders enclosed. Prospects unlimited. Nobody here has shoes."

Dates & Places Used:

TOPIC: Opportunity

Watch the Wreck

Two brothers were being interviewed for a truck-driving team. They were confronted with a hypothetical situation. The interviewer said, "Charlie, imagine you're driving the truck and LeRoy, your brother, is up top asleep. Charlie, your truck is

loaded down with produce. You are going down a steep mountain when all of a sudden your brakes fail. You try your emergency brake and that fails. You try to gear down and you strip all
your gears. Now, without any mechanical means of stopping, you
are accelerating 80–90–100–110–120–130 miles per hour. Now, at
that rate the road suddenly narrows into one lane and goes over a
one-lane bridge. And from out of the horizon you see another
truck coming toward you in exactly the same situation you're in.
At that point, Charlie, what do you do?" Charlie's instant reply
was, "I'd wake up LeRoy." The employer asked him, "Why, at a
time like that, would you wake up LeRoy?" Charlie replied, "Well,
you see, sir, LeRoy ain't never seen a great big wreck."
Dates & Places Used:

644

TOPIC: Opportunity

Opening Line

Douglas Fairbanks, Jr., began a lecture at Flint Center in
Cupertino, California, saying, "I feel like a mosquito in a nudist
colony. I look around and I know it's wonderful to be here, but I
don't know where to begin."
Dates & Places Used:

645

TOPIC: Opportunity

To Make a Buck

The following story is from Ronald Reagan's early autobiography, written before he became governor of California, long before
he became president, entitled *Where Is the Rest of Me?* (p. 215).

I was playing a small town lawyer in a picture called *Storm
Warning* that teed off on the Ku Klux Klan. Some of our first
scenes were shot at night in a small California town that is
rumored to be the center of Klan activity here on the coast. The
studio was understandably nervous and halfway expected some
kind of incident. About three o'clock one morning, shooting a

street scene, I thought maybe the studio was justified in its concern. A little character sidled up to me and whispered out of the corner of his mouth, "I hear this movie is about the Klan." I allowed as how it was, getting ready to yell, "Hey Rube," when his next line stopped me cold. He said, "Well, I'm in the local outfit and if you need to rent some robes, let me know."
Dates & Places Used:

646
TOPIC: Opportunity
Raw Furniture

A sign in a Christmas tree lot the day after Christmas: We sell unfinished furniture!
Dates & Places Used:

647
TOPIC: Optimism
Married Secretaries

An optimist is a man who marries his secretary and thinks he'll be able to continue dictating to her.
Dates & Places Used:

648
TOPIC: Optimism
Optimist and the Fly

The optimist is the kind of person who believes a housefly is looking for a way out. *(George Jean Nathan)*
Dates & Places Used:

649

TOPIC: Optimism

Optimistic Whaler

I'm such an optimist I'd go after Moby Dick in a rowboat and take the tartar sauce with me. *(Zig Ziglar)*
Dates & Places Used:

650

TOPIC: Optimism

Optimistic Planning

There are two prisoners shackled to the wall of a deep dark dungeon.

Spread-eagled, they are securely lashed by manacles and chains and actually hanging suspended, side by side, a few feet above the damp floor of the dungeon. There is only one small window high above their heads, maybe thirty or forty feet up. They are immobile and alone, pinned inexorably to the wall.

One prisoner turns to the other and whispers, "Here's my plan!"
Dates & Places Used:

651

TOPIC: Pacifism

Regrettable Actions

A father and his young son were out for a ride with the horse and buggy (many years ago). It had been a very rainy week, and the roads were extremely muddy. They turned onto a road that had one set of deep ruts in the middle of it which they began to follow. As they came closer to the middle of the mile stretch of road, they saw another horse and buggy coming toward them in the same set of deep ruts. Both buggies stopped horse to horse.

The father quietly told the other man that he would have to back up. The man argued that the father and his son could back up just as easily as he could. They began to argue about it and finally the father looked the other in the face and said, "If you do not back up, I'm afraid I am going to do something I'm going to regret."

The man looked at the father and began backing his horse and buggy down the road. The father and his son remained still, giving the man the opportunity to get out of their way. The son, who had been raised in a Christian tradition that taught that the use of force, violence, and power was not right was astonished. He turned to his father and asked, "Dad, what were you going to do that you were going to regret?"

His father answered, "I was going to back up."

Dates & Places Used:

652

TOPIC: Pacifism

Looking for Loopholes

An old Quaker discovered a burglar in his home late one night. The thief was emptying the contents of the Quaker's safe into a sack. The Quaker tiptoed out, got his shotgun, and tiptoed back. Standing only a few feet from the burglar, he announced his presence. "Friend," he said calmly, "I would not harm thee for the world, but thou art standing where I am about to shoot."

Dates & Places Used:

653

TOPIC: Parents

Sound Advice

Sound travels slowly. Sometimes the things you say when your kids are teenagers don't reach them till they're in their forties.

Dates & Places Used:

654

TOPIC: Parents

Child's Play

Among those things that are so simple that even a child can operate them are parents.
Dates & Places Used:

655

TOPIC: Parents

Don't Let Them Get Away

"I'm really worried," said one little boy to a friend. "Dad slaves away at his job so I'll never want for anything, so I'll be able to go to university if I want to. Mom works hard every day washing and ironing, cleaning up after me, taking care of me when I get sick. They spend every day of their lives working just on my behalf. I'm worried." His friend asked, "What have you got to worry about?" And he replied, "I'm afraid they might try to escape."
Dates & Places Used:

656

TOPIC: Parents

Too Full a Quiver

Back in the days when fathers waited outside for the baby to be born, there were three men waiting for the joyous news. The first was informed by the nurse that his wife had twins. He told the nurse, "Isn't that ironic. I pitch for the Minnesota Twins."

A few minutes later the second man learned his wife had triplets. The coincidence was that he worked for 3-M.

The third man panicked and raced for the door. He was stopped and asked what happened. "I work for a 7–11 store, and I'm getting out of here!"
Dates & Places Used:

657

TOPIC: Pastors

Pastor Dad

The minister's little daughter was sent to bed with a stomach-ache and missed her usual romp with her daddy. A few minutes later she appeared at the top of the stairs and called to her mother, "Mama, let me talk with Daddy."

"No, my dear, not tonight. Get back in bed."

"Please, Mama."

"I said, no. That's final."

"Mother, I'm a very sick woman and I must see my pastor at once."

Dates & Places Used:

658

TOPIC: Pastors

Waiting on God

Several pastors were telling each other how their churches determined how the offerings were received and distributed. One seasoned veteran astounded them all when he said that he left that entirely up to God. He would go into a small room after the service and pray over the money. He would then throw all the money into the air. Whatever God wanted, he could then take. He would take only what God had left.

Dates & Places Used:

659

TOPIC: Pastors

Get Rid of Your Pastor

You may want to put this piece in your weekly newsletter or bulletin, if not used in a sermon. How to get rid of your pastor:

1. Look the pastor straight in the eye while he's preaching and say "Amen" once in awhile, and he'll preach himself to death.

2. Pat him on the back and brag on his good points, and he'll probably work himself to death.

3. Rededicate your life to Christ and ask the preacher for some job to do, preferably some lost person you could win to Christ, and he'll die of heart failure!

4. Get the church to unite in prayer for the preacher, and he'll soon become so effective that some larger church will take him off your hands!

Dates & Places Used:

660

TOPIC: Pastors

The Church Chain Letter

A new church chain letter: Send a copy of this letter to six other churches that are tired of their ministers. Then bundle up your pastor and send him to the church at the top of the list. In six weeks you will receive 16,436 ministers, and one of them should be dandy.

Pastors—Don't show this to your church. They may like the idea.

Dates & Places Used:

661

TOPIC: Pastors

Too Many Pastors

A message was announced over a plane's intercom: "Number four engine has just been shut off because of mechanical trouble. There is nothing to worry about, however; we can still finish the flight with just three engines. Besides, you will be reassured to know that we have four pastors on board." One passenger called the flight attendant and said, "Would you please tell the captain that I would rather have four engines and three pastors?"

Dates & Places Used:

252

TOPIC: Pastors

Perfect Pastor Found

The Perfect Pastor has been found:

He preaches exactly twenty minutes and then sits down. He condemns sin, but never steps on anybody's toes. He works from 8 in the morning to 10 at night, doing everything from preaching sermons to sweeping. He makes $60 per week, gives $30 a week to the church, drives a late model car, buys lots of books, wears fine clothes, and has a nice family. He always stands ready to contribute to every other good cause, too, and to help panhandlers who drop by the church on their way to somewhere. He is 36 years old, and has been preaching 40 years. He is tall on the short side, heavyset in a thin sort of way, and handsome. He has eyes of blue or brown (to fit the occasion), and wears his hair parted in the middle, left side dark and straight, right side brown and wavy. He has a burning desire to work with the youth, and spends all his time with the senior citizens. He smiles all the time while keeping a straight face, because he has a keen sense of humor that finds him seriously dedicated. He makes fifteen calls a day on church members, spends all his time evangelizing non-members, and is always found in his study if he is needed.

Unfortunately he burnt himself out and died at the age of 32.

Dates & Places Used:

TOPIC: Pastors

Jesus Understands

Jesus was walking along one day when he came upon a man crying, and he said, "My friend, what's wrong?" The man replied, "I'm blind; can you help me?" Jesus healed the man, and he went on his way.

Jesus continued along and came upon another man sitting and crying. "Good friend, what's wrong?" He answered, "I'm lame and can't walk; can you help me?" Jesus healed the man, and they both went down the road.

As Jesus continued on, he came upon a third man crying. Jesus said, "Good friend, what's wrong?" He said, "I'm a minister." And Jesus sat down and wept with him.

Dates & Places Used:

664 TOPIC: Pastors

More Humble Pie

A pastor just announced to the congregation that he would be leaving their church. There was a good deal of crying and lots of kind words. As the pastor was talking to one woman who had expressed her sadness at his leaving, he consoled her with these generous words: "Oh, don't feel bad. I'm sure our superintendent will come up with a much better replacement." And she turned and said, "Oh, that's what they said last time. In fact that's what they say all the time. But it never happens!"

Dates & Places Used:

665 TOPIC: Pastors

Housing in Heaven

A bus driver and a minister were standing in line to get into heaven. The bus driver approached the gate, and St. Peter said, "Welcome, I understand you were a bus driver. Since I'm in charge of housing, I believe I have found the perfect place for you. See that mansion over the hilltop? It's yours."

The minister heard all this, and began to stand a little taller. He thought to himself, "If a bus driver got a place like that, just think what I'll get." The minister approached the gate, and St. Peter said, "Welcome, I understand you were a minister. See that shack in the valley?" St. Peter had hardly gotten the words out of his mouth when the irate minister said, "I was a minister, I preached the Gospel, I helped teach people about God. Why does that bus driver get a mansion, and I get a shack?" Sadly, St. Peter responded, "Well, it seems when you preached, people slept. When the bus driver drove, people prayed."

Dates & Places Used:

666

TOPIC: Pastors

Pastor Pig

A man called at the church and asked if he could speak to the Head Hog at the Trough. The secretary said, "Who?" The man replied, "I want to speak to the Head Hog at the Trough!"

Sure that she had heard correctly, the secretary said, "Sir, if you mean our pastor, you will have to treat him with more respect and ask for 'the reverend' or 'the pastor.' But certainly you cannot refer to him as the Head Hog at the Trough!"

At this, the man responded, "Oh, I see. Well, I have $10,000 I was thinking about donating to the building fund."

The secretary exclaimed, "Hold the line; I think the big pig just walked in the door."

Dates & Places Used:

667

TOPIC: Patience

Just in Time

I heard recently about a man who prided himself on being exceedingly punctual. He followed a very precise routine every morning. His alarm went off at 6:30 A.M. He rose briskly, shaved, showered, ate his breakfast, brushed his teeth, picked up his briefcase, got into his car, drove to the nearby ferry landing, parked his car, rode the ferry across to the downtown business area, got off the ferry, walked smartly to his building, marched to the elevator, rode to the seventeenth floor, hung up his coat, opened his briefcase, spread his papers out on his desk, and sat down in his chair at precisely 8:00 A.M. Not 8:01, not even 7:59. Always at 8:00 A.M.

He followed this same routine without variation for eight years, until one morning his alarm did not go off, and he over-slept fifteen minutes. When he did awake, he was panic-stricken. He rushed through his shower, nicked himself when he shaved, gulped down his breakfast, only half-way brushed his teeth, grabbed up his briefcase, jumped into his car, sped to the ferry landing, jumped out of his car, and looked for the ferry. There it was, out in the water a few feet from the dock. He said to himself,

"I think I can make it," and he ran down the dock towards the ferry at full speed. Reaching the edge of the pier he gave an enormous leap out over the water and miraculously landed with a loud thud on the deck of the ferry. The captain rushed down to make sure he was all right.

The captain said, "Man, that was a tremendous leap, but if you would have just waited another minute, we would have reached the dock, and you could have walked on."

Dates & Places Used:

668

TOPIC: Patience

God's Not in a Hurry!

A friend of the great preacher Phillip Brooks, called on him and found him impatiently pacing the floor. His friend asked what the trouble was. Dr. Brooks exclaimed, "The trouble is that I am in a hurry, and God is not!"

Dates & Places Used:

669

TOPIC: Patience

The Patience of Noah

Don't give up. It took Noah six months to find a parking place.

Dates & Places Used:

670

TOPIC: Perfection

True Humility

Only .001 percent of the popluation achieves perfection, which may be why so few people recognize it in us.

Dates & Places Used:

TOPIC: Perfection

Pain of Perfection

A perfectionist is someone who takes infinite pains—and gives them to others.

Dates & Places Used:

TOPIC: Persistence

Tenacity

It has been told that the Chicago Bears were losing a football game at halftime. Their coach Mike Ditka wanted to graphically illustrate his concern for them that they learn to be tough and tenacious. Mike reached his hand into a bucket. He removed his hand with a snapping turtle clamped securely to it. It was not a pretty sight. With the snapping turtle hanging onto his wounded hand, Ditka continued to lecture his astounded team. He assured his team that any one of them could do the same thing if they were really committed and determined.

He then asked for the next volunteer. After an extended time of silence, one of the players named "Refrigerator" stepped forward and volunteered to go next. Ditka thanked him for his courage and told him he could proceed as soon as the turtle was pried loose from his hand. The Refrigerator politely suggested to his coach that there was no reason to remove the turtle. "Just stick out your other hand, and I'll bite that one instead!"

Dates & Places Used:

TOPIC: Persistence

Getting Ready to Win

A man was traveling down the streets of a large city and stopped at a stop light. He looked off to his right and saw two boys fighting in an alley. One boy was quite a bit bigger than the other boy and was consequently knocking the tar out of the little fellow. He would punch the smaller boy, and blood would fly from the boy's nose, but he would get right back up to receive another punch. The traveler decided he had to intervene. He stopped his car and ran over, yelling for the big boy to quit beating up on the little guy.

But it was the little fellow who responded. He said, "Hey mister, mind your own business. I ain't got my second wind yet, and when I do I am going to clobber this guy."

You can't lick a guy who won't stay down. Proverbs says, "The just man falls seven times yet rises up again."

Dates & Places Used:

674 TOPIC: Perspective

Put the Bones Back

A mother tells a cute story about her boy's visit to the doctor with her. While viewing her chest X-rays, the curious child asked what all those "things" were. The doctor told him that those were his mother's bones. With great concern the boy asked, "Are you going to put them back in?"

Dates & Places Used:

675 TOPIC: Perspective

Life in New England

Here are a few cute accounts from the Northeast portion of the USA:
"Lived in this town all your life?" "No. Not yet."

"Can you tell me how to get to Wheelock?" "Well now, if I were going to Wheelock, I don't believe I'd start from here."

"Edward, you know we used to sit a lot closer together back when we was courtin'." "I ain't moved."

"Because I wasn't born in New England, I realize I'll never be considered a native. But since my three children were all born in Putney, Vermont, aren't they natives?" "Well, if your cat happened to have kittens in the oven, would you call 'em biscuits?"

"Jeb, as your doctor, I'm just going to have to tell you to quit drinking. If you don't, you may grow to be stone deaf." "I'll be deaf then. I like what I drink better'n what I hear."

Dates & Places Used:

TOPIC: Perspective

676

Perspective Puzzler

During World War II, a general and his subordinate lieutenant in the States were traveling from their base to a base in another state. They were forced to travel with civilians aboard a passenger train. They found their booth, where two other folks were already seated—an attractive young woman and her grandmother. For most of the trip, they conversed freely.

The train entered a long and rather dark tunnel. Once inside the tunnel, the passengers in this particular car heard two distinct sounds—the first was the smooch of a kiss; the second was the loud sound of a slap.

Now, here are these four people in this booth aboard the passenger train. They possess four differing perspectives. The young woman is thinking to herself how glad she is that the young lieutenant got up the courage to kiss her, but she is somewhat disappointed at her grandmother for slapping him for doing it; the general is thinking to himself how proud he is of his young Lieutenant for being enterprising enough to find this opportunity to kiss the attractive young woman, but he is flabbergasted that she slapped him instead of the lieutenant; the grandmother is flabbergasted to think that the young lieutenant would have the gall to kiss her granddaughter, but she is proud of her granddaughter for slapping him for doing it.

The young lieutenant is trying to hold back his laughter, for he had found the perfect opportunity to kiss an attractive young girl and slap his superior officer all at the same time!

Dates & Places Used:

677

TOPIC: Perspective

More Than a Spot

An economist was asked to talk to a group of business people about the recession. She tacked up a big sheet of white paper. Then she made a black spot on the paper with her pencil, and asked a man in the front row what he saw. The man replied promptly, "A black spot." The speaker asked every person the same question, and each replied, "A black spot."

With calm and deliberate emphasis the speaker said: "Yes, there is a little black spot, but none of you mentioned the big sheet of white paper. And that's my speech."

Dates & Places Used:

678

TOPIC: Perspective

Joy or Fear

An optimist is one who believes he lives in the best of all worlds. A pessimist fears that this is true.

Dates & Places Used:

679

TOPIC: Perspective

Sorrow Abounds

After the Sunday school teacher told the story of the prodigal son to the class, she asked, "Was anyone sorry when the prodigal son returned?"

One boy answered, "Yes, the fatted calf."

Dates & Places Used:

680

TOPIC: Perspective

Normal and Oblong

A gifted Christian communicator was speaking about ways to set the ideas you want to communicate into the context of the audience's lives. When he came into a new community to speak, he always bought a local newspaper and read it through. If there had been a devastating tragedy in that town, the audience would be in a very different mood than if there were an all-city celebration coming up for the high-school state championship basketball team. The speaker said that one Sunday he was to speak in Bloomington, Illinois. He arrived Saturday evening and bought a paper. It seems that there are two small towns or suburbs next to Bloomington—one called "Normal" and the other "Oblong." As the speaker was turning through the paper, he came to the society section, and his eyes were drawn to a headline: "Normal boy marries Oblong girl."

He thought this was hilarious, cut it out and read it from the pulpit the next morning. But no one laughed. The names of the towns were so much a part of their own local language that they couldn't see how funny they might sound to the rest of the world.

Dates & Places Used:

681

TOPIC: Perspective

Canyon or Confusion

Three people were visiting and viewing the Grand Canyon—an artist, a pastor, and a cowboy. As they stood on the edge of that massive abyss, each one responded with a cry of exclamation. The artist said, "Ah, what a beautiful scene to paint!" The minister cried, "What a wonderful example of the handiwork of God!" The cowboy mused, "What a terrible place to lose a cow!"

Dates & Places Used:

682

TOPIC: Perspective

Pushing Boats

Two men who had lived all their lives in the Arctic cold regions traveled to Miami. On the bus to the hotel, they saw people who were waterskiing. Having seen only their kayaks and other hand-propelled boats throughout their lives, one man asked the other, "What makes that boat go so fast?" The other man watched for a few seconds, then replied, "Man on string push it."

Dates & Places Used:

683

TOPIC: Perspective

Last Word on Comet

Can't stargazers do their thing without discombobulating most of the rest of us with something that's a phenomenon to them and usually invisible to us? Halley's Comet is only the latest of those frequent once-in-a-lifetime heavenly happenings that have millions shivering outside, suffering eyestrain, and acquiring a pain in the neck. Is it too much to hope that astronomers can gaze without continuously trying to turn the rest of us on? As the woman who traveled to an Inca ruin in Peru to best view Halley's Comet said, "That's it? That's all there is? I came four thousand miles to see this crummy little fuzzball?"

Dates & Places Used:

684

TOPIC: Perspective

Surgical Advice

A woman who worked for a veterinarian was about to have knee surgery. She was nervous about the surgery and decided to ask her veterinarian boss if he had any advice for her. Without much thought he advised, "Just turn your worries into prayers, get plenty of rest, and don't lick your incision."

Dates & Places Used:

685

TOPIC: Persuasion

Ways to Shop

During a busy Christmas shopping season a little boy was standing in the middle of the aisle of one of the large department stores, crying, "I want my mommy!" As people would go by they would say, "There, there, little boy. Your momma will find you." And a number of them had given him pocket change to help assuage his tears. But he kept sobbing, with tears running down his cheeks. Finally someone from the department store came along and said, "I know where your mommy is, son." And the little boy looked up and responded, "So do I, just keep quiet."

Dates & Places Used:

TOPIC: Persuasion

A Glorious Send-Off

A boy's pet turtle fell over and lay motionless. The boy ran in to tell his salesman father. The father sized up the situation, put the turtle in a little box, and proceeded to share his faith with his son.

In his most convincing sales manner, he told of the joys of eternal life and the beauty surrounding the heavenly throne. He also told about the marvelous wake that they would hold for the late departed turtle, and said that the boy could invite his friends over for ice cream and cake. The boy gradually brightened up. The father decided to close by inviting the boy out to bury the turtle. When they opened the box, there was the turtle walking around as if nothing had happened. With a cheery glow on his face, the boy looked up at his father and said, "Dad, let's kill him!"

Dates & Places Used:

TOPIC: Persuasion

Say It as if You Mean It

Helena Modjeska (1844–1909) was a popular actress with great emotional style and superb ability. She demonstrated this

ability by giving a dramatic reading in Polish, her native tongue, at a dinner party. Her listeners, who didn't understand the language, were in tears by the time she had finished. She had just recited the Polish alphabet.
Dates & Places Used:

688 TOPIC: Persuasion
Country Persuasion

Out in the country people trade and buy livestock, much in the same way that city folks buy provisions for themselves in the supermarket. As in the city, a farmer sometimes comes across a deal he can't refuse. To prove this point, my old boyhood friend Fred tells this story about his own experience.

"I tell you what I'm going to do," said Fred to his friend Louis. "For a hundred dollars, I'm going to get you an elephant. What do you think about that?" Louis replied, "I think it sounds crazy. I don't want an elephant. I don't even like elephants." Fred said, "Don't be so stubborn. This is the deal I'm offering you; a full-grown elephant for just one hundred dollars." Louis protested, "But I don't want a full-grown elephant for no hundred dollars. For one thing, where would I keep it? And the mess they make. No sir. Count me out. An elephant I do not need." Fred eyed his friend closely. "Tell you what I'll do. For a hundred and fifty dollars, I'll get you two elephants!" Louis said, "Now you're talking sense."
Dates & Places Used:

689 TOPIC: Persuasion
Hitchhiker Religion

A sign carried by a hitchhiker: "Whither Thou Goest, I Will Go."
Dates & Places Used:

690

TOPIC: Persuasion

Motivation

Linus is on his way to school with a bunch of spring flowers in his hand. Charlie Brown meets him along the way and immediately figures out what's going on—Linus is taking flowers to the teacher. So Charlie Brown inquires: "Flowers for the teacher, Linus? You know, Linus, you'll never get anywhere with Miss Othmar by trying to use bribery." Linus turns around, confronts Charlie Brown, and says, "Bribery? This isn't bribery. I prefer to think of it as pump priming."

Dates & Places Used:

691

TOPIC: Persuasion

Gift of Imagination

In Berkeley, near the campus of the University of California, a ramp goes up the freeway. Just about the time vacations begin, that ramp is loaded with college kids hitching rides. They have signs saying, "Sacramento" or "L.A." or names of other destinations. They hold up these signs for the passing motorist to see and respond to. But one man was particularly impressed when he saw a young man with a sign saying simply "MOM IS WAITING." How could he resist giving him a ride?

Dates & Places Used:

692

TOPIC: Pessimism

Big Bad Grass

All you need to grow fine, vigorous grass is a crack in your sidewalk.

Dates & Places Used:

693

Share a Brush

A little girl is out in the backyard brushing the dog's teeth, and her father stops by and says, "What are you doing?" She says, "Well, I'm brushing Scuffy's teeth." She pauses and says to her father, "Don't worry, Dad. I'll put your toothbrush back like I always do."
Dates & Places Used:

694

Tough to Hide True Feelings

An Easterner walked into a Western saloon and saw a dog sitting at a table playing poker with three men. He asked, "Can that dog really play cards?" One of the men answered, "Yeah, but he ain't much of a player. Whenever he gets a good hand he wags his tail."
Dates & Places Used:

695

Beyond This Vale of Tears

A little girl's cat had died. Her mother attempted to console her by saying, "Tabby is in heaven now." The little girl looked up and asked, "But Mom, what would God want with a dead cat?"
Dates & Places Used:

696

Cats and Love Return

The cat and the love you give away come back to you.
Dates & Places Used:

697

Life Happens

Life is what happens to you while you're busy planning more important things.

Dates & Places Used:

698

TOPIC: Planning

Set Up for Life

I had a note from my brother-in-law the other day. He's in the catering business. He says business is terrific. In fact, he said that he now has enough money to last him the rest of his life—as long as he dies by next Tuesday.

Dates & Places Used:

699

TOPIC: Politeness

Levels of Love

A little girl stayed for dinner at the home of her friend. The vegetable was buttered broccoli, and the mother asked if she liked it. The child replied very politely, "Oh yes, I love it." But when the bowl of broccoli was passed, she declined to take any. The hostess said, "I thought you said you loved broccoli." The girl replied sweetly, "Oh, yes ma'am, I do, but not enough to eat it!"

Dates & Places Used:

700

TOPIC: Politics

Not What You Pay For

If you think you're getting too much government, just be thankful you're not getting as much as you're paying for.
Dates & Places Used:

701

TOPIC: Politics

Have Your Way

Politics is the art of letting people have your way.
Dates & Places Used:

702

TOPIC: Politics

Creating Chaos

A surgeon, an engineer, and a politician were debating which of their professions was the oldest. The surgeon said, "Eve was made from Adam's rib, and that, of course, was a surgical procedure. Obviously, surgery is the oldest profession."

The engineer countered with, "Yes, but before that, order was created out of chaos, and that most certainly was an engineering job."

The politician smiled and said triumphantly, "Aha! And just who do you think created the chaos?"
Dates & Places Used:

703

TOPIC: Politics

Senate Prayers

When Edward Everett Hale was Chaplain of the Senate, someone asked him, "Do you pray for the senators, Dr. Hale?" He replied, "No, I look at the senators and pray for the country."
Dates & Places Used:

704

TOPIC: Politics

Which Side

In Washington, D.C., a tourist asked a passerby on C Street, "Which side is the State Department on?"

The reply, "Ours, I think."

Dates & Places Used:

705

TOPIC: Politics

Sure-Fire Test for Lying

Earl Long, former eccentric governor of Louisiana, once said of another politician: "You know how you can tell that fella's lying? Watch his lips. If they're movin', he's lying."

Dates & Places Used:

706

TOPIC: Politics

Egocentric Steering

A newly elected politician was visiting Washington, D.C. to get acquainted. He was visiting in the home of one of the ranking senators who was trying to interpret the bizarre wonder of the capital. As they stood looking out over the Potomac River, an old, rotten, deteriorating log floated by on the river. The old-timer said, "This city is like that log out there." The fledgling politician asked, "How's that?" The senator replied, "Well, there are probably over 100,000 grubs, ants, bugs, and critters on that old log as it floats down the river. And I imagine every one of them thinks that he's steering it."

Dates & Places Used:

707

Amazing or Baloney

A friend attributed his popularity to one particular word. "Years ago," he said, "upon hearing a statement with which I disagreed, I used to say 'Baloney,' and people began to avoid me like the plague. Now I substitute 'Amazing' for 'Baloney,' and my phone keeps ringing, and my list of friends continues to grow."
Dates & Places Used:

708

TOPIC: Popularity

Self-Concern

We would be far less concerned about what other people think of us if we only realized how seldom they do!
Dates & Places Used:

709

TOPIC: Possibility

Canine Limits

Don't say that nothin' is impossible until you've tried to teach your dog to eat an artichoke.
Dates & Places Used:

710

TOPIC: Power

Bzzzzzzz

A logging foreman sold a farmer a chainsaw guaranteed to cut down fifty trees in a single day. A week later, a very unhappy farmer came to report that the power saw must be faulty—it

averaged only three trees a day. The foreman grabbed the saw, pulled the cord, and the saw promptly went, "Bzzzzzzzzz." The startled farmer demanded, "Hey! What's that noise?"
Dates & Places Used:

711

TOPIC: Praise

Predetermined Affirmation

Everyone needs recognition for his accomplishments. One little boy was no exception to this rule. He said to his father, "Dad, let's play darts. I'll throw, and you say, 'Wonderful!'"
Dates & Places Used:

712

TOPIC: Praise

Act of Applause

Bishop Fulton J. Sheen was greeted by a burst of applause when he made his appearance as a speaker at a meeting in Minneapolis. He responded by saying: "Applause before a speaker begins is an act of faith. Applause during the speech is an act of hope. Applause after he has concluded is an act of charity."
Dates & Places Used:

713

TOPIC: Praise

The Proof Is In

Rule number two in public speaking: After a flattering introduction, never tell the audience you don't deserve it. They'll find out soon enough.
Dates & Places Used:

714

Ruined by Praise

The trouble with most of us is that we would rather be ruined by praise than saved by criticism.

Dates & Places Used:

715

Franklin on Prayer

When Benjamin Franklin was a child, he found the long prayers used by his father before and after meals very tedious. One day, after the winter's provisions had been salted, he said, "I think, Father, if you were to say grace over the whole cask, once for all, it would be a vast saving of time."

Dates & Places Used:

716

Needs and Wants

Sometimes we don't know the difference between what we need, and what we want. We want so much, but God gives us what we truly need. I heard the following story in an episode from the TV show, *St. Elsewhere:*

One sunny summer day, a grandmother and her grandson were walking along the ocean. The little boy, the apple of his grandmother's eyes, was dressed in his Sunday best from hat to shoe. Suddenly a huge wave broke onto the shore and swallowed the boy up, and he disappeared from sight. The old woman prayed fervently that the Lord would send back her grandson unharmed. She pledged to be eternally in his service if he would do that. Miraculously, the little boy was returned to shore unharmed and safe, albeit thoroughly soaked, and with his hair

disheveled. The grandmother looked up to heaven and said, "You know, Lord, he did have a hat."
Dates & Places Used:

717 TOPIC: Prayer
Trash-Basket Forgiveness

It's easy to get mixed up when you're four years old and in church. This particular four-year-old prayed: "And forgive us our trash baskets as we forgive those who put trash in our baskets."
Dates & Places Used:

718 TOPIC: Prayer
Asleep at Last

A rabbi said to a precocious six-year-old boy: "So your mother says your prayers for you each night. Very commendable. What does she say?" The little boy replied, "Thank God, he's in bed!"
Dates & Places Used:

719 TOPIC: Prayer
Parrot's Prayer Answered

A clergyman owned a parrot with an acquired vocabulary of cuss words from a previous owner. It was embarrassing. A woman in his congregation suggested a remedy. She would put him with her well-behaved parrot. Her female parrot said nothing except, "Let's pray." The birds were put together. The pastor's bird took one look at the lady parrot and chirped, "Hi, Toots, how about a little kiss?" The lady parrot responded gleefully, "My prayers have been answered."
Dates & Places Used:

TOPIC: Prayer

Disputed Power of Prayer

There was a small Kentucky town that had two churches and one whiskey distillery. Members of both churches complained that the distillery gave the community a bad image. On top of this the owner of the distillery was an atheist. They tried to shut down the place but were unsuccessful. At last they decided to hold a joint Saturday night prayer meeting. They would ask God to intervene. Saturday night came, and all through the prayer meeting a terrible electrical storm raged. To the delight of the church members lightning struck the distillery, and it burned to the ground. Next morning, the sermons in both churches were on "The Power of Prayer." Fire insurance adjusters promptly notified the distillery owner they would not pay for his damages. The fire was caused by an "act of God," they said, and coverage for "acts of God" was excluded in the policy.

Whereupon the distillery owner sued all the church members, claiming they had conspired with God to destroy his building. The defendants denied absolutely that they had done anything to cause the fire. The trial judge observed: "I find one thing about this case that is very perplexing. We have a situation where the plaintiff—an atheist—is professing his belief in the power of prayer, and the defendants—church members—are denying the power of prayer."

Dates & Places Used:

TOPIC: Prayer

Be Careful What You Pray

It was a blistering hot day, the house was full of guests, and things weren't going too well. Finally, the hostess got everyone seated for dinner and asked her seven-year-old daughter to say grace. "But mother," said the little girl, "I don't know what to say." "Yes you do," said her mother, "just say the last prayer you heard me use." Obediently, the child bowed her head and recited hesitantly: "Oh, Lord, why did I invite these people on such a hot day?"

Dates & Places Used:

TOPIC: Prayer

722

Atomic Prayer

A sign in a high school restroom read: "NOTICE! In the event of an atomic attack, the federal ruling against prayer in this school will be temporarily suspended."

Dates & Places Used:

TOPIC: Prayer

723

Urgent Prayer

A husband and wife from California were motoring through Texas. They saw a tornado coming and, of course, they were afraid. The husband pulled the car off to the side of the road and stopped. The couple got out and crouched beside it. The twister was moving directly toward them but, at the last second, veered off across a field, then hit and totally demolished a small wooden house. The man and woman, still shaking with fright, got up and ran toward the house, which now consisted of little more than kindling wood and a hole in the ground. They looked down into the hole and saw an old man holding on for dear life to a piece of timber, his eyes tightly closed. The woman called down to him, "Hey down there, are you all right?" The old man opened his eyes, looked around cautiously and said, "I guess so." The woman asked, "Was there anyone else with you?" The old man replied, "Just me and God, and we were having an urgent conversation."

Dates & Places Used:

TOPIC: Prayer

724

Better Boston Prayers

A young minister, learning that a woman from Boston who was visiting in town had been taken ill, stopped in to cheer her up. "I'd like to say a brief prayer for your recovery," he suggested.

The woman responded, "That won't be necessary, young man, I'm being prayed for in Boston."
Dates & Places Used:

725

TOPIC: Prayer

Powerful Positions

Three ministers were talking about prayer in general and the appropriate and effective positions for prayer. As they were talking, a telephone repairman was working on the phone system in the background. One minister said that he felt the key was in the hands. He always held his hands together and pointed them upward as a form of symbolic worship. The second suggested that real prayer was conducted on one's knees. The third suggested that they both had it wrong—the only position worth its salt was to pray while stretched out flat on your face.

By this time the phone man couldn't stay out of the conversation any longer. He interjected: "I found that the most powerful prayer I ever made was while I was dangling upside down by my heels from a power pole, suspended forty feet above the ground."
Dates & Places Used:

726

TOPIC: Prayer

Animal Crackers Thanks

Little five-year-old Joey was thanking God for the food in his Bible class. "Dear God, thank you for my mommy, my daddy, my brother, my sister, grandfather, etc . . . and thank you for my teacher. And God, thank you for the animal crackers."

Joey paused, and everyone began to squirm and get restless. We waited and waited, and finally his teacher quietly asked Joey if there was anything wrong. Joey slowly raised his head and in a very low whisper asked, "Are we going to have anything to drink?" His teacher said no and immediately he bowed his head and said, "Amen."

This was not a ritualistic roll-through prayer.
Dates & Places Used:

727

TOPIC: Predictability

Sure Thing

It seems that no matter what you do, someone always knew you would.

Dates & Places Used:

728

TOPIC: Prejudice

Careless Conclusion

A young American at a banquet found himself seated next to a Chinese diplomat. Not knowing what to say to a Chinese person, the young man pointed to the first course and asked, "Likee soupee?" The diplomat nodded and smiled.

Later, the Chinese diplomat, Wellington Koo, was called on to speak and delivered an eloquent address in flawless English. As he sat down to the sound of applause, he turned to the young American and said, "Likee speechee?"

Dates & Places Used:

729

TOPIC: Preparation

The Direct Message

Ian Pitt-Watson told the truth to his congregation: "Because I'm leaving on Tuesday for Korea, I am not as well prepared as I ought to be. And I am reminded of the pastor who thought, when he had difficulty preparing a particular sermon, 'Perhaps the Holy Spirit will tell me what to say on Sunday morning.' This thought returned to him several times during the week, and when at last he stood silently before his congregation, he turned to the Holy Spirit for guidance, and a celestial voice said to him, 'Tell the people you are unprepared!'"

Dates & Places Used:

730 Harvey Firestone

Mr. Firestone's pride in his products was inherited by his sons. In 1947, I attended the wedding in Akron of Harvey Jr.'s daughter, Martha, to Edsel Ford's son, William Clay. The groom's party drove from Detroit in new Lincolns, which were duly parked in the Firestone executive garage.

I was standing with Harvey Jr. when the manager of the garage asked if Harvey had noticed that all the Lincolns of the Ford party were mounted with Goodyear tires. Would Mr. Firestone like to kid Mr. Ford about this? "No," said Harvey Jr. with a big grin. "Say nothing to Mr. Ford. Just jack up all the Lincolns, take off the Goodyears, and put on ours!" As the manager hurried off to do just that, Harvey Jr. turned to me with a twinkle. "I'm not going to have a daughter of mine married on Goodyear tires."

Dates & Places Used:

731 Classy Mutt

Two well-bred female AKC-approved dogs were proudly strutting down the street with their noses held high in the air. Along came a big alley dog, a mutt. Embarrassed at being in the company of such a no-account dog, one of the dogs said, "We must go. My name is Miji, spelled M-I-J-I." The other one said, "My name is Miki, spelled M-I-K-I." The alley dog put his nose up in the air also and said, "My name is Fido, spelled P-H-Y-D-E-A-U-X."

Dates & Places Used:

732 Sons All Look the Same

During a high school half-time show, a father sitting behind us on the bleachers boasted, "That's my son!" The boy who had

been playing the trumpet solo so well up until that point then proceeded to make many mistakes. "Well," came the voice behind us, "maybe not. They all look alike from up here."
Dates & Places Used:

733 TOPIC: Pride

Forgive Us Both

An Atlanta minister tells the story of a clergyman who was given a very flowery introduction. When the clergyman stood up to present his message, he said, "May the Lord forgive this man for his excesses, and me for enjoying them so much."
Dates & Places Used:

734 TOPIC: Pride

A Better Day

Alcibiades was telling Pericles, forty years his senior, how best to govern Athens. This did not amuse Pericles. He said, "Alcibiades, when I was your age, I talked just as you do now." Alcibiades replied, "How I should like to have known you, Pericles, when you were at your best."
Dates & Places Used:

735 TOPIC: Pride

Join the Crowd

Harvard economist, author, and television personality John Kenneth Galbraith served in government under John Kennedy. One day the *New York Times* ran a profile on Galbraith, and it appeared on a morning when he was having breakfast with President Kennedy, who asked Galbraith what he thought of the article. Galbraith said it was all right but he couldn't understand why they had to call him arrogant. The president replied, "I don't see why not. Everybody else does."

Dates & Places Used:

736

TOPIC: Pride

Prophetic Boasting

A friend was really tired of hearing Muhammad Ali boast about his physical prowess. His constant claiming "I am the best!" was wearing thin. So a colleague asked him how he did at golf. Ali replied, "I'm the best. I just haven't played yet."

Dates & Places Used:

737

TOPIC: Priorities

Selective Perception

Margaret Reinitz tells the following story: While I was shopping one Saturday, I sprayed my wrists with an expensive scent from a perfume counter's tester bottle. I then continued my shopping, exulting in the delicious fragrance. That evening as I was preparing our usual Saturday hamburgers, my husband said he had to run an errand and asked if I would like to ride along. When I grabbed my jacket, I noticed that the elegant scent of perfume still clung to the sleeves. I slid into the front seat of the car next to our nine-year-old son. He sniffed and exclaimed, "Boy, you smell good, Mom!"

I replied, "Yes, I know! That's the perfume I sprayed on my wrists while I was shopping today."

He answered, "No, it isn't. That's hamburgers!"

Dates & Places Used:

TOPIC: Priorities

Impact Is What Matters

There was an Irish attorney who was making the best he could of a rather shaky case. The judge interrupted him on a point of law. The judge asked, "Surely, your clients are aware of the doctrine of *e minimis non curat lex?*" The lawyer's sarcastic response was: "Be assured, my lord, that in the remote hamlet where my clients have their humble abode, it forms the sole topic of conversation."
Dates & Places Used:

TOPIC: Priorities

Far from Everything

Former Under Secretary of the Interior John C. Whitaker kept his perspective by telling of an eighty-five-year-old woman who had lived her life in one spot in Nova Scotia. The population there swells to nine in summer and stays steady at two during the winter.

Whitaker, who has been fishing there every year since he was twelve, flew in one day. Miss Mildred welcomed him into her kitchen and said, "Johnny, I hate to admit I don't know, but where is Washington?" When Whitaker realized that she wasn't kidding, he explained: "That's where the president is. That's like where you have the prime minister in Ottawa." Then she asked how many people lived there, and Whitaker said there were about two million. She said, "Think of that, two million people living so far away from everything."
Dates & Places Used:

TOPIC: Priorities

Crisis in Sports

When you're playing for the national championship, it's not a matter of life or death. It's more important than that. *(Duffy Daugherty)*
Dates & Places Used:

741

TOPIC: Problems

No Problem Too Big

In one of the *Peanuts* comic strips, Charlie Brown says, "There's no problem so big that I can't run away from it."
Dates & Places Used:

742

TOPIC: Problems

Peaceful Shifting

The one who smiles when things go wrong is just going off shift.
Dates & Places Used:

743

TOPIC: Problems

Keeping Problems Away

Andy Capp walks home from the pub, arm in arm with a friend, singing, "Dear-old-pals." As he enters his house, he calls out, "Yoo-hoo! It's me," and then passes out on the floor.

His wife walks over to him and covers him with a blanket. Andy says, "Thanks sweet'eart."

His wife says, "Don't mention it." Then to the audience she says, "Never take your problems to bed with you."
Dates & Places Used:

744

TOPIC: Problems

Skunk Removal

A woman once called the police station to report a skunk in her cellar. She was told to make a trail of bread crumbs from the basement to the yard, and then wait for the skunk to follow it out of the basement. A while later the woman called again and reported that she had done as she was told, and now she had two skunks in her basement.

Dates & Places Used:

745

TOPIC: Problems

Perhaps a New Vocation

A man moved from the city to the country planning to live a simpler life. He bought a farmhouse with some land around it. After he moved in, he bought a hundred baby chicks. They all died. The man was disappointed, but he bought another hundred baby chicks. All of these chicks died as well. The man was now confused and looking for answers. He wrote to the county agricultural extension office and explained his problem. He told how he wanted to become a successful chicken farmer and needed to know what he was doing wrong. He asked if he could possibly be planting his chicks too close together or perhaps too deep.

The county extension office responded by letter that they could not answer his questions until he sent in a soil sample.

Dates & Places Used:

746

TOPIC: Prodigal Son

The Valley Version

So like there was this old dude who had two sons. The youngest one was like, you know, a total fox fer sure; the older one was a terminal zod. So this young dude is like totally bored and stuff cuz there was nothin' to do. So he goes to his old man and sez, "Like I'm sure I'm gonna stick aroun' this hole the rest of my life. I want my share of your mega-bucks." His daddy coughs up his share of the family bucks, and like this young fox goes totally spaz fer sure and scarfs down a ton of doritos, rolfing all night long till he's totally bagged out. So he lands himself a job babysitting for this pig farm, and like he gets so grossed out lookin' at the grody pig glop that he climbs into his own head and starts thinkin' 'bout gettin' back to his own room and stuff. "Like even my old man's flunkies get freebies, and I'm stuck here in gag city, feelin' like some kinda mondo shanky Melvin." So like he pulls it together and bums a ride to his old turf and piles out in front of his gate. But his dad hears the dogs barkin' and stuff and runs down the driveway and like plants a really gloppy kiss on this fox's neck: I mean like he's really stoked to see 'im. "I've messed up to the man," says the son. "Let me stick around and do jobs for my rent." But his dad throws him this totally awesome party and lays this terminally gorgeous set of clothes on him. But his older brother is ripped off because he never got a party. "I stick around this place all my life; my room is super-neat, and my buddies don't drive on the lawn or do drugs, and you throw this really tubular party for this total airhead; I mean, give me a break!" "You don't understan'," sez the old man. "I mean your little brother was a waste case, like totally, and now he's family."

Dates & Places Used:

747 TOPIC: Profanity

Severe Judgment

A woman purchased a parrot whose previous owner had taught him profanity and decided that she would reform him. He began to learn a number of Christian words and phrases. The righteous owner caught him cursing one day and grabbed him and said, "I'll teach you to never talk that way again." She put him in the deep freeze and shut the door. A few minutes later she took him out and asked, "Have you learned your lesson?" The bird shivered and replied, "Yes, Ma'am."

After a couple of months the lesson was forgotten: She returned the parrot to the freezer, but forgot him for some time. He almost froze to death. She leaned him in his cage to thaw out. When he began to move and talk a little, she asked him again, "Did you learn your lesson?" "YES, MA'AM," he retorted. Then he sat there quietly for a few more minutes shivering and said, "May I ask you a question?" She answered, "Yes." The parrot said, "I

thought I knew all the bad words there were but just what did that turkey in there say?"
Dates & Places Used:

748 TOPIC: Profanity

Watch Your Words

A mother was concerned about her eldest son's use of profanity. She was counseled to slap the boy each time he cursed. The next morning as her sons came to the table, she asked what they wanted for breakfast. The eldest said, "I want some blankety, blank Post Toasties." The mother slapped him as hard as she could. As he sat dazed on the floor, she turned to the younger son and asked what he wanted for breakfast, to which he replied, "Well, one thing's for sure: I sure don't want any Post Toasties!"
Dates & Places Used:

749 TOPIC: Progress

So Far So Good!

Many people live their lives like the high-rise workman who was carelessly walking on an upper beam one day and fell off. As he was falling, a man on the 21st floor cried out, "How are you doing?" The man responded, "So far so good."
Dates & Places Used:

750 TOPIC: Progress

Progressive Delays

A woman placed an order with a large mail order company. Several weeks later she received this response: "Thank you for

your order. Recent improvements in our shipping procedures may cause a delay in shipping."
Dates & Places Used:

751

TOPIC: Projections

Computers

Computer forecasts are no more reliable than the assumptions on which they are based. If, in 1895, we had projected the number of horses needed for transportation in the United States in 1995, the computer would have told us that every American citizen would be buried under eleven feet of manure.
Dates & Places Used:

752

TOPIC: Providence

The Ways of God

A man sitting under a walnut tree was wondering why God had placed a large pumpkin on a small vine and a little walnut on a large tree. While he was philosophizing, a walnut fell from the tree and hit the man on the head. The man rubbed his head ruefully and said, "I'm glad there aren't pumpkins up there."
Dates & Places Used:

753

TOPIC: Providence

Know Your Blessings

Bill was sitting in his house during a torrential downpour. As the floodwaters reached the bottom of his front door, some friends came along in a rowboat and called to him to climb in. But Bill said, "No, I'm trusting in the Lord. I'll be OK. I'm staying here." The rain kept coming, and the floodwaters kept rising, until Bill was on the second floor, and then he was soon sitting on the roof. Along came a helicopter. The pilot dropped down a rope ladder and called to Bill to climb aboard. But Bill said, "No, I'm trusting in the Lord. I'm staying here." The waters kept rising, and old Bill drowned. Arriving in heaven, Bill said to the Lord, "Lord, I just don't understand it. I trusted in you, and I still ended up drowning." And the Lord replied, "Well, Bill, I don't understand it either. First I sent you a boat, and then I sent you a helicopter, and you didn't take either one!"

Dates & Places Used:

754
TOPIC: Psychiatrists
Out of Order

A man went to visit a psychiatrist. He said, "I've got two problems." The psychiatrist said, "Okay, tell me all about it." The man began, "Well, I think I am a Pepsi Vending Machine." The shrink sat the man right down and started going through his bag repertoire, but nothing seemed to help.

Finally, out of exasperation, the doctor jumped to his feet, took three quarters from his pocket, forced them down the man's throat, grabbed him by the head and shook him till he swallowed the money. Triumphantly, he said, "Okay, give me a Pepsi."

The man replied, "I can't, Doc. That's my second problem; I'm out of order."

Dates & Places Used:

755
TOPIC: Psychiatrists
The Why of Fun

A psychiatrist received a postcard from one of his patients. It read, "I am having a great time. I wish you could be here to tell me why."

Dates & Places Used:

756

Start Out Right

Begin every day with a good breakfast, and you'll always be late for work.

Dates & Places Used:

757

Bird Catchers

How do you catch a "Unique" bird? You "NEEK" up on him!"
How do you catch a "Tame" bird? The "TAME" way.

Dates & Places Used:

758

Purpose

Fear not that your life shall come to an end, but rather that it shall never have a beginning.

Dates & Places Used:

759

Help Yourself

Make the most of yourself, for that is all there is of you.

Dates & Places Used:

288

760

TOPIC: Purpose

Motivation That Works

The loaded station wagon pulled into the only remaining campsite. Four children leaped from the vehicle and began feverishly unloading gear and setting up the tent. The boys then rushed to gather firewood, while the girls and their mother set up the camp stove and cooking utensils. A nearby camper marveled to the youngsters' father: "That, sir, is some display of teamwork." The father replied, "I have a system. No one goes to the bathroom until the camp is set up."

Dates & Places Used:

761

TOPIC: Qualifications

Misplaced Experts

Too bad that all the people who know how to run the country are busy driving taxicabs and cutting hair. *(George Burns)*

Dates & Places Used:

762

TOPIC: Quality

What Are You Making?

While on a trip to Switzerland, an American businessman was watching a Swiss clockmaker carving the case of an ornate cuckoo clock. As the businessman watched the clockmaker carve out the case, he was astounded at his slow rate of progress. The businessman finally said, "My good man, you'll never make much money that way."

"Sir," the clockmaker replied, "I'm not making money, I'm making cuckoo clocks."

Dates & Places Used:

763

TOPIC: Quality

A Bad Bulb

A three-watt bulb has been burning in a northern California fire station continually for eighty-five years. General Electric would like to examine it to make sure they never make that mistake again.
Dates & Places Used:

764

TOPIC: Questions

Buried Potatoes

A young boy was helping his grandfather dig potatoes. After a while, the child began to tire. "Grandpa," he asked wearily, "what made you bury these things anyway?"
Dates & Places Used:

765

TOPIC: Questions

The Wrong Questions

Why do people have to ask, "Did you lose your ball?" or, "Did you find it yet?" when you're out in the rough looking for it? What do they think you're doing out there—checking on the fire ants or something? Why do people ask a person who's trying to dig out of a snowbank, "Are you stuck?" One feels like answering, "No, my car died, and I want to give it a decent burial." Or, wet, disgusted, irritated, with a flat tire on a rainy night beside a busy road, why is one asked, "Have you got a flat tire?" "Oh, no," you may feel like replying, "of course not, I always rotate my tires at night on a busy road when it's raining."
Dates & Places Used:

TOPIC: Recognition

Silent Suffering

It is easier to suffer in silence if everyone knows about it.

Dates & Places Used:

767

TOPIC: Recommendations

Muddled Note

Horace Greeley, famous editor of the *New York Tribune*, was noted for having about the most illegible handwriting there was. Often he couldn't even read it himself if it was a few hours "cold." One day he wrote an editorial just before the paper went to press, and the typesetter could hardly read it, and because it was too late for correction, it appeared in print with a number of rather outstanding errors. When Greeley read it, he was furious. He fired the typesetter on the spot. He even wrote him a scorching letter in which he denounced him for his stupidity. But the note was in such a terrible hand the typesetter couldn't read it.

But since he had been told in person that he was fired, he set out to look for another job at the office of a rival newspaper. The foreman at the other paper asked him if he had any recommendations. "Sure," said the man, "I've got a letter from Mr. Greeley." And he produced the letter in which Greeley called him all sorts of names. The foreman glanced at it, but couldn't read it either. He asked, "How much are you making with Greeley?" The typesetter named a figure. The foreman replied, "I'll give you $15 a week more. Start tomorrow morning."

Dates & Places Used:

768

TOPIC: Rejection

Buying Friends

UCLA football coach Pepper Rodgers was in the middle of a terrible season. It even got so bad that it upset his home life. He

recalls, "My dog was my only friend. I told my wife that a man needs at least two friends, and she bought me another dog."
Dates & Places Used:

769 TOPIC: Rejection
Worth More Than a Locket

W. Paul Jones tells of a woman who shared her story of her childhood as a polio victim:

"When my mother left me in Sunday School, I always asked to wear her locket. She thought I liked the locket. That wasn't it at all. I knew I wasn't worth coming back for, but I knew she would come back for her locket."
Dates & Places Used:

770 TOPIC: Rejoicing
Timing Eggs

The late Archbishop Temple, when he was primate of England, once told this story. One morning, in a house where he was a guest, he heard the cook singing lustily, "Nearer, My God to Thee." He was impressed that she was singing hymns, and he spoke of it to his host. The host replied, "Oh, yes. That's how she boils the eggs—three verses for soft boiled and five for hard." The archbishop thought the cook was expressing her faith. All she was doing was timing her eggs.
Dates & Places Used:

771 TOPIC: Relativity
Einstein's Analogy

It is reported that Albert Einstein's secretary once asked him to explain to her the theory of relativity.

He replied, "Two hours with a beautiful woman seems like two minutes. Two minutes on a hot stove seems like two hours. That is relativity!"

Dates & Places Used:

772 TOPIC: Relevance

Sharing Experiences

A mother was writing an excuse for her first-grader, who had been home with a stomachache.

As the child observed her writing, he said, "Okay, but don't say I threw up. I want to save that for 'Show and Tell.'"

Dates & Places Used:

773 TOPIC: Religion

Zealous Evangelism

There is a story, probably apocryphal, about Clare Booth Luce and her zeal for Catholicism. Apparently she was visiting Rome and had obtained a private audience with the pope. After they had had an appropriate time alone, the papal assistant rejoined the pope and Mrs. Luce to bring the interview to an end. He found the pope sort of trapped in a corner, pleading, "Please, Mrs. Luce, I'm already a Catholic!"

Dates & Places Used:

774 TOPIC: Remarriage

Third-Time Charm

A man in his middle years was on a Caribbean cruise. On the first day out he noticed an attractive woman about his age who smiled at him in a friendly way as he passed her on the deck. This pleased him. That night he managed to get seated at the same table with her for dinner. As the conversation developed, he commented that he had seen her on the deck that day and had appreciated her friendly smile.

When she heard this, she smiled again and commented, "Well, the reason I smiled was that when I saw you I was immediately struck by your strong resemblance to my third husband." At this, he perked up his ears and said, "Oh, how many times have you been married?" She looked down at her plate, smiled demurely, and answered, "Twice."

Dates & Places Used:

775

TOPIC: Repentance

Let Me In!

When my daughter Michelle was six years old, we went to a hotel in Vail, Colorado. My children were having great fun exploring all the features of the hotel in detail. While my son and I were watching television in the bedroom, and my wife was taking a shower, Michelle was in the other room "exploring." Michelle began to knock on the door in the other room. I turned toward the room and told her to stop knocking on the bathroom door while Mom was taking a shower.

A couple minutes later we heard the faint knocking again. I told her to stop it; this time with a little more force in my voice. Once again she began to knock on the door, and now her knocking was accompanied by a muffled scream, "Let me in!"

I was tired of listening to my daughter bother her mother like this. I flew off the bed and went into the other room. No one was there, yet the knocking continued. She had locked herself outside the room and was beginning to panic. I apologetically opened the door and granted her immediate entrance.

Dates & Places Used:

776

TOPIC: Repentance

Repent!

A new pastor preached his first sermon at his new church. He preached a wonderful sermon: "Repent, repent, repent! The kingdom of God is at hand. Go and repent." Everyone loved the sermon, and some even said it was the best sermon they had ever heard.

On his second Sunday in the pulpit, the new pastor preached the same sermon, "Repent, repent, repent! The kingdom of God is at hand. Go and repent." Since most of the parishioners did not remember last week's sermon, once again many responded that it was the best sermon they had ever heard.

On his third Sunday, the pastor again preached the same sermon, word for word. This time, his listeners began to stir and were disturbed. They approached the governing board of the church and directed them to look into the matter.

On the fourth Sunday the new minister preached the same sermon once again, "Repent, repent, repent! The kingdom of God is at hand. Go and repent." The church board called in the new pastor for a full explanation. His answer: Yes, he was able to preach other sermons. Yes, he did have other sermons. Yes, he did want to preach other sermons. The problem? He would preach another sermon as soon as the congregation repented!

Dates & Places Used:

777

TOPIC: Repentance

Order of Repentance

It is much easier to repent of sins that we have already committed than to repent of those we intend to commit.

Dates & Places Used:

TOPIC: Repentance

Timely Repentance

A rabbi was teaching his students a lesson on preparing for death and on repentance. One of the students asked, "Rabbi, when should a man repent?" The rabbi responded, "Repent a day before your death." His students were confused. "How can a man know the day of his death?" they asked. His answer: "He cannot, and since he may die tomorrow, it is all the more necessary for him to repent today."

Dates & Places Used:

779

TOPIC: Requests

The Dog Doesn't Know

After a hard day at work, a father was very patiently listening to his seven-year-old son scratch away on his violin while the dog howled dismally nearby. The father was trying to be as loving and understanding as a father is supposed to be, but the screeching of the violin and the howling of the dog were beginning to be just a little too much for his already jangled nerves.

Trying to be that good father, as lovingly as he possibly could, he said, "Son, can't you play something the dog doesn't know?"

Dates & Places Used:

780

TOPIC: Requests

How to Get a Car

The art of negotiation is learned at an early age. You'd be amazed how many teens get a car by asking for a motorcycle.

Dates & Places Used:

781

TOPIC: Requests

Waiting for God

A man asked God how long a million years was to him. God replied, "It's just like a single second of your time, my child." So the man asked, "What about a million dollars?" The Lord replied, "To me, it's just like a single penny." The man gathered himself up and said, "Well, Lord, could I have one of your pennies?" And God said, "Certainly, my child, just a second."

Dates & Places Used:

782

TOPIC: Requests

A Special Request

A certain pastor conducts an expanded altar call at the end of his sermons. He asks those who wish to make spiritual decisions to come forward, as well as those with prayer requests or some other questions. One Sunday his three-year-old daughter responded to his invitation. She waited patiently while others ahead of her made their requests. When her turn came, her father leaned down to ask for her request. She whispered, "Can we go to the restaurant after church?"

Dates & Places Used:

783

TOPIC: Requests

Make Requests Specific

Communication should be specific. An example of this is found in the January 25, 1982, edition of *Fortune*. It's a "Personal" ad found in the *New York Review of Books* that read: "HOUSEHUSBAND sought by attractive professor in small-town New England. Freelance nonfiction writer, funny, middle-aged tennis-playing socialist would be ideal." This woman knew what she wanted.

Dates & Places Used:

TOPIC: Resistance

Second-Guessing God

A man told his mother about a friend who died and left three small children.

His mother sympathetically said, "Why couldn't it have been me? I'm ninety-three years old, and she was so young. I've served the Lord all my life, and I'm ready to go." He consoled, "Mother, God left you here on earth for a purpose. He must have something else he wants you to do." She retorted, "Well, I'm telling you right now, I'm not going to do it."

Dates & Places Used:

TOPIC: Resistance

Teaching a Pig to Sing

A consultant was brought in to train and motivate the corporate troops. He got up to speak, and it soon became obvious that there was great resistance among his audience. They were conveying with their body language and their lack of enthusiasm that they were not with him. The speaker paused for a moment to gain their attention and said, "This reminds me a great deal of trying to teach a pig to sing. It costs a lot of money, and it makes the pig mad." The ice was broken, and the communication began.

Dates & Places Used:

TOPIC: Respect

Like a Son

A promising young executive quit his job, and before leaving, stopped in to say goodbye to the boss.

The boss lamented, "I'm sorry to see you go. Actually, you've been like a son to me—sassy, impatient, demanding, and loud."

Dates & Places Used:

787

TOPIC: Respect

Turn Out the Light

The famous inventor Thomas Edison was known for his patience and perseverance. He worked nonstop, day and night on the electric light bulb.

Finally, late one evening it happened. The light went on. It worked. He rushed upstairs to tell his sleeping wife.

Her response? "Tom, would you please turn out the light and come to bed?"

Dates & Places Used:

788

TOPIC: Responses

Rope's End

When you're at the end of the rope, tie a knot, hang on, and swing!

Dates & Places Used:

789

TOPIC: Responses

One Up

A salesman with a reputation for one-upsmanship, always having a snappy retort, never at a loss for words, was transferred from New York to the company's West Coast office.

His new colleagues knew his reputation and decided to take him down a peg. They went to a farm that supplies exotic animals to motion picture companies and rented an old, gentle, toothless lion. While the salesman was out of his apartment, they led the lion in and made him lie down on the living room sofa. Then they went into the bedroom and waited with the door slightly ajar to witness his reactions.

Soon the salesman arrived home. He walked in, saw the lion on the sofa, walked to the closet and hung up his jacket, then strolled to the door of the bedroom. He gave the door three businesslike raps and called out, "Christians, five minutes!"

Dates & Places Used:

790

Churchill's Gratitude

We all know people who spend too much time saying too little. Winston Churchill once dealt with such a person in a most unique way. The man said to Churchill, "You know, Sir Winston, I've never told you about my grandchildren." Churchill responded by clapping the man on the shoulder and replying, "I realize it, my dear fellow, and I can't tell you how grateful I am!"

Dates & Places Used:

791

Ask Him

A trial lawyer was famous for his courtroom techniques and legal arguments. His opponents feared him; his clients loved him. He was always sure to win the case. He began writing in law journals concerning how these techniques could be acquired. He used a standardized lecture to be used for speaking engagements.

He traveled with his secretary, a bright young man who was proud to be associated with this renowned lawyer. After several months of listening to the same lecture, the bold secretary announced to the lawyer that he had heard the same speech so many times that he could give that speech himself. This so intrigued the lawyer that the switch was arranged.

It was agreed that the next time they were out of town, and no one would recognize them, they would exchange duties. The lawyer stood in the back of the room while the secretary addressed a room of expectant lawyers.

The secretary waxed eloquent, demonstrating techniques and addressing intricate details with precision. At the end of his speech the secretary was given a standing ovation. It was truly a splendid speech! The moderator indicated that there were still a few minutes left on the program and asked the appreciative audience if they had any questions for their honored guest.

One lawyer ventured to ask a question concerning the legal precedents for one of the techniques referred to early in the speech. The lawyer in the back of the room felt his heart sink. He could easily field the question, but there was no way to let his secretary know the answer. They were about to be exposed! The secretary began to laugh. With just a tinge of mockery he responded, "Why, that is such a simple and well-known precedent all of you should know the answer! Even the common layperson should know the answer to that question. In fact, to demonstrate my premise, I am going to let my secretary give you your answer."

Dates & Places Used:

792 TOPIC: Responsibilities

Almost the Same

A certain church held a Sunday service patterned after those in colonial America. The pastor dressed in long coat and knickers, and the congregation was divided by gender: men on the left side of the aisle and women on the right.

At collection time, the pastor announced that this, too, would be done in the old way. He asked the "head of the household" to come forward and place the money on the altar. The men instantly rose. To the amusement of the entire congregation, many of them crossed the aisle to get money from their wives.

Dates & Places Used:

793 TOPIC: Responsibilities

Carry the Load

If you have no ulcers, you're not carrying your share of the load.

Dates & Places Used:

794

Property Rights

A man bought a small farm and was visited by his neighbor. He asked him, "Can you tell me where the property line runs between our farms?" The neighbor asked, "Are you talking owning or mowing?"

Dates & Places Used:

795

To Fix the World

One day when a father came home, he sat down to relax and read the paper. His son had other ideas. The playful boy continually pestered his father. The frustrated father tired of his son's nagging and took a page of the paper with a picture of the world and tore it into pieces. "Son, go into the other room and put the world back together. Moments later the boy returned. He had taped the world back together. The surprised father asked, "How did you do that so quickly?" "It was easy," said the boy. "You see, on the other side of the world was a picture of a man, and as soon as I got the man straightened out, the world was OK too!"

Perhaps the way to fix our broken world, a world that has been shattered into a million pieces by the deadly hammer of sin, is to put the broken man back together first.

Dates & Places Used:

796

A Specific Job

This ad was taken from a recent church music publication:
Position Wanted: Organist-Choirmaster, lifelong, militantly loyal, dyed-in-the-wool traditional RC, seeks fulltime position in pre-Vatican II urban parish (will consider Tridentine) blessed

with large church building designed by P. C. Keely, 19th-century American pipe organ of three or four manuals, and, most importantly, using or willing to implement the BACS hymnal (Hymns, Psalms & Spiritual Canticles). All-male or professional mixed choir a must (no volunteers!) as is freedom from outside interference by liturgy committees, religious educators or other so-called vested interests. Prefer Massachusetts (except Fall River diocese), will consider other areas in Northeast. Write . . .

Dates & Places Used:

797 TOPIC: Resurrection
Part-Time Tomb

Someone asked Joseph of Arimathaea, "That was a great tomb. Why did you give it to someone else to be buried in?" "Oh," said Joseph, "he only needed it for the weekend."

Dates & Places Used:

798 TOPIC: Resurrection
Out of This Hole!

A five-year-old girl returned from Sunday school class, and was asked by her mother what she had learned from this Easter Sunday lesson. The daughter excitedly retold the whole story. She told of the death of Jesus and how he was buried in a tomb. Later an angel came and looked in the tomb and asked Jesus what he wanted. "I want out of this hole," Jesus said.

Dates & Places Used:

799

TOPIC: Resurrection

Now the Good Part

As a family watched the Easter story on television, the child was deeply moved. As Jesus was tortured and killed, tears rolled down her cheeks. She was absolutely silent until after Jesus had been taken down from the cross and put into the tomb. Then she suddenly grinned and shouted, "Now comes the *good* part!" We first hear about the sufferings and death of Jesus. Now comes the good part! The tomb is empty! Jesus is risen from the dead!

Dates & Places Used:

800

TOPIC: Resurrection

Stay Out of the Way!

The call to worship had just been pronounced, starting Easter Sunday morning service in an East Texas church. The choir started the processional, singing "Up from the Grave He Arose" while marching in perfect step down the center aisle to the front of the church. The last woman was wearing shoes with very slender heels. Without a thought for her fancy heels, she stepped onto the grating that covered the hot air register in the middle of the aisle. Suddenly the heel of one shoe sank into the hole in the register grate. In a flash she realized her predicament. Not wishing to hold up the whole processional, without missing a step, she slipped her foot out of her shoe and continued marching down the aisle. There wasn't a hitch. The processional moved with clocklike precision. The first man after her spotted the situation and without losing a step, reached down and pulled up her shoe, but the entire grate came with it!

Surprised, but still singing, the man kept on going down the aisle, holding in his hand the grate with the shoe attached. Everything still moved like clockwork. Still in tune and still in step, the next man in line stepped into the open register and disappeared from sight. The service took on a special meaning that Sunday, for just as the choir ended with "Allelujah! Christ arose!" a voice was heard under the church shouting, "I hope all of you are out of the way 'cause I'm coming out now!"

The little girl closest to the aisle shouted, "Come on, Jesus! We'll stay out of the way."
Dates & Places Used:

801

TOPIC: Retirement

Retirement Breaks

The worst thing about retirement is having to drink coffee on your own time.
Dates & Places Used:

802

TOPIC: Retirement

Retirement Plans

A newly hired consultant breezed into the personnel manager's office and interrupted his conversation with another employee to ask how many of the company's employees were approaching retirement age.

The personnel manager said, "All of them. Not one of them is going the other way."
Dates & Places Used:

803

TOPIC: Reunions

Change and Perspective

At a college reunion, thirty years after graduation, one man said to another, "See that fellow over there? Well, he's gotten so bald and so fat he didn't even recognize me!"
Dates & Places Used:

804

TOPIC: Revenge

Point of Purchase

A woman went to a post office to buy a stamp during the Christmas rush. This particular post office was not known for the kindness of its clerks. The stamp was pushed across the counter with such force that it landed on the floor about two feet from the counter. The woman calmly picked up the stamp and placed the money for the stamp on the floor in place of the stamp.

Dates & Places Used:

805

TOPIC: Revenge

Helping Others Learn

I was amused by the story I read in *Bits and Pieces* about Jack's mother who ran into the bedroom when she heard him scream and found his two-year-old sister pulling his hair. She gently released the little girl's grip and said comfortingly to Jack, "There, there. She didn't mean it. She doesn't know that hurts." Mom was barely out of the room when the little girl screamed. Rushing back in, she said, "What happened?" "She knows now," little Jack explained.

Dates & Places Used:

806

TOPIC: Revenge

Avenging Enemies

If thine enemy wrong thee, buy each of his children a drum.

Dates & Places Used:

807

TOPIC: Revenge

Get Even

A man died and left his great wealth to his secretary. Naturally, his wife was furious. She went to have the inscription on his tombstone changed, but was too late. To change it now she would need to buy a new stone. She thought for a moment. She certainly didn't want to spend any more of her money, so she said, "Right after 'Rest In Peace' I want you to chisel in these additional words: 'Till We Meet Again.'"

Dates & Places Used:

808

TOPIC: Revenge

Sweet Revenge

An elderly lady driving a big, new, expensive car was preparing to back into a parallel parking space when suddenly a young man in a small sports car zoomed in ahead of her. The woman angrily asked why he had done that when he could tell she was trying to park there. His response was simply "Because I'm young, and I'm quick." The young man then entered the store. When he came back out a few minutes later he found the elderly lady using her big new car as a battering ram, backing up, and then ramming it into his car. He very angrily asked her why she was wrecking his car. Her reponse was "Because I'm old, and I'm rich!"

Dates & Places Used:

809

TOPIC: Revenge

Zipper Vengeance

A husband and wife were having a quarrel over the breakfast table. The quarrel remained unfinished, as it was time to get to work. The wife, having trouble with the zipper on her dress, asked for assistance. In a huff, the husband freed the zipper and then angrily ran it up and down rapidly several times, then left.

That afternoon, when the wife returned from work, there was a car in the driveway with a man lying on his back underneath the car, except for his lower half. Remembering the breakfast incident, she went over, grasped the zipper on his fly, and zipped it down and up several times and stomped into the house. There, to her surprise, sat her husband drinking coffee. In great embarrassment she explained to her husband what she had done. He rushed outside to find his neighbor out cold. When the wife had grasped his zipper, he had reflexively tried to sit up and knocked himself out. No wonder vengeance is not ours.

Dates & Places Used:

---

810 · TOPIC: Rewards
Change for a Reward

Fortunate was the Cleveland Heights woman who lost her purse in a shopping center. An honest lad found it and returned it to her. "That's funny," commented the woman, "before I lost my bag, there was a twenty dollar bill in it. Now I find two fives and ten one dollar bills."

"That's right lady," agreed the honest lad. "The last time I found a lady's purse, she didn't have any change for a reward."

Dates & Places Used:

---

811 · TOPIC: Rewards
Beatitude Exceptions

Reported to be seen on a sign outside a church in Houston, Texas: "The meek shall inherit the earth." Underneath it, a graffitist had scrawled (appropriately, perhaps, in oil-rich Texas): "But not the mineral rights."

Dates & Places Used:

812

TOPIC: Rewards

Within Limits

Linus and Lucy were talking. Linus said, "I've been thinking. Charlie Brown has really been a dedicated baseball manager. He's devoted his whole life to the team. We should give him a testimonial dinner." Lucy replied, "How about a testimonial snack?" ("Peanuts")
Dates & Places Used:

813

TOPIC: Righteousness

Too Good

A traffic officer pulled a motorist over to the curb and demanded to see his driver's license. The driver produced a license, which the officer studied suspiciously for several minutes before returning it and waving him on. The officer explained, "You were driving so carefully, I was certain you had an invalid license."
Dates & Places Used:

814

TOPIC: Risk

A Space-Age Mustard Seed

An American astronaut lay strapped into his capsule, ready to be launched, when a reporter asked via radio: "How do you feel?"
"How would you feel," the astronaut replied, "if you were sitting on top of 150,000 parts, each supplied by the lowest bidder?"
Dates & Places Used:

815

TOPIC: Risk

The Big Black Door

A general of the Persian army always gave his condemned prisoners a choice, the firing squad or the black door. Most chose the firing squad. The prisoners were never told what was on the other side of the door. Few ever chose the unknown of the black door. When asked what was on the other side of the black door, the general answered, "Freedom, and I've known only a few men brave enough to take it."

Dates & Places Used:

816

TOPIC: Risk

An Explosive Situation

As an explosives salesperson, Dan had to be extremely careful with his products as well as with the customers he dealt with. Most of his territory was farmland and mines, and most of the customers needed explosives to clear the land. Since Dan had covered the same area for several years, he knew most of his customers on a first-name basis. One day Dan met a new customer, a man who had just bought a farm and needed some dynamite to clear some stumps from the field. The new customer asked if he could be billed for the explosives.

"Well," asked Dan, "have you ever used dynamite before?"

"No, I haven't," replied the new customer.

"Then I'm afraid I'll have to ask for cash in advance."

Dates & Places Used:

817

TOPIC: Risk

Changing the Odds

Dr. Jerome Frank, Professor of Psychiatry at Johns Hopkins University tells of a particular airline flight:

Whenever I am flying, and I engage people in conversation, a confession is almost always forthcoming when they find out I am a psychiatrist. A few years ago, before all of the modern security measures were installed at the nation's airports, a man I was sitting next to on a coast-to-coast flight told me, "You know, I used to be deathly afraid of flying. It all started after that man brought a bomb on board a flight to Denver to kill his mother-in-law. I could never get it out of my mind that someone on board one of my flights might be carrying a bomb." I asked, "Well, what did you do about it?" He replied, "Well, I went to one of those special schools for people who are afraid of flying, and they told me there was only one chance in a hundred thousand that someone would be on board my flight with a bomb. That didn't make me feel much better. The odds were still too close. But then I reasoned that if there was only one chance in a hundred thousand that one bomb would be on the plane, there was only one chance in a billion that two bombs would be on board. And I could live with those odds."

So I asked, "But what good would that do you?"

He quickly replied, "Ever since then, I carry one bomb on board myself just to improve the odds."

Dates & Places Used:

TOPIC: Risk

Marital Gamblers

Marriage is a lottery in which a man stakes his liberty, and a woman her happiness. *(Mme. De Rieux)*

Dates & Places Used:

TOPIC: Risk

Three Shoestrings

Did you hear about the fellow who went into business on a shoestring and tripled his investment? Now he's trying to figure out what to do with three shoestrings!

Dates & Places Used:

820

TOPIC: Risk

Suicidal Businesses

In both skydiving and the semiconductor business, you start out by committing suicide and then try to save yourself.

Dates & Places Used:

821

TOPIC: Rivalry

In Time We Look Sillier

Two men in seminary competed for top honors. Their rivalry became the talk of the campus. After graduation they went their separate ways, one to the parish, the other to the military chaplaincy. Many years passed when by chance they met at an airport. The first had become a bishop with robes and a portly protrusion to match. The second had achieved the rank of general. The bishop spoke first to the general: "Porter, where do I go to get flight 569?" The chaplain replied, "Frankly, I wouldn't recommend that you fly in your condition, madam!"

Dates & Places Used:

822

TOPIC: Romance

Love at Second Sight

Some folks believe in love at first sight; others believe in taking another look.

Dates & Places Used:

823

TOPIC: Romance

The Confusion Begins

A boy's first dilemma is when he determines that he likes girls better than he likes frogs and dogs, but he doesn't know why.

Dates & Places Used:

824

TOPIC: Romance

No Searching

A man and wife were walking in a crowd. The husband delighted his wife by taking her hand. She asked, "You don't want to lose me?" He replied, "I don't want to have to look for you."

Dates & Places Used:

825

TOPIC: Russia

A Ten-Year Drain

It seems a Russian citizen wanted to buy a car a few years ago. He went to the official agency and put his money down. He was told by the clerk that he could take delivery of his automobile in exactly ten years. The purchaser asked the clerk, "Morning or afternoon?" The official replied, "Ten years from now, morning or afternoon, what difference does it make?" The car buyer said, "Well, the plumber's coming in the morning."

Dates & Places Used:

826

TOPIC: Russia

No God, No Food

A communist party official asked a farmer how things were going, and the farmer replied that the harvest was so bountiful that the potatoes would reach the "foot of God" if piled on top of one another. The commissar says, "But this is the Soviet Union, there is no God here." The farmer replied, "There are no potatoes, either."

Dates & Places Used:

827

TOPIC: Sabbath

Working on Sunday

A Christian man was once urged by his employer to work on Sundays: "Doesn't your Bible say that if your ox falls into a ditch on the Sabbath, you may pull him out?"

"Yes," replied the other, "but if the ox had the habit of falling into the same ditch every Sabbath, I would either fill up the pit or sell the ox."

Dates & Places Used:

828

TOPIC: Sacrifice

We All Have Our Jobs

The city editor had just been informed that a wire had fallen across Main Street in a storm. He assigned two reporters to the story. "No one knows whether the wire is live or not," he said, "so one of you is to touch it, and the other is to write the story."

Dates & Places Used:

829

TOPIC: Sacrifice

Bridge the Gap

On one of the earlier editions of the television show "America's Funniest Home Videos" there was the segment from Japan showing a brother and sister coming to a break in the sidewalk. It was a long step across, and the gap was about two feet deep. The boy made it quite easily, but his sister was too fearful and refused to even try. After several attempts to convince her that she could make it, the little fellow stretched out across the gap, forming a human bridge with his body. His sister safely crawled across the span. In what ways are we willing to lay down our lives for others?

Dates & Places Used:

830

TOPIC: Sales

Going Out of Business

This sign appeared in the window of a store in New York City: "Don't be fooled by imitators who claim to be going out of business. We have been going out of business longer than anyone on this block."

Dates & Places Used:

831

TOPIC: Sales

Know Your Customer

A young salesman walked up to the receptionist and asked to see the company's sales manager. Ushered into the office, he said, "I don't supppose you want to buy any life insurance, do you?"

"No," replied the sales manager curtly.

"I didn't think so," said the salesman dejectedly, getting up to leave.

"Wait a minute," said the sales manager. "I want to talk to you." The salesman sat down again, obviously nervous and confused. "I train salesmen," said the sales manager, "and you're the worst I've seen yet. You'll never sell anything until you show a little confidence and accentuate the positive. Now, because you're obviously new at this, I'll help you out by signing up for a ten-thousand-dollar policy." After the sales manager had signed on the dotted line, he said helpfully, "Young man, one thing you'll have to do is develop a few standard organized sales talks."

"Oh, but I have," replied the salesman, smiling. "This is my standard organized sales talk for sales managers."

Dates & Places Used:

832

TOPIC: Sales

Overpriced Puppy

A little boy was trying to sell a puppy. Day after day the boy continued to try to sell the little dog. A salesman walked by the boy's table daily on his way to and from work. He began to pity the poor fellow who just didn't quite understand the basic skills of selling. He stopped one day and explained to the boy that he needed to SEE IT BIG. He had to promote this little puppy as something more than it appeared to be. He needed to give it a bath, groom it, put up a nice sign, and raise his price.

The next day on his way to work he saw that the boy had taken his advice. Just one problem; he had gone a little too far. He had raised the price of the dog to $1,000.

As he returned from work that afternoon, he planned to explain to the boy that his price was a bit too high. But the boy was no longer at the table. On the table was his sign with "SOLD" written on the front. The salesman could not believe what he saw.

The salesman ran to the door and rang the doorbell. When the boy came to the door, the man asked him what had happened to the puppy. The boy told him he had sold him for a thousand dollars and then thanked the man for the advice. The man asked the boy how he could possibly sell the dog for $1,000. "It was simple: I traded it for two $400 cats and a $200 rabbit."

Dates & Places Used:

833 TOPIC: Sales

Selling Insurance

After his tour of duty overseas a certain officer was appointed to a stateside induction center where he advised new recruits about their government benefits, especially G.I. insurance. Soon he had an almost one hundred percent sales record.

This was a remarkable rate of success. His supervisors were amazed. Rather than ask him how he accomplished this sales record, one of the officers stood in the back of the room while this man was giving his sales presentation. This certain officer explained the general provisions and benefits of G.I. insurance to the new recruits. He then added his own perspective to the presentation by saying, "If you buy the G.I. insurance, go into battle and are killed, the government will have to pay $35,000 to your beneficiaries. If you don't buy G.I. insurance, go into battle and are killed, the government will only have to pay a maximum of $3,000."

He concluded, "Now which bunch of soldiers do you think are going to be sent into battle first?"

Dates & Places Used:

834

Let Him In

At age two a little girl began to learn all the traditional fairy tales, like Goldilocks and the Three Bears and The Three Little Pigs. Her mother and father taught her the familiar Bible stories as well. The girl's young mind was like a sponge, and she took all of these in.

One day her mother read to her Revelation 3:20. When the mother finished the verse, she asked, "If Jesus is knocking at your heart's door, will you open the door and let him in?"

Without a moment's hesitation, the little girl responded, "Not by the hair on my chinny-chin-chin."

Dates & Places Used:

835

TOPIC: Salvation

Step One

Many people hope to be elected to heaven who are not even running for the office.

Dates & Places Used:

836

TOPIC: Satisfaction

Finally Satisfied

A person with six children is better satisfied than a person with six million dollars. The reason for this is that the man with six million dollars wants more.

Dates & Places Used:

837

TOPIC: Security

Jungle Wisdom

A reporter was interviewing an African safari guide. He asked, "Is it true that jungle animals won't harm you if you carry a torch?"

The guide replied, "That depends on how fast you carry it."

Dates & Places Used:

838

TOPIC: Security

Sports Job Security

Maybe you've seen the new book called *Sports Quotes*. It has some great short quotations. Here's a sampler:

I have a lifetime contract. That means I can't be fired during the third quarter if we're ahead and moving the ball. *(Lou Holtz)*

Dates & Places Used:

839

TOPIC: Self

Selfish Optimist

An optimist is someone who tells you to cheer up when things are going his way.

Dates & Places Used:

840

TOPIC: Self

Why We Listen

No one listens unless it is that person's turn next. *(Ed Howe)*

Dates & Places Used:

841

TOPIC: Self-control

Silent Fool

It is better to remain silent and be thought a fool than to open one's mouth and remove all doubt.
Dates & Places Used:

842

TOPIC: Self-control

Busted Smiles

A boy was reprimanded for laughing out loud during school. "Teacher, I didn't mean to. I was smiling, and the smile busted."
Dates & Places Used:

843

TOPIC: Self-control

Better Than Latin

Learn to say no. It will be of more use to you than to be able to read Latin. *(Charles Spurgeon)*
Dates & Places Used:

844

TOPIC: Self-image

All Is Well

Charlie Brown tells Lucy about his birdhouse project: "Well, I'm a lousy carpenter. I can't nail straight. I can't saw straight, and I always split the wood. I'm nervous, I lack confidence, I'm stupid, I have poor taste and absolutely no sense of design." And

then in the last frame he concludes, "So, all things considered, it's coming along okay." ("Peanuts")
Dates & Places Used:

845

TOPIC: Self-image

Close to Perfect

The closest to perfection a person ever comes is when he fills out a job application form.
Dates & Places Used:

846

TOPIC: Self-image

Famous Mothers

Alexander the Great's mother: "How many times do I have to tell you—you can't have everything you want in this world." Franz Schubert's mother: "Take my advice, son. Never start anything you can't finish." Achilles's mother: "Stop imagining things. There's nothing wrong with your heel." Sigmund Freud's mother: "Stop pestering me! I've told you a hundred times that the stork brought you!" Boy George's mother: "Do you enjoy being different? Why can't you be like Nancy, your brother?"
Dates & Places Used:

847

TOPIC: Self-image

Identity Crisis

One day Charlie Brown was talking to his friend Linus about the pervasive sense of inadequacy he feels all the time. Charlie moaned, "You see, Linus, it goes all the way back to the beginning. The moment I was born and set foot on the stage of life they took one look at me and said, 'Not right for the part.'" ("Peanuts")
Dates & Places Used:

848

If Sermon Offends Thee

A preacher came to the breakfast table with a cut on his cheek. His wife asked him what had happened. He replied that he was concentrating on his sermon while shaving and cut his face. His wife said, "Maybe you should concentrate on your shaving and cut your sermon."

Dates & Places Used:

849

Long-Winded Driving

A pastor and his wife were driving to visit Grandma and Grandpa for Christmas. Their daughter Rachel asked the inevitable question, "Are we almost there?"

The father said, "No, we are still 150 miles away."

She asked, "Well, how long is that?"

"Well Rachel, it's about three more hours."

She didn't say anything for a few moments as she thought about what three hours must be. She leaned forward from the backseat to the front, making sure she could see her mother's face and said, "Mommy, is that as long as one of Daddy's sermons?"

Dates & Places Used:

850

A Hair-Raising Sermon

A certain pastor typically preached up to two hours. One Sunday he was going strong for some time when one of his regular members got up and left. A while later the same man returned. Later the pastor asked him where he had gone during the sermon. The member said he'd gone to get a haircut. The pastor asked why he hadn't gotten one before he came to church. The member replied, "Before I came, I didn't need one."

Dates & Places Used:

TOPIC: Sermons

Mindless Messages

A well-meaning woman, greeting her pastor at the back door, told him that his sermons on television meant so much more to her husband now, since he had lost his mind.
Dates & Places Used:

TOPIC: Sermons

Prepare or Rely

The preacher began his sermon by saying, "I am not well prepared this week. It has been a terribly busy week, and I just didn't have much time to prepare my sermon. We'll have to rely on the Holy Spirit. Next week I'll try to come better prepared."
Dates & Places Used:

TOPIC: Sermons

The Profit in Sermons

"I never heard a sermon but what I got some good out of it. However, I had some mighty close calls."
Dates & Places Used:

TOPIC: Sermons

An Adaptable Fiction

Imagine yourself going down the road of life, and you come to a vital crossroads. Standing there at the crossroads are the following three figures: a pastor who never finishes his sermon until late Saturday night, a pastor who always has his sermon finished and polished by Thursday noon, and the Easter Bunny. Which of these three would you ask for directions?

The answer is: The pastor who never finishes his sermon until late Saturday night. The other two are both figments of your imagination.

Dates & Places Used:

855

TOPIC: Sermons

Not Much Missed

After a worship service a woman spoke to her new pastor. She said, "I'm deaf, and I can't hear a word you say, but I still come to get my plate full."

Hoping to console, the pastor said, "Well, maybe you haven't missed much."

She replied, "Yes, that's what they all tell me."

Dates & Places Used:

856

TOPIC: Sermons

Stay Alert

The easiest way to stay awake during a sermon is to deliver it.

Dates & Places Used:

857

TOPIC: Sex

An F in Sex

A little girl asked, "Grandma, how old are you?" The grandmother replied, "You shouldn't ask people that question. Most grownups don't like to tell their age." The next day she asked how much her grandmother weighed. The grandmother replied, "You shouldn't ask grownups how much they weigh. It isn't polite."

The next day the little girl was back with a big smile on her face. She said, "Grandma, I know how old you are. You're 62. And you weigh 140 pounds." The grandmother was a bit surprised and said, "My goodness, how do you know?" The girl smiled and said, "You left your driver's license on the table, and I read it." The girl continued, "Grandma, I also saw on your driver's license that you flunked sex."
Dates & Places Used:

858

TOPIC: Sex

Battle of the Sexes

Nobody will ever win the battle of the sexes. There's too much fraternizing with the enemy. *(Henry Kissinger)*
Dates & Places Used:

859

TOPIC: Sex

No Need to Share

A couple who lived in a small condominium with their young daughter were shopping for a house. As they walked through a three-bedroom model, the daughter seemed enthralled. "This is perfect, Mommy!" she exclaimed. "There's enough bedrooms so you and Daddy won't have to share!"
Dates & Places Used:

860

TOPIC: Sex

Guess What They Did

Robert Strand tells the following story:
The topic of the well-attended Wednesday evening Bible study was faith and obedience. Abraham and Sarah were cited as Old Testament examples. I said, "Abraham looked old, felt old, acted

old, and was old. Sarah looked old, felt old, acted old, and was old. The angel had brought good news to this aged couple, 'You are going to have a baby at your house.'"

Then there was a pregnant pause for effect, and again, with great presence of mind, I asked, "What do you suppose Abraham and Sarah went home and did after the angel finished with this message?"

The first shock was one of absolute silence. Then the titters started, which in turn were transformed into gales of laughter. The only thing left to do was to pronounce the benediction.

Dates & Places Used:

861 TOPIC: Shame

Shameful Students

A woman agreed that her children were doing better in school, but she was still planning to attend PTA meetings under an assumed name.

Dates & Places Used:

862 TOPIC: Sharing

Sharing with Whom?

A woman who was shopping took a break for some coffee and cookies. She sat in the one unoccupied chair across from a man reading a newspaper. She sipped her coffee and reached for a cookie, only to see the man across from her also taking a cookie. She glared at him; he just smiled at her, and she resumed her reading.

Moments later she reached for another cookie, just as the man also took one. Now feeling quite angry, she stared at the one remaining cookie—whereupon the man reached over, broke the cookie in half and offered her a piece. She grabbed it and stuffed it into her mouth, as the man smiled at her again, rose, and left. The woman was really steaming as she angrily opened her purse, her coffee break now ruined, and put her magazine away. And there she saw her bag of cookies.

All along she'd unknowingly been helping herself to the cookies belonging to the gracious man whose table she'd shared!
Dates & Places Used:

863 TOPIC: Shopping
Synchronized Wallets

A family was doing their Christmas shopping at the mall. As they prepared to split up to do some separate shopping, the father said, "Let's synchronize our watches. We'll meet in the parking lot at six o'clock." All four adjusted their watches. The mother then turned to her husband, and with hand outstretched, said, "OK. Now we'll all synchronize our wallets!"
Dates & Places Used:

864 TOPIC: Sickness
Really Sick

No one is sicker than a man who is sick on his day off or a child on a day when there is no school.
Dates & Places Used:

865 TOPIC: Sin: Consequence
No One to Tell

One Saturday night a pastor said to himself, "No way I can face that congregation tomorrow. I'm going golfing." So, he phoned his assistant and told him he wasn't feeling well and wouldn't be at church. Then the pastor arose very early that Sunday morning and drove out to the local course. Up in heaven, St. Peter nudged God and said, "You see your servant down there, Lord? You see what he's doing?" God replied, "Mm-hmm." "Well, aren't you going to do anything about him?" God replied, "Don't worry." The truant pastor was the first one to the tee that morning. He teed up his ball, took a swing, and—oh my, what a shot! It was the best drive he'd ever hit. As he watched, with disbelief and joy, the ball bounced high on the apron and rolled on the green directly to the flag. The pastor ran up to the green to find the ball in the cup. His very first hole-in-one! He danced around the green all excited. Meanwhile, St. Peter tugged at the Lord's sleeve. "God, I thought you were going to take care of this guy! Now he's gone and gotten a hole-in-one." God replied, "I took care of him. Who do you think he's going to tell?"

Dates & Places Used:

866

TOPIC: Sin

Sins of Omission

The Sunday school teacher asked her class: "What are sins of omission? After some thought one little fellow said, "They're the sins we should have committed but didn't get around to."

Dates & Places Used:

867

TOPIC: Sin

Siding with the Devil

While a man dressed in a devil costume was walking to a Halloween costume party, it began to rain torrentially. The man ran for the first cover he could find. It happened to be a church in the middle of a service. He ran directly into the sanctuary to the shock of all in attendance.

The congregation panicked. All cleared the room, except for one unfortunate woman who was trapped beneath the feet of this confused fellow. With fear and trembling the woman pleaded, "You know I've been on your side all along!"

Dates & Places Used:

868

TOPIC: Sin

Old Sins

A middle-aged woman phoned her daughter in not a little exasperation. "Dear," she said, "have you spoken to your grandmother recently? I've tried to call her every evening this week, and there's been no answer. She really should be at home. I'm beginning to worry!"

The daughter thought a second and said, "Oh. They're having a revival at the retirement village this week. I'll bet that's where Grandmom has been when you've called."

"Revival!?" the woman repeated. "What on earth do they need with a revival? What kind of sins could they possibly have at a retirement village, for crying out loud?"

The daughter wisely shot back, "*Old* ones, Mother, *old* ones."

Dates & Places Used:

869

TOPIC: Sincerity

Hidden Joy

A gifted public speaker was asked to recall his most difficult speaking assignment. He said, "That's easy. It was an address I gave to the National Conference of Undertakers. The topic they gave me was 'How to Look Sad at a Ten-Thousand-Dollar Funeral.'"

Dates & Places Used:

870

TOPIC: Singing

Personalized Hymns

As a growing boy, I spent a lifetime singing what I considered boring hymns. Not appreciating the words as written, my friends and I would revise the words, such as . . .

"I was sinking deep in sin—Wheeee!"

"Love lifted me . . ." (as we would raise ourselves in our seats)

"Do you know that you've been born again and again and again?"

"Broader than the scope of my transmission . . ."

The price to be paid for this adolescent sacrilege is to never be able to sing "Wonderful Grace of Jesus" without thinking about going through all four gears of the transmission before finishing the chorus.

Dates & Places Used:

871 TOPIC: Skepticism

Not All Is Possible

For those who say nothing is impossible, ask them to put skis over their shoulders and try walking through a revolving door.

Dates & Places Used:

872 TOPIC: Sleep

Embarrassing Snoring

A man asked his doctor if there was anything that could be done for his snoring. The doctor asked if it disturbed his wife. The man answered, "No, just the rest of the congregation."

Dates & Places Used:

873 TOPIC: Smiles

Smile!

A little girl asked her grandmother how she felt. She said she felt fine. The little girl asked, "Well, if you feel good, why don't you tell your face?"

Dates & Places Used:

874

TOPIC: Speech

The Mouth Trap

The mouth is the grocer's friend, the dentist's fortune, the orator's pride, and the fool's trap.

Dates & Places Used:

875

TOPIC: Speech

Mouth Not a Door

Maybe the eyes are the windows of the soul, but that still doesn't make the mouth the door to the brain.

Dates & Places Used:

876

TOPIC: Speech

Talking Too Fast

The trouble with people who talk too fast is that they often say something they haven't thought of yet.

Dates & Places Used:

877

TOPIC: Speech

Turn Off the Sound

When your mind goes blank, remember to turn off the sound.

Dates & Places Used:

878

TOPIC: Sports

Play Like the Pros

Australian golfer Greg Norman was playing in the Australian Open. He sliced the ball into the woods out of play. He did the same on his next shot. He brought it out and dropped it again. This time he hit it into the rough, got to the green, and with three putts scored an 8 on a par 5. Paul Harvey commented, "I always wanted to play like Greg Norman, and now I can."
Dates & Places Used:

879

TOPIC: Sports

When Losing Is Good

Show me a man who is a good loser, and I will show you a man who is playing golf with his boss.
Dates & Places Used:

880

TOPIC: Sports

How It's Explained

John Heisman defines a football on the first day of practice: "A prolate spheroid, an elongated sphere, in which the outer leather casing is drawn tightly over a somewhat smaller rubber tubing . . . better to have died a small boy than to fumble this."
Dates & Places Used:

881

TOPIC: Staff

Things Could Be Worse

When Jesus started his church, the pastor (Jesus) was executed. The chairman of the board (Peter) was cursing, swearing, and denying his position. The treasurer (Judas) committed suicide after embezzling funds. The other board members (the disciples) ran away. The only ones left were a few from the Ladies Fellowship. You see, your church is not all that bad!

Dates & Places Used:

882 TOPIC: Status

Almost Persuaded

A dignified, wealthy Englishman had long dreamed of playing Sandringham, one of Great Britain's most exclusive golf courses. One day he made up his mind to chance it. Entering the clubhouse, he asked at the desk if he might play the course. The club secretary inquired, "Member?" To which he replied, "No, sir." "Guest of a member?" "No, sir." The answer came back, "Sorry."

As he turned to leave, he spotted an acquaintance in the lounge. It was Lord Parham. He approached and, bowing low, said, "I beg your pardon, your Lordship, but my name is Higginbotham of the London solicitors, Higginbotham, Willinby, and Barclay. I should like to crave your Lordship's indulgence. Might I play this beautiful course as your guest?" His Lordship gave Higginbotham a long look, put down his paper and asked, "Church?" "Church of England, sir, as was my late wife." "Education?" "Eton, sir, and Oxford." "Sport?" "Rugby, sir, and spot of tennis." "Service?" "Brigadier, sir, Coldstream Guards, and Victoria Cross." "Campaigns?" "Dunkirk, El Alamein, and Normandy, sir." "Languages?" "Private tutor in French, fluent German, and a bit of Greek." His Lordship considered this briefly, then nodded to the club secretary and said, "Nine holes."

Dates & Places Used:

883 TOPIC: Strategy

Serve Both Ways

A woman was interviewing a prospective servant and asked, "Can you serve company?" The applicant replied, "Yes, mum,

both ways." The woman looked puzzled and asked, "What do you mean, both ways?" "So's they'll come again, or stay away."
Dates & Places Used:

884

TOPIC: Stress

Easy Duz It

A boy entered a grocery store one day and asked the grocer for a box of Duz detergent. The grocer was puzzled and asked why he would want a box of Duz. The boy was going to wash his cat. "Young man, you shouldn't wash your cat with this kind of soap," the grocer protested. But the boy insisted it would be OK.

A few days later, the boy returned, and the grocer asked about the cat. "Oh, he died." The grocer responded, "Well, son, I warned you not to wash your cat with that Duz detergent!" The boy replied, "The soap didn't hurt him a bit! The spin cycle got him."
Dates & Places Used:

885

TOPIC: Stubbornness

Impregnable Bias

One of the most frustrating conversations in theatrical history is recorded by *Theatre Arts* magazine: A subscriber dialed "information" for the magazine's number. "Sorry," drawled the woman, "but there is nobody listed by the name of '*Theodore Arts.*'" The subscriber insisted, "It's not a person; it's a publication. I want Theatre Arts." The operator's voice rose a few decibels. She repeated, "I told you, we have no listing for Theodore Arts." By now the subscriber was hollering, "Confound it, the word is Theatre: T-H-E-A-T-R-E." The operator came back with crushing finality: "*That* is not the way to spell Theodore."
Dates & Places Used:

886

TOPIC: Subjectivity

Objective Party

There are two sides to every question—as long as it doesn't concern us personally.

Dates & Places Used:

887

TOPIC: Substitute

First in Line

President Woodrow Wilson had a lively sense of humor. Early James, director of the Wilson House Museum in Washington, D.C., says the following story fits the Wilson personality and is very likely true:

A New Jersey man telephoned the White House at three o'clock in the morning and asked to speak to the president on a matter of national importance. The operator rang and woke Wilson. When the man got through to the president he told him, "The collector of customs here in New Jersey has died." The president replied, "I'm sorry to hear that, but why are you calling at this hour?" The reply came back, "Because I want to replace him." President Wilson responded, "Well, if the undertaker has no objection, neither do I."

Dates & Places Used:

888

TOPIC: Success

Keep Jumping

A young man asked a successful salesman for the secret of his success in selling. The salesman said, "You just have to jump at every opportunity that comes along." The young man asked how he would know an opportunity was coming. The salesman responded, "You can't. You have to keep jumping."

Dates & Places Used:

889

TOPIC: Success

The Source of Success

A newspaper reporter was interviewing an old rancher and asked him to what he would attribute his success as a rancher. With a twinkle in his eye the man replied, "It's been about 50 percent weather, 50 percent good luck, and the rest is brains."
Dates & Places Used:

890

TOPIC: Success

The Look of Success

The greatest help to a man struggling to succeed is to look as if he has already succeeded.
Dates & Places Used:

891

TOPIC: Success

Success of the Ruthless

A line from Daddy Warbucks in the musical "Annie":
"You don't have to be good to the people you meet on the way up if you don't plan to go down again."
Dates & Places Used:

892

TOPIC: Success

Figuring the Profit

A small businessman from the old country kept his accounts payable in a cigar box, his accounts receivable on a spindle, and his cash in the cash register. His son said, "I don't see how you can run your business this way. How do you know what your profits are?" The businessman replied, "Son, when I got off the boat, I had only the pants I was wearing. Today your sister is an art teacher, your brother is a doctor, and you're an accountant. I have a car, a home, and a good business. Everything is paid for. So you add it all up, subtract the pants, and there's your profit.

Dates & Places Used:

893 TOPIC: Sunday School

Deep Sacrifice

Many of us sacrifice like the little girl who, after hearing a Lenten sermon on sacrifice, decided to give up something for this special religious season. Her mother said, "You know, it should be something that you really like." The little girl thought for a moment and then said, with a twinkle in her eye, "Well, Mom, I guess it will have to be Sunday school, 'cause I like that better than anything else."

Dates & Places Used:

894 TOPIC: Sympathy

Mixed Message

A Philadelphia legal firm sent flowers to an associate in Baltimore upon the opening of its new offices. Through some mixup the ribbon that bedecked the floral piece read "Deepest Sympathy." When the florist was duly informed of his mistake, he let out a cry of alarm. "Good heavens," he exclaimed, "then the flowers that went to the funeral said, 'Congratulations on Your New Location!'"

Dates & Places Used:

895

TOPIC: Talent

Amazing Virtuosity

Pianist Victor Borge was once asked if he played any other musical instruments. Borge answered, "Well, yes, I have another piano."
Dates & Places Used:

896

TOPIC: Talk

Eating Words:

Man does not live by words alone, despite the fact that sometimes he has to eat them. *(Adlai Stevenson)*
Dates & Places Used:

897

TOPIC: Talk

A Knowing Hush

If no one ever spoke unless he knew what he was talking about, a ghastly hush would descend upon the earth. *(Alan Herbert)*
Dates & Places Used:

898

TOPIC: Talk

Really????

Husband to wife: "I know you believe you understand what you think I said, but I'm not sure you realize that what you heard is not what I meant."
Dates & Places Used:

899

TOPIC: Tardiness

Secret of Shorter Days

Employee to irate boss: "Of course I have a good reason for being late! It makes the day seem shorter."

Dates & Places Used:

900

TOPIC: Tardiness

Too Late to Tell

Boss to tardy employee: "You're twenty minutes late again! Don't you know what time our people start work here?"

Employee: "No sir, they've always already started by the time I get here."

Dates & Places Used:

901

TOPIC: Tattling

Trust in God

A counselor from a seventh grade camp was discussing with twelve-year-old Scott about Scott's experience with trying out "snuff" on the Q.T. with two other boys the night before. "I got really sick on the stuff," said Scott.

The counselor asked, "What did you think of the whole experience?"

Scott replied, "I won't ever try it again, but don't tell Bill, the director."

The counselor questioned Scott: "But God knows what you did. What's the difference between God's knowing and Bill's knowing?"

Scott explained, "God won't tell my parents!"

Dates & Places Used:

TOPIC: Taxes

Simplified Taxes

Congress is simplifying the tax forms this year. There are only four lines:

1. What was your income last year?
2. What were your expenses?
3. How much do you have left?
4. Send it in.

Dates & Places Used:

TOPIC: Taxes

Priorities for Success

People owe it to themselves to become a success. After that, they owe it to the IRS.

Dates & Places Used:

TOPIC: Taxes

IRS Foxholes

A cartoon once showed a small boy talking to his toys in the playroom, explaining that his dad phoned and asked him to pray for him. It seems he had been called in for a tax audit. One of the characters observed, "There are no atheists in the IRS waiting room."

Dates & Places Used:

TOPIC: Teachers

Bogus Wisdom

A famous guru had many disciples who hung onto his every word. Some were less fortunate and gathered on the porch of his home to hear his teachings, and yet others gathered in the road to hear the repeated words of the teacher. When the guru was dying, the three groups anxiously waited for his last words of wisdom. The disciples inside the house said, "Dear teacher, give us your dying words of wisdom," The guru whispered, "Life is like a river." The other disciples at a distance asked, "What did he say? What did he say?" The ones closest in repeated, "Life is like a river." This was passed on faithfully throughout the crowd of disciples.

Everyone nodded their heads at these words of wisdom, but one of the men at the far end of the road frowned and asked aloud, "Life is like a river? What does that mean?" So this question passed back through the disciples from group to group until it came back to where the guru lay dying, "Life is like a river? What does that mean?" And the guru struggled to lift his head off the pillow and replied, "OK. So maybe life isn't like a river."

Dates & Places Used:

906

Pain in the Neck

Several parts of the body tried to determine who would be boss: The brain said, "Since I already coordinate every function of the body I am the logical choice to be boss." The heart objected, saying, "Without my pumping blood throughout the body, none would be able to function, so I should be boss." The eyes said, "Without us the body would not know where it was going. We should be boss." The mouth said, "I speak for the body. I should be boss." One by one, each member of the body gave his reason as to why he should be boss. Finally the neck spoke up and said that he should be boss. "You!" said the brain. "Why you? You don't do anything to begin with." "Yeah," said the heart. "We wouldn't even miss you if you weren't here." This made the neck very mad, and he became tense. His muscles knotted up, and he began to exert excruciating pain. So intense was the pain, that the brain couldn't think. The eyes became blurry, and the heart had to work so hard that it became tired and began to skip a beat every now and then. After a week of this, all the parts of the body agreed that the neck could be boss.

The moral of the story? You don't have to be a brain, or have a heart to be boss; all you have to do is be a pain in the neck.
Dates & Places Used:

907

TOPIC: Teamwork

Short-Sighted Memory

An aging golfer still loved to golf but was unable to see the ball after he hit it. A golf pro suggested that the aging golfer team up with a certain old man, who would be just the right partner for him. "He's got the eyes of a hawk."

The golfer took the advice of the pro and sought the man out. The two men went out together, and on the very first tee the aging golfer hit a long drive. He asked his new partner, "Were you able to see where it went?"

His partner responded, "Sure did, but I can't remember where I saw it go."
Dates & Places Used:

908

TOPIC: Teamwork

Turtle Top

Someone has said, "One thing is for sure, if you see a turtle on top of a fence post you know he had help getting there."
Dates & Places Used:

909

TOPIC: Teamwork

Our Recital

A famous organist was giving a recital with an organ that was supplied by air by way of a hand pump. A young boy was hired to pump the organ for this occasion. All was going along fine until the lad put his head around the side of the organ and whispered: "We're doing pretty good, aren't we?"

"What do you mean by 'we'?" objected the organist. A few minutes later, in the midst of a beautiful strain, the organ suddenly stopped playing music. Desperately the organist tried all the stops. No use. Then again he saw the head of the boy bob around the corner, a broad smile on his face. He said, "Now do you know who I mean by 'we'?"

Dates & Places Used:

910
TOPIC: Teamwork

That's the Spirit

A little boy appeared at the door, selling postcards for a dime. He was asked what he was going to do with the money he was earning. He said, "I'm raising $100,000 for our new church building." The startled customer replied, "Do you expect to raise it all by yourself?" He answered, "Oh, no sir; there are two of us!"

Dates & Places Used:

911
TOPIC: Teamwork

Unaware

An airliner, stacked over a major airport, contacted the tower and was told to hold at three thousand feet. The pilot responded that he was indeed holding at three thousand feet. Another voice cut in. "You can't be holding at three thousand feet. I'm holding at three thousand feet." The first pilot interrupted, "I certainly can, you turkey, you're my co-pilot."

Dates & Places Used:

912

The Old Is Now New

A boy told his dad, "They've got a magic record player at school." "Yes?" quizzed his father. "Yep," replied the little one, "It doesn't need electricity to play. All you do is wind up the crank."
Dates & Places Used:

913

Phoneless Cord

There's a brand-new invention for people who want to relax in an atmosphere of quiet tranquility. It's a phoneless cord.
Dates & Places Used:

914

Woody Allen Wisdom

We have been told that Woody Allen stated at the conclusion of a recent commencement address: "Science has taught us how to pasteurize cheese—but what about the H-Bomb? Have you ever seen what happens when one of those things falls off a desk accidentally?" Woody Allen says modern man has no peace of mind; he finds himself in the midst of a crisis of faith. He is what we fashionably call "alienated." He has seen the ravages of war, he has known natural catastrophes, he has been to singles bars. As Woody sums it up, "And yet can technology really be the answer when my toaster has never once worked properly in four years? I followed the instructions and pushed two slices of bread down in the slots, and seconds later they rifled upward. Once they broke the nose of a woman I loved very dearly."
Dates & Places Used:

915

TOPIC: Teens

Nature's Wisdom

Adolescence is perhaps nature's way of preparing parents to welcome the empty nest.
Dates & Places Used:

916

TOPIC: Teens

Progress in Doctrine

A speaker conducted a successful seminar entitled "Rules for Raising Children." Then he got some kids of his own, and he changed the title to "Suggestions for Raising Children." When his kids reached their teen years, he discontinued the seminar.
Dates & Places Used:

917

TOPIC: Teens

Teenage Awareness

First mother of a teenager: "My daughter doesn't tell me anything. I'm a nervous wreck!" Second mother of a teenager: "My daughter tells me everything, and I'm a nervous wreck!"
Dates & Places Used:

918

TOPIC: Teens

A Sign of Growing Up

When children stop asking where they came from and start refusing to tell you where they are going, you know they're growing up.
Dates & Places Used:

919

Teen-Free Car

Three men were discussing what is most essential in a car: "Dependability." "Styling." "Economy." Just then a fourth man, who recently had bought his family a new car, entered the room. They decided to pose the question to him. They said, "Just what is the thing you'd like most to get out of your new car?" And he immediately responded, "My teenage son."
Dates & Places Used:

920

TOPIC: Teens

Teen's Poor Eyesight

Parents of two teenagers are worried about their children's failing eyesight. Their daughter can't find anything to wear in a closet full of clothes, and their son can't find anything good to eat in a refrigerator full of food.
Dates & Places Used:

921

TOPIC: Teens

Experience Not Needed

The best substitute for experience is being a teenager.
Dates & Places Used:

922

TOPIC: Teens

Teenage Reason

There's nothing wrong with teenagers that reasoning with them won't aggravate.
Dates & Places Used:

923

TOPIC: Teens

Parenting Teens

Mark Twain's philosophy: When a kid turns thirteen, stick him in a barrel, nail the lid shut, and feed him through the knothole. When he turns sixteen, plug the hole.

Dates & Places Used:

924

TOPIC: Teens

Raising Problem Kids

A college sophomore who had spent most of the school year in one kind of trouble or another received the following card from his parents who were vacationing in Greece: "Dear Son, we are now standing high on a cliff from which the ancient Spartan women once hurled their defective children to the rocks below. Wish you were here."

Dates & Places Used:

925

TOPIC: Ten Commandments

One Commandment at a Time

H. L. Mencken once said, "Say what you will about the Ten Commandments, you must always come back to the pleasant fact that there are only ten of them." This practical observation reminds one of the man who shook hands with the pastor after the service and thanked him for his sermon on the Ten Commandments. "Reverend, you sure preached a good sermon. In fact, I've made up my mind that for the next ten weeks, I'm gonna keep one of them Ten Commandments each week until I get through all ten of 'em."

Dates & Places Used:

926

TOPIC: Tests

Outstanding Legs

A certain college student needed a small two-hour course to fill out his schedule. The only one that fit was Wildlife Zoology. He had some reservations as he heard the course was tough, and the teacher a bit different. But as it was the only choice, he signed up. After one week and one chapter, the professor passed out a test for the class. It was a sheet of paper divided into squares, and in each square was a carefully drawn picture of some bird legs. Not bodies, not feet, just different birds' legs. The test simply asked them to identify the birds from the picture of their legs.

Well, the student was absolutely floored. He didn't have a clue. He sat and stared at the test and got madder and madder. Finally, reaching the boiling point, he stomped up to the front of the classroom and threw the test on the teacher's desk and exclaimed, "This is the worst test I have ever seen, and this is the dumbest course I have ever taken."

The teacher looked up at him and said, "Young man, you just flunked the test." Then the teacher picked up the paper, saw that the student hadn't even put his name on the paper and said, "By the way, young man, what's your name?" At this the student bent over, pulled up his pants, revealed his legs, and said, "You identify me."
Dates & Places Used:

927

TOPIC: Thanksgiving

Just a Minute

A food editor of the local newspaper received a telephone call from a woman inquiring how long to cook a 22-pound turkey.

"Just a minute," said the food editor, turning to consult a chart.

"Thank you very much," replied the novice cook, and hung up!
Dates & Places Used:

928

TOPIC: Thanksgiving

No Soap

In regions of Mexico hot springs and cold springs are found side by side, and because of the convenience of this natural phenomenon the women often bring their laundry, boil their clothes in the

hot springs, and then rinse them in the cold springs. A tourist watching this procedure commented to his Mexican guide: "They must think Mother Nature is generous to freely supply such ample, clean hot and cold water." The guide replied, "No, señor, there is much grumbling because she supplies no soap."
Dates & Places Used:

929

TOPIC: Thanksgiving

Sampler on Thanks

Things to be thankful for: that only you and God know all the facts about you . . . that even if you can't pay your bills, at least you do not have to be one of your creditors . . . that in case your job is a little harder than you like, it is worth remembering that you can't sharpen a razor on velvet . . . the doors of opportunity before you and for friends who oil the hinges.
Dates & Places Used:

930

TOPIC: Thanksgiving

Born a Turkey

Snoopy is getting dog food for his Thanksgiving Day dinner, and he is aware that everyone else in the family is inside having turkey. He meditates and talks to himself: "How about that? Everyone is eating turkey today, but just because I'm a dog I get dog food."

He trots away and positions himself on top of his doghouse and concludes: "Of course, it could have been worse, I could have been born a turkey." ("Peanuts")
Dates & Places Used:

931

The Future

The best thing about the future is that it comes only one day at a time. *(Abraham Lincoln)*
Dates & Places Used:

932

TOPIC: Time

Time Spent

It actually takes a lot of energy to live. If we are not careful, we will use it all up living.

A man may be allotted threescore and ten years. If he is, he will spend twenty-three years and four months of it asleep. He will work nineteen years and eight months. He will spend ten years and two months in religion and recreation. He will spend six years and ten months eating and drinking. Six years will be spent in traveling. Four years are spent in illness. In this time he will spend two years dressing.

Come to think of it, no wonder we are tired.
Dates & Places Used:

933

TOPIC: Time

Getting Organized

I write down everything I want to remember. That way, instead of spending a lot of time trying to remember what it is I wrote down, I spend the time looking for the paper I wrote it on.
Dates & Places Used:

349

934

TOPIC: Time

Frog's Perspective

One frog to another: "Time's fun when you're having flies."
Dates & Places Used:

935

TOPIC: Time Management

Beetle in Hand

When we attempt to do too many things at once, we often get rattled and accomplish even less. The story is told of young Charles Darwin in *Great Lives, Great Deeds* that one day he was eagerly holding one rare beetle in his right fist, another in his left, and then suddenly he caught sight of a third beetle which he simply knew he must have for his collection. What to do? In a flash he put one of the beetles in his mouth for safe-keeping and reached for the third beetle with his now free hand. But the mouth-imprisoned beetle squirted acid down young Darwin's throat so that in a fit of coughing he lost all three beetles.
Dates & Places Used:

936

TOPIC: Tough

We're Talking Tough

Dad: "Son, when I was in the Army, we had a drill sergeant who was so tough he used to wear a wig." Son: "What's so tough about that?" Dad: "He used to keep it on with a nail."
Dates & Places Used:

937

TOPIC: Trash

When Push Comes to Love

While eating at a fast-food restaurant, a little boy took his tray to the garbage can to throw away the trash. He studied the lid of the receptacle for a few moments and came running back to his mother and proudly announced that he knew how to spell "garbage": P–U–S–H!

His mother asked him if he knew what L–O–V–E spells. The boy said he did not. The mother hugged her son and told him that was how she felt about him.

Dates & Places Used:

938

TOPIC: Travel

Buffalo Shuttle

A man once went up to the airline counter and asked for a ticket to New York City. The airline clerk asked, "By Buffalo?"

"I guess that's OK," the customer replied, "if the saddle's comfortable."

Dates & Places Used:

939

TOPIC: Travel

Not Meant to Fly

If God had really intended men to fly, he'd make it easier to get to the airport.

Dates & Places Used:

940

TOPIC: Travel

Tours to Israel

Here is a new historical twist to Holy Land Tours: The Moses Tour leaves Cairo, Egypt, once every forty years. Featured cuisine: quails, strange white stuff, and water from our Rock fountain. Dessert: milk and honey at end of tour. The Elijah Tour–sometimes you may feel alone atop lovely Mount Carmel. Only one way airfare necessary. Return in a chariot of fire. Qualification: must eat like a bird. The Saul of Tarsus Tour–ride the donkeys to Damascus. Strange visions in magic hours on the road. Live in four-star dungeons, probable shipwreck on bonus adjunct rider tour to Rome. Bring materials for letter writing. The Isaiah Tour–if you hear a voice saying, "Go," you'll enjoy Servant Airlines' tour to different northern cities. The Noah Tour. Not for claustrophobics, a special 365 day cruise around the world. Paradise, Paramedics, Paratroopers. A para-everything. Visit gopherwood ark building factory. The Ruth Tour–wherever we go, you'll go. Wherever we eat, you'll eat. Our tour will be your tour. The Balaam Tour–play the original donkey videogame with special voice module. The Sarah Tour–lots of laughs. Don't go if eighty-nine years old. May return with extra family members. The Jonah Tour leaves Cleveland, Ohio; destination Los Angeles, California. Arrives Israel by no choice of your own. This tour is "made in the shade." You'll know your tour guide in the airport under the sign "We won't go!" The Simon Peter Tour–ride the fishing boats on the Sea of Galilee, water-walking option available, see the famous memorial of the falling sheet on the rooftop in Jaffa, view the videocassette of the original version of "True Confessions." Visit the 1995 Jerusalem rooster-crowing contest. The Jesus of Nazareth Tour–who knows where he will lead? His words to us are "Follow me."

Dates & Places Used:

941 TOPIC: Treasurers
An Extra Squeeze

The strong man at a circus sideshow gave an exhibition of his strength by squeezing an orange to pulp, then offered a reward to anybody who could get another drop of juice out of it. A thin, sallow, undersized man stepped up, took the orange, squeezed it, and out came several more drops of juice. The astonished strong man asked him how he could perform such a feat. "I've been a church treasurer for thirty years." he said, "and I'm experienced at that sort of thing."

Dates & Places Used:

942 TOPIC: Treasurers
Denomination Credit

Two country fellows met on a back road one afternoon. One was going down the road with a possum-hunting dog, and the other said to him, "How much will you take for the dog?" The owner quoted the price of $100 and declared the dog was an excellent hunter. The other fellow accepted the price, wrote out a check on the spot, and handed it over. The owner shook his head and gave the check back. "The check's good," the buyer said. "I'm a trustee in the Methodist Church." So the owner took the check and handed over the dog. A little bit later he met his uncle and asked him. "Uncle Josh, what does it mean to be a trustee in the Methodist Church?" Uncle Josh replied, "I'm not sure, but I think it's something like being a deacon in the Baptist Church." "Oh, no," the man said, "there goes my dog."

Dates & Places Used:

943 TOPIC: Trials

It's Going to Be a Bad Day

It's going to be a bad day when you see a "60 Minutes" news team in your office. You call Suicide Prevention, and they put you on hold. You turn on the news, and they're showing emergency routes out of the city. Your twin sister forgot your birthday. Your car horn goes off accidentally and remains stuck as you follow a group of Hell's Angels on the freeway. Your boss tells you not to bother to take off your coat. Your income-tax check bounces. You put both contact lenses in the same eye.

Dates & Places Used:

944 TOPIC: Trials

Trouble Changes

With me, a change of trouble is as good as a vacation. *(David Lloyd George)*

Dates & Places Used:

945

Run Like Crazy

In *The Gospel in Hymns*, published in 1950, is a story about Phillips Brooks, author of "O Little Town of Bethlehem":

One April Fool's Day, Brooks saw a boy on Boylston Street in Boston trying to reach a doorbell. Brooks walked up the steps, saying, "Let me help you, my little man!" He pushed the button; the boy scampered down the steps, saying, "Now run like crazy!"

Dates & Places Used:

946

Trinity

My wife was trying to get across a doctrine of the Trinity to her Sunday school class of first graders. Laboriously, she dragged out references to God the Father and God the Son, but was getting nowhere with the third person of the Trinity, until our young son volunteered, a bit uncertainly: "God the Wife?"

Dates & Places Used:

947

The Whole Sad Story

A story is told of a man who could not give a convincing explanation about his broken arm. He kept muttering some story about accidentally sticking his arm through his car window that he thought was down.

That's the public version. In private he confesses that it happened when his wife brought some potted plants inside that had been out on the patio all day. A garter snake had hidden in one of the pots and later slithered out across the floor where the wife had spotted it.

"I was in the bathtub when I heard her scream," he related. "I thought my wife was being murdered, so I jumped out to go help her. I was in such a hurry I failed to even grab a towel. When I ran into the living room, she yelled that a snake was under the couch. I got down on my hands and knees to look for it, and my dog came up behind me and cold-nosed me. I guess I thought it was the snake and I fainted. My wife thought I'd had a heart attack and called for an ambulance. I was still groggy when the ambulance arrived, so the medics lifted me onto a stretcher. When they were carrying me out, the snake came out from under the couch and frightened one of the medics. He dropped his end of the stretcher, and that's when I broke my arm."

Dates & Places Used:

948

TOPIC: Trust

Fencing In Is More Credible

In the late 1800s a rancher walked into the general store of a frontier town on the Great Plains and asked the owner for credit for supplies. "Doin' any fencin' this spring, Josh?" asked the storekeeper. "Sure am, Will," said the rancher. "Fencin' in, or fencin' out?" "Fencin' in. Taking in another three hundred and fifty acres across the creek." "Good to hear it, Josh. You have the credit. Just tell Henry out back what you need." A visitor, overhearing the conversation, commented to the storekeeper that this certainly was an unusual credit system. "It works," said the owner. "If a man's fencing out, he's running scared with what he's got. If he's fencin' in, he's got hope. I always give credit to a man who's fencing in."

Dates & Places Used:

949

TOPIC: Trust

Expecting the Worst

Helen Hayes, the actress, tells the following story in her autobiography:

It was Thanksgiving day, and she was cooking her first turkey dinner for her family. Before serving it she announced to her husband, Charles MacArthur, and their son James: "Now I know this is the first turkey I've ever cooked. If it isn't any good, I don't want anybody to say a word. We'll just get up from the table, without comment, and go out to a restaurant to eat." Then she returned to the kitchen.

When she entered the dining room bearing the turkey, she found her husband and son seated at the table with their hats and coats on. Obviously they didn't have much faith in her ability to cook a turkey!

At times we are like that with regard to God. We have problems, we pray to God for help, and then we sit back and expect the worst to happen. We don't have much faith in him; we don't really trust him.

Dates & Places Used:

950

TOPIC: Trust

Second Opinion

A man fell off a cliff and, at the last minute as he fell, happened to grab hold of a shrubby bush. As he dangled in space, he was filled with terror and called out toward heaven, "Is there anyone up there?" A calm, powerful voice came out of the sky, "Yes, there is." The tourist pleaded, "Can you help me? Can you help me?" The calm voice replied, "Yes, I can. Simply let loose of the bush, and everything will turn out fine." There was a tense pause, then the tourist yelled, "Is there anyone else up there?"

Dates & Places Used:

951

TOPIC: Trust

The Human Dilemma

This sign was seen at the desk of a country inn in England: "Please introduce yourself to your fellow guests since we are one big happy family. Do not leave valuables in your room."

Dates & Places Used:

952

TOPIC: Truth

On a Shaky Limb

Charles Swindoll once told of a time in graduate school when he was overzealous with an answer to a question. The professor let him continue until his position became weaker and weaker. In Swindoll's words, "He stared right through me, frowned, then replied, 'Mr. Swindoll, if you continue any further out on that limb, I'm going to saw you off with a hard set of facts.'"

Dates & Places Used:

953

TOPIC: Truth

Get the Whole Story

A farmer in Bloomington bought a horse, and was told, honestly, by the seller that the horse had one fault: He liked to sit on avocados. The farmer said, "Well, that's all right; there aren't any avocados around here." So, he put down his money, mounted the horse and started home. On the way they had to cross a stream. In the middle the horse sat down and wouldn't budge. The farmer walked back to the horse dealer and explained what happened. "Well, now you never said nothin' about water, so I didn't tell you." The farmer said, "Didn't tell me what?" The horseman explained, "If he can't get avocados, he sits on fish."

Dates & Places Used:

954

TOPIC: Understanding

Sympathetic Ear

Franklin D. Roosevelt decided to find out if anybody was paying attention to what he was saying. As each person came up to him with extended hand, he flashed that big smile and said, "I murdered my grandmother this morning." People would automatically respond with comments such as "How lovely!" or "Just

continue with your great work!" Nobody listened to what he was saying, except one foreign diplomat. When the president said, "I murdered my grandmother this morning," the diplomat responded softly, "I'm sure she had it coming."
Dates & Places Used:

955 TOPIC: Undertakers
Work with People

A reporter asked the young woman why she wanted to be a mortician. "Because," she said, "I enjoy working with people."
Dates & Places Used:

956 TOPIC: Undertakers
Better Business

A *Wizard of Id* cartoon shows the king chatting with the undertaker. The king asks the undertaker, "Doesn't this business get to you after a while?" The undertaker admits, "There are depressing days." The king says, "I would think so." And then in the last frame, the undertaker finishes his remark, ". . . but then someone dies, and I snap out of it!"
Dates & Places Used:

957 TOPIC: Uniqueness
Individual Commuter

An individualist is one who lives in the city and commutes to the suburbs. (*Michael Meaney*)
Dates & Places Used:

TOPIC: Uniqueness

Looks Like Trouble

A cartoon once showed the foreman of a jury at the door of the jury room giving the lunch order to the bailiff. You know the jury is in for a long time when you hear the order: "Eleven cheeseburgers and one hot dog. Eleven coffees and one hot chocolate. Eleven fruit pies and one prune Danish."

Dates & Places Used:

TOPIC: Uniqueness

Uniqueness of Snoopy

Snoopy the dog is sitting by the side of the road, watching all of the kids going by. Snoopy is reflecting to himself. He says, "I wonder why it is that some were born people, and others were born dogs. It just isn't fair." And then in the last frame he concludes, "Why was I the lucky one?" ("Peanuts")

Dates & Places Used:

TOPIC: Unity

The Fatal Blow

Weary of discord, Mark Twain said, "So I built a cage, and in it I put a dog and a cat. After a little training I got the dog and the cat to the point where they lived peaceably together. Then I introduced a pig, a goat, a kangaroo, some birds, and a monkey. And after a few adjustments, they learned to live in harmony together. So encouraged was I by such successes that I added an Irish Catholic, a Presbyterian, a Jew, a Muslim from Turkestan, and a Buddhist from China, along with a Baptist missionary that I captured on the same trip. And in a very short while there wasn't a single living thing left in the cage!"

Dates & Places Used:

961

TOPIC: Unity

Lions and Lambs

Visitors to the zoo were surprised to see the exhibit labeled "Coexistence" containing a lion and some lambs. The zookeeper explained there was nothing to it. "All I have to do every now and then is add a few fresh lambs."

Dates & Places Used:

962

TOPIC: Vacations

Timing Is Everything

A salesman from the Chicago area was in Miami when he called his manager. He explained the difficult situation saying, "I'm stuck here in the middle of a hurricane. All of the airports are closed, the airlines don't know when the next planes will take off. The highways are flooded, and the buses and trains aren't even running. What do I do?" The boss came back immediately with: "Start your two-week vacation as of this morning."

Dates & Places Used:

963

TOPIC: Vacations

Rich Isn't

Rich isn't just a state of mind. It's not having to arrange your vacation so that you arrive home on pay day.

Dates & Places Used:

964

TOPIC: Vacations

Vacation Is

A vacation is that brief period of time between trying to get ahead so you can leave and trying to catch up when you get back.

Dates & Places Used:

965

TOPIC: Vacations

The Gift of Imagination

Four couples rented a summer house for two months. Each couple took a two-week vacation there and took the combined thirteen children of the four families with them. One couple was bragging on this clever plan to a friend when the friend said, "I don't think two weeks in a cabin with thirteen children would be much of a vacation." "Oh no," they replied. Those two weeks were absolutely terrible. The vacation was the six weeks at home without the children.

Dates & Places Used:

966

TOPIC: Values

Short-Sighted Pig

A pig ate his fill of acorns under an oak tree and then started to root around the tree. When warned that his digging would kill the tree, he answered, "Let it die. Who cares as long as there are acorns?"

Dates & Places Used:

967

TOPIC: Visitation

All-Purpose Verses

A young pastor had rung a parishioner's doorbell and was waiting to be received, but no one came to the door. He sensed that someone was at home, so he kept ringing. As a final departing act he wrote Revelation 3:20 on the back of one of his calling cards and stuck it under the door: "Behold, I stand at the door and knock. If any one will hear my voice and open the door I will come in." Two days later the pastor received his calling card back in an envelope with a brief note attached that simply contained the text from Genesis 3:10: "I heard the sound of thee in the garden, and I was afraid because I was naked; so I hid myself."

Dates & Places Used:

968

TOPIC: Violence

Hunting Husband

Soon after a woman obtained a cat from the Humane Society, she phoned back to say they would not keep it. "I'm awfully sorry," she said. "It's a dear, and we are fond of it, but the cat is a bird killer, and we just can't have a bird killer. I'm sure my husband would be glad to make a contribution to the Humane Society for your trouble," she added, "but he's up north shooting deer."

Dates & Places Used:

969

TOPIC: Violence

The End of Ideas

Two Chinese men were arguing heatedly in the midst of a crowd. A stranger expressed surprise that no blows were being struck. His Chinese friend replied, "The man who strikes first admits that his ideas have given out."

Dates & Places Used:

970

TOPIC: Vision

The Wright Vision

In the year 1870 the Methodists in Indiana were having their annual conference. At one point, the president of the college where they were meeting said, "I think we live in a very exciting age." The presiding bishop said, "What do you see?" The college president responded, "I believe we are coming into a time of great inventions. I believe, for example, that men will fly through the air like birds." The bishop said, "This is heresy! The Bible says that flight is reserved for the angels. We will have no such talk here." After the conference, the bishop, whose name was Wright, went home to his two small sons, Wilbur and Orville. And you know what they did to their father's vision.

Dates & Places Used:

971

Easy Objectivity

Two boys entered the dentist's office. One boy said, "I want a tooth taken out, and I don't want any gas, and I don't want it deadened; we're in a hurry!" The dentist said, "You're a brave young man. Which tooth is it?" The boy turned to his smaller friend and said, "Show him your tooth, Albert."

The world is full of volunteers like that. We're anxious to have something happen to someone else! We don't mind if God changes the world as long as he doesn't bring any pain into our lives.

Dates & Places Used:

972

Designated Giving

The congregation was taking up a special collection to add to the salaries of pastors who received very inadequate salaries because they worked in very small churches that simply couldn't pay more. On the face of one check was written, "For some inadequate pastor." Pastor, does your paycheck seem to send you this kind of message? Or are you being paid with the coin of another realm?

Dates & Places Used:

973

A Better Year

In 1930 Babe Ruth earned $80,000. When asked if he thought it was fair that he received more than President Hoover, he said, "Well, I had a better year."

Dates & Places Used:

TOPIC: Wages

Paid in Like Currency

According to Garrick Utley on a recent news report from Russia the joke going the rounds of the factory workers is: "They pretend to pay us. We pretend to work."

Dates & Places Used:

TOPIC: Waiters

Know Your Place

Before the waitress could open her mouth, Grandpa announced, "I'm Bob, and I'll be your customer for the next hour."

Dates & Places Used:

TOPIC: War

Hide—No; Win—Yes

During the Civil War a Union soldier from Ohio was shot in the arm. His captain saw he was wounded and barked out an order, "Gimme your gun, Private, and get to the rear!"

The private handed over his rifle and ran toward the north, seeking safety. But after going only about two or three hundred yards, he came upon another skirmish. So he ran to the east, and found himself in another part of the battle. Then he ran west, but encountered more fighting there.

Finally, he ran back to the front lines shouting, "Gimme back my rifle, Cap'n. There ain't no rear to this battle nowhere!"

When it comes to the troubles of the world, life is unfair, and "there ain't no rear to this battle nowhere!" When it comes to living, you just can't run away and hide. The Easter proclamation, though, is Good News. The Easter proclamation is the good part, gooder than Good Friday. The Easter proclamation is that you can't run and hide, but you CAN win! Through the power of God, that raised Jesus from the dead, you CAN win!

Dates & Places Used:

977

TOPIC: War

Peace, Peace

A retired couple was alarmed by the threat of nuclear war, so they undertook a serious study to find the safest place on the globe. They studied and traveled, traveled and studied. Finally they found THE PLACE. And on Christmas they sent their pastor a card from their new home—in the Faulkland Islands—just prior to the conflict between Argentina and Great Britain.

Dates & Places Used:

978

TOPIC: War

Cost of Peace

Washington is full of peace monuments built after every war.

Dates & Places Used:

979

TOPIC: Wealth

Formula for Success

A man was being honored as his city's leading citizen. Called on to tell the story of his life, he said, "Friends and neighbors, when I first came here thirty years ago, I walked into your town on a muddy dirt road with only the suit on my back, the shoes on my feet, and all of my earthly possessions wrapped up in a red bandanna tied to a stick, which I carried over my shoulder. Today I'm the chairman of the board of the bank. I own hotels, apartment buildings, office buildings, three companies with branches in forty-nine cities, and I am on the boards of all the leading clubs. Yes, friends, your city has been very good to me." After the banquet a youngster asked the great man, "Sir, could you tell me what you had wrapped in that red bandanna when you walked into this town thirty years ago?" The man said, "I think, son, it was about a half million dollars in cash and $900,000 in government bonds."

Dates & Places Used:

980

TOPIC: Wealth

Comparative Values

A woman was walking along the river with a friend. A frog hopped up right beside her. It sounded like the frog was talking. She listened carefully. The frog croaked out, "If you kiss me, I'll turn into a Texas oilman, and I'll be grateful to you forever." Quickly she snatched up the frog and stuffed it into her purse. Her friend asked why she just grabbed it like that, instead of kissing it to take advantage of the offer. She replied, "That's easy. These days, a talking frog is worth a lot more than a Texas oilman!"

Dates & Places Used:

981

TOPIC: Wealth

Red Alert

The story is told in Russia about the late Premier Leonid Brezhnev, who wanted to impress his old mother from the Ukraine. First he showed her through his sumptuous apartment in Moscow. She said nothing. Then he drove her in his chauffeured black limousine out to his dacha in Usovo, showed her the marble reception rooms, and seated her to a fine lunch of caviar and crab. She still appeared unimpressed. So he flew her in his private helicopter to his hunting lodge in Zavidovo, where a fire crackled in the huge fireplace of the banquet room. She seemed increasingly ill-at-ease. At last he burst out, "Well, Mamma, what do you think?" She said with some hesitation, "It's nice, Leonid, but what if the Communists come back?"

Dates & Places Used:

TOPIC: Wealth

Buying Better Treatment

Money can't buy you friends, but your enemies treat you better.

Dates & Places Used:

TOPIC: Wealth

Prove It Yourself

Money can't buy happiness, we're told. But a lot of people would like the chance to prove it for themselves.

Dates & Places Used:

TOPIC: Wealth

Fun Anticipation

I can't think of anything that's as much fun to own as it is to look forward to owning.

Dates & Places Used:

985

TOPIC: Wealth

Poverty Perspective

In Hollywood, there is an exclusive school attended by children of movie stars, producers, and directors. Asked to write a composition on the subject of poverty, one little girl started her literary piece: "Once there was a poor little girl. Her father was poor, her mother was poor, her governess was poor, her chauffeur was poor, her butler was poor. In fact, everybody in the house was very, very poor."

Dates & Places Used:

986

TOPIC: Wealth

Communicating Poverty

Poverty is hereditary. You can get it from your children *(also true of insanity)*.

Dates & Places Used:

987

TOPIC: Weddings

No Old Flames

I was escorted to a wedding by my twenty-four-year-old bachelor son. He appeared unaffected by the ceremony until the bride and groom lighted a single candle with their candles and then blew out their own. With that he brightened and whispered, "I've never seen that done before." I whispered back, "You know what it means, don't you?" His response: "No more old flames?"

Dates & Places Used:

TOPIC: Weddings

Too Much Work

The pastor of a big city church ran an ad for a caretaker-housekeeper. The next day, a well-dressed young man appeared at the pastor's door. But before he could say more than "Hello, I came to see about . . . ," the pastor began questioning him.

"Can you sweep, make beds, shovel walks, run errands, fix meals, balance a checkbook, and baby-sit?" the churchman asked.

"Whoa," the young man said, "I only came to see about getting married, but if it's that much work, I'm not interested."

Dates & Places Used:

TOPIC: Wills

Stewardship Note

At presbytery, yesterday, one of my colleagues passed along this definition of the seven decades of man: Spills, Drills, Thrills, Bills, Ills, Pills, and Wills. His point was, we really shouldn't put off the Wills until the last decade. It may be too late.

Dates & Places Used:

TOPIC: Women

Needs

Every girl has certain needs. From birth to age 18 she needs her parents. From age 18 to 35 she needs good looks. From age 35 to 55 she needs a good personality. After 55, she needs CASH!

Dates & Places Used:

991

TOPIC: Words

Church Daffynitions:

Bulletin Board—a feeling of monotony caused by a repetitive bulletin format

Organ Donor—any person who contributes a large amount of money to the purchase of a church organ

Cistern—ones we should be lifting up when we are not upholding the brethren

Hymns—opposite of "hers"

Church Register—the vent cover over the church furnace

"Dropped from the Register"—the process of church discipline using the "trial by fire" method

Pious—having made too many trips to the dessert table at the potluck

Pastorate—past tense of "pastor eat," which is an imperative statement seldom required at potlucks

Pride—process used to detach church members from the television set to attend an evening service

Dates & Places Used:

992

TOPIC: Words

It's a Puzzle

What do butterflies get in their stomachs when they are nervous?

Dates & Places Used:

993

TOPIC: Words

Shrink Resistant

A young man was buying a shirt in a department store. The shirt label said, "Shrink Resistant." He asked the clerk what that meant. The clerk said, "The label means that the shirt will shrink, but it doesn't want to."

Dates & Places Used:

994

Careful How You Put It

The following have actually been found in church bulletins:

"This being Easter Sunday, we will ask Mrs. Smith to come forward and lay an egg on the altar."

"The ladies of the church have cast off clothing of every kind, and they may be seen in the church basement on Friday afternoon."

"This afternoon there will be a meeting in the South and North ends of the church. Children will be baptized at both ends."

Dates & Places Used:

995

TOPIC: Words

Converts or Traitors

Small boy: "Dad, what is a religious traitor?" Father: "A person who leaves our church and joins another." Boy: "And what is a person who leaves another church and joins ours?" Father: "A convert, son, a convert."

Dates & Places Used:

996

TOPIC: Words

Confusion Class

Pastor Travis Schmidt of Boyd, Minnesota tells of some confirmation confusion. The children of his churches generally must attend a confirmation class before receiving communion. Most parents do not bring their young children to the altar during communion to receive a blessing from the minister. However, as Pastor Schmidt tells the story:

During one particular worship service, my wife, Jennifer, had a little girl helping her watch our two-year-old son, Joshua. She asked the young girl if she would like to receive a blessing from the minister during communion. The girl said she would. So at

the appropriate time they came forward together to receive a blessing. That was when one of this girl's cousins nudged her father. The whole congregation heard her very serious question: "Daddy, how come Allison gets to go up to the altar during communion? After all, she hasn't been confused yet."
Dates & Places Used:

997

TOPIC: Work

Degrees of Happiness

An ancient Chinese proverb says, "If you wish to be happy for one hour, get intoxicated. If you wish to be happy for three days, get married. If you wish to be happy for eight days, kill your pig and eat it. If you wish to be happy forever, learn to fish."
Dates & Places Used:

998

TOPIC: Work

Wrong Work Is Better

Anyone can do any amount of work, provided it isn't the work he is supposed to be doing at the moment. *(Robert Benchley)*
Dates & Places Used:

999

TOPIC: Work

Helpful Adjustment

A child's father kept bringing home office work just about every night. Finally his first-grade son asked why. Daddy explained that he had so much work he couldn't finish it all during the day. The boy reasoned, "Then, why don't they put you in a slower group?"

Dates & Places Used:

1000

TOPIC: Work

Raising Boys

Adrian Rogers, former president of the Southern Baptist Convention, tells about the man who made his sons work in the cornfields while their peers spent the afternoon at the swimming hole. Someone scolded the father saying, "Why do you make those boys work so hard? You don't need all that corn."

The wise father replied, "Sir, I'm not raising corn. I'm raising boys."

Dates & Places Used:

1001

TOPIC: Worship

Presents Fill Temple

A dear elderly lady was teaching the four- and five-year-old Sunday school class at our church. During one of the lessons, they were learning about the building of the temple. She explained to the students that when the temple was finished, the presence of the Lord filled the temple. Instantly the eyes of each child got wide and full of excitement.

She soon discovered, however, that the source of their excitement was not joy that God had come to dwell in the temple, but rather, delight at imagining that huge building filled with *presents* from God!

Aren't we often much like those children? We are easily more excited about our *presents* from God than being *in the presence* of God.

Dates & Places Used:

Index of Subtopics

(Each illustration number is cross-referenced from two to six times. Numbers indicate entry number, not page.)

Abilities: 895
Abortion: 541
Absolutes: 524
Abuse: 41
Acceptance: 768, 769, 775
Accidents: 50, 200, 208, 335, 496, 522, 643, 947
Accommodation: 506
Accomplishment: 235, 483, 708, 758
Accuracy: 7, 952
Achievement: 970
Action: 19, 203, 211, 223, 330, 356, 529, 579, 888
Activism: 18
Activity: 30, 529, 932
Adversity: 976
Advertising: 172, 283, 296, 510, 646, 691, 796, 830, 832
Advice: 286, 357, 408, 653, 684, 745
Aesthetics: 624
Affection: 148, 823
Affirmation: 711
Age: 3, 30, 31, 56, 89, 90, 183, 232, 234, 240, 327, 354, 380, 443, 561, 575, 577, 581, 594, 605, 622, 632, 802, 803, 808, 868, 904, 990
Aggression: 375, 378
Aging: 31, 580, 907
Agreement: 906, 958
Alcohol: 378
Alibis: 341
Alliances: 389
Alliterations: 489
Ambiguities: 994
Ambition: 171, 244, 888
Ancestors: 490
Anecdotes: 184
Anger: 65, 175, 187, 273, 301, 420, 563, 743, 804, 808, 809
Animals: 684, 973
Annoyance: 671, 779
Anticipation: 372, 686, 984
Anxiety: 9, 917
Apathy: 485

Apparel: 146
Appeals: 691
Appearances: 49, 62, 85, 87, 88, 89, 99, 238, 280, 289, 365, 369, 401, 588, 602, 631, 682, 890
Applause: 712
Application: 503, 845, 853
Appreciation: 243, 441, 787
Approach: 831
Archaeology: 241
Army: 584, 956
Arrogance: 189, 734
Art: 188
Assertiveness: 375
Assistance: 11, 79, 210, 316, 334, 401, 452, 829, 908, 910, 979
Association: 689
Assumptions: 46, 92, 682, 751, 770
Atheists: 720, 722, 826
Attendance: 141, 373, 478, 865, 893, 995
Attention: 158, 167, 612, 619, 785, 972
Attitudes: 33, 46, 80, 162, 173, 231, 358, 383, 393, 427, 431, 474, 481, 504, 520, 616, 625, 642, 649, 788, 804, 839, 862, 873, 879, 891, 928
Authority: 105, 404, 634, 676

Babies: 8, 93, 656
Backgrounds: 265
Balance: 7
Bankruptcy: 245
Baptists: 86
Bargains: 622, 688
Basics: 500
Beauty: 44, 571, 602
Bed: 859
Behavior: 46, 383, 616
Beliefs: 262, 363, 720
Benefit: 14, 240, 853
Bethlehem: 131
Bias: 504, 675, 724, 728
Bible: 92, 101, 312, 502, 509, 633, 925, 940, 967
Bible Knowledge: 131, 304

Bills: 294, 370, 903
Birth Control: 366
Birth: 598
Bitterness: 136, 563
Blame: 342, 361
Blessings: 325, 558, 568, 889, 929, 939
Blindness: 418
Blondes: 99
Bloopers: 122, 220, 232, 860
Boasting: 189, 219, 534, 727, 736, 845
Body: 498
Bombs: 817
Boredom: 19, 514, 533, 850
Boss: 189, 647, 879
Boxing: 55
Brain: 498
Bravery: 453
Breakfast: 756
Breaks: 801
Brevity: 180, 523, 848
Bribes: 690
Budget: 244, 863, 941
Business: 83, 338

Calm: 789
Camping: 279, 760
Cards: 132
Careers: 698, 846
Cars: 169, 267
Catholics: 265, 467, 593, 773
Cats: 695, 696
Caution: 243, 300, 566, 822, 935
Census: 355
Certainty: 85
Change: 66, 69, 147, 263, 276, 345, 437, 438, 439, 486, 613, 667, 776, 788, 803, 944
Chaos: 702
Character: 398, 786, 881
Charlie Brown: 930
Cheating: 197, 278, 429
Children: 15, 21, 23, 34, 41, 43, 93, 114, 125, 128, 129, 130, 144, 148, 165, 188, 200, 233, 234, 241, 274, 279, 304, 306, 311, 333, 365, 366, 370, 372,

402, 412, 413, 429, 434, 435, 461, 464, 499, 502, 514, 589, 595, 597, 603, 604, 607, 608, 609, 610, 617, 618, 636, 653, 654, 655, 656, 657, 674, 693, 699, 721, 732, 772, 782, 786, 798, 799, 834, 836, 846, 859, 916, 918, 924, 937, 965, 986, 1000

Choice: 815

Choir: 67, 800

Chores: 607

Christmas: 308, 407, 459, 484, 508, 641

Church Growth: 881

Church: 68, 69, 109, 166, 267, 478, 485, 659, 660, 769, 893, 899, 900, 991, 995, 996

Civilization: 636

Clarity: 309, 767

Cleanliness: 265

Clothes: 47, 633, 920

Coffee: 120

College: 336, 431, 548, 655

Comfort: 167, 313, 661

Comics: 57

Commands: 634

Commercialism: 308

Commission: 866

Commitment: 2, 141, 207, 229, 364, 409, 976, 987, 988

Committees: 81, 180, 579

Commonality: 114

Common Sense: 752

Communication: 11, 38, 44, 47, 54, 64, 74, 81, 100, 133, 136, 142, 143, 264, 284, 309, 345, 353, 371, 400, 421, 447, 502, 503, 507, 508, 544, 552, 553, 562, 575, 593, 617, 748, 767, 783, 785, 821, 857, 860, 885, 898, 911, 917, 922, 927, 938, 994

Communion: 120

Communism: 825, 826, 981

Community: 511

Companionship: 391, 450

Comparison: 169, 190, 337, 428, 472, 605, 670, 736, 747, 878, 930, 970, 980

Compassion: 213, 258, 395, 517, 582, 703, 891, 954, 968

Competence: 150

Competition: 59, 190, 259, 360, 378, 605, 694, 736, 821

Complaints: 74, 104, 301, 631, 683, 928

Complicity: 945

Compliments: 430

Compromise: 526

Computers: 549, 751

Conception: 541

Conclusions: 62, 65, 159

Conditions: 12, 754, 811

Confession: 479, 512, 776

Confidence: 77, 85, 302, 583, 643, 673, 814, 844, 949

Confidential: 901

Confirmation: 996

Conflicts: 39, 166, 393, 615, 704, 858, 960, 993

Confusion: 58, 142, 303, 551, 996

Congress: 246

Conscience: 293, 538

Consequences: 127, 185, 192, 208, 249, 445, 572, 614, 865

Consideration: 37, 395, 404, 427, 452, 466, 955

Consistency: 83, 111, 126, 291, 465, 867

Contemplation: 113

Contentment: 4, 95, 174, 432, 836, 878, 928, 997

Contest: 190

Contracts: 858

Contradictions: 109

Control: 706

Convenience: 250, 278, 392, 810

Conversation: 390, 707, 840

Conversion: 66, 426, 773

Conviction: 32, 255, 426, 538, 651, 652, 720, 827

Cooking: 177, 578, 604, 610, 770, 927, 949

Cooperation: 60, 449, 711, 760, 793, 829, 906, 909, 910, 911, 960

Counselors: 155, 408

Country: 511

Courage: 215, 316, 378, 453, 501, 672

Courtship: 569, 774

Creation: 108, 119, 176, 586, 633, 702, 752, 939, 959

Creativity: 290, 482, 652, 685, 962, 974

Credit: 816, 948

Crime: 199, 945

Criticism: 20, 71, 168, 173, 175, 176, 177, 223, 299, 671, 683, 714, 761

Crops: 826

Crucifixion: 516

Cruelty: 41, 292, 527, 891

Crying: 104

Culprit: 436

Cures: 499

Customers: 972

Cynicism: 227

Danger: 217, 492, 817

Darkness: 418

Dating: 220, 824

Deafness: 444

Death: 216, 237, 328, 419, 495, 525, 887

Debt: 39, 83, 387, 494, 948

Decay: 182

Deceit: 185, 252, 277, 380

Decency: 601

Deception: 22, 90, 278, 336, 340, 399, 510, 521, 539, 540, 685, 687, 701, 830, 869

Decisions: 32, 81, 151, 180, 352, 457, 561, 594, 749

Dedication: 655, 812, 828

Defeat: 205, 420

Deferral: 791

Definitions: 125, 128, 156, 274, 387, 456, 591, 595, 701, 866, 880, 964, 994, 995, 996

Delays: 749

Delegation: 828

Delinquents: 924

Deliverance: 492

Denial: 293

Denominations: 86, 118, 146, 446, 555, 960

Dependence: 710, 908, 950

Depression: 75

Design: 959

Desire: 248, 372, 481, 716, 983, 993

Despair: 237, 401, 495, 583, 847

Destination: 285

Destiny: 285

Details: 225, 528, 548, 550, 726, 744, 979

Devil: 364, 867

Differences: 226, 383, 388, 615

Difficulty: 144, 567
Dinosaurs: 241
Diplomacy: 253, 288, 651, 701, 779
Direction: 501, 744
Disappointment: 344, 664
Disaster: 63
Discipleship: 329
Discipline: 115, 417, 436, 589, 602, 604, 748, 916, 1000
Discovery: 482, 752
Discretion: 13, 112, 179, 779, 816
Disgrace: 479
Disrespect: 105
Dissatisfaction: 248
Divorce: 48, 155, 568
Doctors: 150, 471, 525, 674, 684
Doctrine: 416, 946
Dog: 693
Donations: 172, 488, 638
Doubt: 741, 813
Drama: 687
Dreams: 975
Dress: 45, 369
Driving: 193, 300, 302, 333, 522, 613, 669, 957
Drunkenness: 82, 319
Duty: 67, 211, 332, 567, 596, 598, 607, 998

Early: 52
Easter: 797, 798, 799, 800
Education: 51, 149, 307, 428, 518, 539, 547, 857, 861, 999
Efficiency: 1, 272, 715
Effort: 332
Ego: 534, 706
Elections: 106, 331, 835
Embarrassment: 97, 872, 947
Emotion: 373, 694
Empathy: 322, 805, 954
Emphasis: 677
Employees: 171, 497, 515, 756, 786
Employment: 801, 802, 864
Encouragement: 237, 313, 361, 451, 929
Endorsement: 380
Endurance: 884
Enemies: 90, 389, 394, 491, 982
Energy: 19, 30, 611, 932, 998

Engagement: 292
Enjoyment: 442
Entertainment: 545
Enthusiasm: 611, 659
Entrance: 775
Epitaphs: 239, 807
Equality: 376
Errors: 35, 362, 463, 589
Escape: 945
Eternity: 109, 781
Eulogy: 398
Evangelism: 426, 834
Exaggeration: 733
Example: 126, 320, 519
Excellence: 59, 194, 204
Exceptions: 221
Excess: 733
Excitement: 644
Excuses: 27, 68, 69, 70, 153, 185, 214, 219, 221, 250, 282, 316, 373, 394, 429, 431, 476, 537, 539, 540, 566, 587, 750, 754, 967, 973
Exemptions: 236
Exercise: 281
Expectations: 287, 345, 374, 443, 531, 569, 589, 596, 660, 662, 664, 716, 810, 949
Expenses: 294, 486, 903
Experience: 351, 354, 359, 570, 805
Experts: 57, 78, 142, 150, 156, 223, 277, 683
Explanations: 250, 430, 553
Exploitation: 348
Exposed: 249, 540
Expressions: 454, 992

Facts: 952
Failure: 204, 205, 258, 315, 325, 352, 410, 429, 551, 745, 857, 878
Faith: 222, 228, 414, 583, 588, 650, 814, 860, 949, 950
Faithfulness: 67, 111, 130, 152, 229, 365, 386, 500, 554, 807, 827, 881, 987, 995
Fame: 235, 455
Family: 15, 145, 231, 282, 366, 371, 462, 494, 618
Farming: 51, 367, 745
Fathers: 200, 274, 405, 657, 732, 786

Fear: 150, 198, 216, 217, 218, 219, 228, 302, 414, 611, 613, 627, 645, 678, 741, 789, 817, 981
Fellowship: 114, 316, 318, 449
Feminism: 946
Fertility: 128
Fighting: 192, 193, 673
Finances: 78, 107, 377, 792, 892, 902, 904, 941
Fishing: 151, 377, 649, 997
Flattery: 690, 713, 733
Flesh: 535
Flexibility: 77, 181, 526, 831
Flying: 316, 600, 817
Focus: 289, 390, 677, 795
Fondness: 242
Food: 209, 216, 268, 275, 279, 281, 287, 343, 412, 446, 699
Foolishness: 262, 350, 397, 456, 543, 559, 590, 629, 841, 874, 875, 876, 896, 897, 905, 914, 966
Forgetfulness: 28, 98, 580, 581
Forgiveness: 40, 196, 582, 615, 717, 743, 775, 777
Fortune: 530, 556, 557, 558, 889, 930, 947
Fragrance: 737
Fraud: 57, 592
Freedom: 808, 815, 818, 963
Friendship: 46, 61, 80, 106, 163, 326, 433, 451, 511, 707, 768, 951, 982
Frugality: 138, 527, 863
Frustration: 885
Fun: 933
Function: 5
Funds: 298
Funerals: 206, 869
Futility: 246, 456, 550, 978, 984
Future: 110, 229, 305, 310, 328, 894, 975, 989

Gain: 819
Gambling: 559
Gender: 374, 376
Generations: 20, 327, 576, 621, 622, 630
Gifts: 55, 127, 133, 134, 172, 213, 405, 421, 422, 585, 597, 610, 806, 881, 1001
Giving: 266, 296, 297, 298, 401, 403, 488, 564, 637,

638, 666, 690, 696, 862,
941, 969
Goals: 6, 76, 170, 214, 285,
381, 501, 611, 650, 697,
719, 774, 910
God: 109, 123, 188, 234, 583
Godliness: 435
God's Will: 255
Golf: 191, 202, 420, 736,
865, 879, 907
Good Works: 448
Gospel: 330, 799
Gossip: 875, 897
Government: 246, 700, 703
Grace: 393, 473, 487, 775,
862
Grades: 547, 926
Grandchildren: 493
Grandmothers: 555
Gratitude: 488, 928
Great Commission: 329
Greed: 201, 275, 403, 572,
638, 810, 811, 935, 981
Grief: 238, 242
Growth: 918, 925, 948
Guests: 236, 470
Guilt: 40

Habits: 203, 276, 300, 422,
438, 519, 535, 536, 827,
953
Halloween: 867
Handicaps: 31, 165, 418, 907
Handwriting: 767
Happiness: 53, 291, 452,
482, 570, 742, 818, 842,
873, 997
Harmony: 906
Hatred: 388
Healing: 471, 663, 684, 724
Health: 20, 22, 28, 29, 96,
293, 294, 295, 520, 793,
864, 920
Heart: 29
Heaven: 233, 234, 328, 331,
450, 472, 665, 695, 835,
894
Hell: 233, 328, 449, 894
Help: 228, 313, 320, 449,
663, 908
Heredity: 47, 493
Hesitation: 302, 532
History: 121, 122, 940
Holiness: 538
Holy Spirit: 729, 852
Home: 470

Honesty: 38, 179, 194, 247,
249, 398, 409, 429, 494,
512, 537, 566, 721, 942
Honor: 395, 787, 812
Hope: 237, 287, 583, 984
Horse: 362
Hospitality: 883
Humanity: 184, 456
Humility: 3, 164, 186, 318,
480, 664, 855, 916
Humor: 117, 225, 377, 584,
588, 606, 618, 656, 680,
743, 859
Hunger: 920
Hunting: 257, 757
Hurry: 260, 273, 668
Husbands: 56, 342
Hymns: 625, 870
Hypocrisy: 535, 560

Idealism: 531, 567, 569, 662,
734
Ideas: 546, 974
Identity: 61, 318, 847, 861,
926
Idiots: 301
Ignorance: 355, 485
Imagination: 65, 975
Immortality: 235, 240
Impaired: 165
Imperfect: 168
Importance: 740
Impossibility: 871
Impressions: 427
Improvement: 420, 531,
613, 750
In-Laws: 161
Inadequacy: 663, 847
Inappropriate: 101
Incarnation: 135, 459
Income: 161, 244
Independence: 462, 915
Individuality: 957, 958, 959
Infinity: 240, 781
Inflation: 107
Influence: 192, 719
Information: 355
Inheritance: 811
Instruction: 271, 286, 344,
714
Insults: 164, 855
Insurance: 335, 833
Intelligence: 1, 263, 493,
571, 630, 889
Intentions: 6, 8, 744
Interest: 56, 103, 389, 464,
998

Interpretation: 113, 121,
122, 353
Introductions: 644
Inventions: 381, 912, 975
Investments: 819, 980
Invitations: 782, 834
Involvement: 151
Irony: 992
IRS: 903, 904
Isolation: 977
Itemization: 10

Jealousy: 483
Jesus: 130, 484, 797
Jobs: 323, 347, 382, 786,
838, 845
Jokes: 474, 506
Joy: 53, 742, 842, 873, 997
Judgment: 71, 113, 168, 224,
225, 301, 424, 747, 749,
812
Jury: 199
Justice: 7, 193, 201, 202,
249, 513, 582, 808, 926,
959

Kindness: 64, 395
Kissing: 14, 31, 84, 676
Knowledge: 125, 183, 261,
355, 500, 639

Labels: 993
Language: 90, 311, 728, 746,
843, 992
Late: 52
Laughter: 474, 475, 842
Law: 108, 290, 484, 523,
722, 925
Lawyers: 169, 738
Laziness: 323, 382
Leaders: 320, 905
Leadership: 79, 187, 211,
381, 542, 682, 706
Learning: 21, 218, 261, 312,
349, 351, 627
Leftovers: 578
Lent: 893
Lessons: 63, 332, 351
Letters: 93, 124, 132, 767
Lies: 22, 27, 219, 222, 249,
250, 252, 253, 277, 336,
380, 587, 705, 830
Life: 75, 111, 225, 349, 351,
442, 449, 611, 628, 697,
758, 847, 904
Light: 608
Limitations: 337, 384
Listening: 322, 444, 545,
840, 954
Literalism: 259, 505

Liturgy: 118, 120, 267
Loans: 816, 948
Logic: 221, 262, 275, 321,
    358, 377, 465, 543, 559,
    688
Lord's Prayer: 717
Loss: 63, 245, 295, 399, 815,
    823, 879
Lottery: 367
Love: 2, 3, 31, 54, 165, 167,
    229, 242, 554, 696, 822,
    824, 829, 937
Loyalty: 449, 732
Luck: 159, 399, 556, 559,
    568, 592

Machines: 88
Management: 26, 261, 533
Manger: 129
Manhood: 193
Manipulation: 654
Manners: 464, 466, 601,
    616, 699
Mark Twain: 923
Marriage: 5, 31, 37, 58, 48,
    54, 56, 152, 155, 157,
    177, 209, 220, 242, 291,
    342, 345, 400, 407, 419,
    460, 466, 468, 477, 495,
    544, 552, 562, 586, 628,
    647, 774, 792, 807, 818,
    859, 898, 987, 988
Maturity: 24, 25, 49, 351,
    352, 354, 434, 435, 462,
    632, 734, 915, 918, 921
Meals: 715
Meanings: 108, 206, 306,
    503, 505, 507, 510
Mediocrity: 171, 204, 623
Membership: 882
Memory: 28, 82, 100, 196,
    272, 300, 312, 458, 907,
    934, 978
Men: 628, 858
Mental Health: 163, 755
Mercy: 517
Messages: 143, 767
Messes: 127
Methods: 831
Miracles: 174
Mischief: 945
Misers: 490
Mission: 166, 329
Mistakes: 6, 7, 35, 63, 92, 97,
    100, 116, 132, 186, 201,
    220, 224, 243, 272, 273,
    295, 303, 339, 349, 350,
    352, 411, 447, 469, 532,

539, 590, 608, 633, 641,
    721, 752, 744, 763, 809,
    851, 884, 894, 994
Misunderstanding: 73, 133,
    154, 155, 238, 239, 284,
    353, 447, 457, 467, 505,
    508, 575, 645, 823, 885,
    938
Mockery: 870
Moderation: 384, 442, 812
Modern Art: 58
Money: 107, 133, 161, 244,
    245, 247, 266, 293, 351,
    367, 587, 399, 405, 432,
    433, 463, 486, 487, 490,
    506, 554, 617, 638, 685,
    698, 836, 863, 892, 902,
    942, 979, 982, 983, 990
Morality: 386
Mothers: 41, 89, 104, 125,
    241, 331, 370, 395, 527,
    578, 589, 602, 691, 846,
    917, 937, 949
Motivation: 106, 170, 172,
    218, 312, 439, 463, 506,
    690, 719, 723, 760, 770,
    833, 883
Motives: 562, 725, 755
Mouth: 841
Mundane: 542
Murder: 334, 954
Music: 101, 630, 632, 779,
    806, 895, 909

Names: 434, 558
Nativity: 128, 129
Nature: 961
Needs: 60, 91, 107, 213, 433,
    607, 657, 716, 990
Negative: 175, 174, 177, 299
Neglect: 37, 455
Negotiation: 380, 688, 780
Nerves: 917, 992
Newlyweds: 209
Noah: 669
Noise: 8, 585, 806
Nonviolence: 973
Normal: 94
Nose: 289
Notes: 339
Novelty: 912

Obedience: 34, 115, 270,
    317, 509, 589, 597, 602,
    784, 925
Obesity: 280
Objections: 811, 887
Occupations: 310, 681
Offense: 40

Offerings: 403, 564, 565,
    629, 658, 792
Omission: 866
Omnipotence: 119
Omnipresence: 412, 413,
    414, 415
Opinions: 102
Opportunity: 453, 473, 676,
    815, 983
Optimism: 227, 468, 642,
    647, 673, 678
Options: 23
Order: 702
Organization: 934, 935
Outlines: 489
Overcoming: 418, 650

Pain: 5, 16, 256, 404, 475,
    805, 936, 968
Painting: 269
Palm Sunday: 117
Parents: 4, 15, 34, 148, 200,
    227, 230, 231, 339, 366,
    434, 461, 519, 576, 618,
    635, 636, 653, 674, 718,
    772, 861, 901, 916, 919,
    922, 923, 924, 965, 986
Partnership: 911
Past: 987
Pastors: 102, 266, 347, 408,
    443, 460, 469, 499, 603,
    850, 854, 855, 856, 865,
    967, 969
Patience: 17, 43, 260, 322,
    463, 563, 634, 849, 931,
    968
Peace: 269, 416, 481, 743,
    789, 913, 977, 978
Peers: 708
People: 387, 955
Perception: 42, 365
Perfection: 168, 191, 223,
    428, 662, 845
Perfectionism: 205
Performance: 627
Persecution: 483
Persistence: 207, 215, 453,
    888
Personality: 955
Perspective: 42, 58, 71, 73,
    75, 87, 88, 116, 123, 139,
    144, 263, 275, 353, 383,
    431, 475, 556, 597, 674,
    717, 737, 759, 794, 795,
    803, 839, 851, 912, 956,
    985
Pessimism: 29, 33, 73, 76,
    110, 227, 299, 324, 368,

369, 440, 482, 678, 681, 683, 709, 871, 943
Pests: 78, 138, 515, 626, 648, 787
Pets: 209, 251, 305, 371, 461, 558, 601, 614, 686, 696, 709, 768, 884
Philosophy: 75, 113
Phones: 370, 913
Phonies: 311, 905
Piano: 627
Piety: 346
Places: 447
Planning: 23, 76, 107, 356, 411, 528, 650, 751, 774, 825, 966, 989
Pledges: 296
Plumbers: 825
Poem: 137
Poise: 348
Police: 333, 516, 813
Politeness: 506
Politics: 253, 479, 531, 702
Possessions: 245, 400, 574, 794, 919, 984
Possibilities: 481
Potatoes: 826
Potlucks: 446
Poverty: 486, 985, 986
Power: 79, 119, 438, 724, 909
Practicality: 51, 134, 523, 547
Practice: 359
Praise: 54, 95, 96, 178, 398, 718
Prayer: 12, 92, 93, 123, 124, 228, 316, 364, 409, 412, 573, 585, 619, 703, 718, 753, 781
Preaching: 848, 856
Precision: 796
Preferences: 255, 379, 620, 621, 624, 630, 699, 737, 771, 783, 790, 893, 953
Pregnancy: 860
Prejudice: 114, 504, 645, 696, 705, 882
Preparation: 271, 361, 852
Presence: 1001
Presentations: 791
Presents: 1001
Presumption: 62, 138, 153, 348, 416, 488, 727, 728, 753, 761, 765, 905
Pretence: 57, 72, 252, 357, 480, 521, 971
Prices: 64, 98, 487, 832

Pride: 45, 146, 178, 187, 189, 457, 471, 480, 521, 554, 670, 706, 711, 714, 727, 735, 761, 766, 840, 886
Priorities: 14, 68, 91, 98, 254, 257, 272, 390, 396, 528, 697, 722, 787, 833, 836, 843, 880
Private: 693
Prizes: 82, 605
Problems: 29, 324, 368, 485, 709, 915, 922, 947, 953
Prodigal: 679
Profanity: 579, 747
Profits: 567, 892
Progress: 110, 248, 375, 548, 762, 763, 844, 912, 914
Promises: 409, 458, 494, 592
Promptness: 756
Protestants: 467
Providence: 332, 513, 585, 668, 720, 931
Provision: 781
Psychiatrists: 195
Psychology: 454
Publicity: 358
Puns: 47, 84, 129, 157, 337, 339, 421, 458, 515, 991
Purchases: 10
Purpose: 108, 317, 338, 362, 379, 397, 410, 476, 529, 579, 619, 695, 764, 774, 784, 846, 880, 899, 939, 972
Pursuit: 439

Quality: 194
Questions: 791

Race: 362
Raffles: 400
Rationalization: 700
Reading: 311
Ready: 52
Reality: 72, 346, 551, 567, 569, 961
Reasons: 27, 42, 254, 335, 341, 358, 394, 495, 725, 764, 922
Rebellion: 115
Recognition: 491
Recruits: 584
Regions: 675
Regret: 35, 238, 268, 531
Rejection: 641, 769
Rejoicing: 625
Relativity: 524
Relaxation: 609, 801, 913
Releasing: 4

Relevance: 60, 91, 156, 236, 612, 680, 738, 739, 790, 886
Relief: 50, 718
Religion: 346
Religious Differences: 267
Reluctance: 599
Repentance: 39, 350, 420, 437, 679, 746, 775
Representation: 704
Reprobation: 747
Reputation: 455, 735
Requests: 80, 154, 689, 691, 796
Resistance: 212
Respect: 264, 419
Responses: 136, 549, 584, 776, 834
Responsibility: 185, 214, 314, 637, 761, 964, 998
Rest: 30, 609, 965
Restoration: 788
Results: 199, 208, 445, 665
Resurrection: 251, 305
Retirement: 26, 698, 868
Retribution: 971
Revenge: 33, 193, 292, 331, 385, 563, 926
Revival: 868
Rewards: 305, 428, 445, 465, 665, 713
Riddle: 676, 992
Ridicule: 434
Rights: 158
Risk: 160, 216, 217, 257, 512, 950
Rituals: 118, 120
Roles: 374, 596, 792
Romance: 2, 858
Routine: 667
Rules: 202, 436, 527, 635
Rural: 511
Rushed: 441

Sacrifice: 450, 679, 784, 893
Safety: 837
Saint: 435
Salaries: 73, 161, 181, 463, 658, 902, 963, 969, 970
Sales: 10, 171, 190, 325, 425, 575, 606, 620, 629, 642, 646, 686, 688, 698, 701, 707, 754, 763, 773, 789, 816, 819, 820, 888, 890, 910, 962
Salvation: 66, 330, 426, 448, 778, 795
Sanity: 986

Santa: 147
Satisfaction: 95, 268, 432
Schedules: 440, 667, 825, 932
Scholarships: 473
School: 861
Science: 4, 241, 771
Search: 823
Seclusion: 977
Secretaries: 647
Secrets: 24, 423, 479, 512
Security: 406, 661
Self-Control: 195, 276, 417, 423, 651, 863
Self-Image: 15, 77, 708, 759, 769
Self-Improvement: 759
Self-Righteousness: 731
Sense: 543
Sensitivity: 527, 553, 968
Separation: 391
Sermons: 97, 102, 489, 514, 612, 712, 729, 782, 785, 851, 872
Service: 204, 972
Sex: 94, 824
Shame: 282, 319, 424, 974
Share: 859
Shopping: 134, 308
Shortsightedness: 966
Shout: 34
Siblings: 145
Sickness: 16, 37, 237
Sight: 256, 907
Signs: 606, 689
Silence: 13, 24, 841, 897
Similarity: 145
Simplicity: 902
Sin: 116, 197, 249, 364, 386, 391, 417, 425, 437, 438, 536, 560, 572, 590, 594, 679, 692, 746, 747, 776, 777, 925
Sincerity: 276, 385, 437, 725, 777
Singing: 139, 623, 625, 770
Single: 568
Size: 160
Skiing: 871
Skill: 191, 895
Slander: 425
Slavery: 655
Sleep: 74, 856
Smiles: 440, 742, 842
Snacks: 279
Snobs: 882
Snoring: 82
Socialism: 981

Society: 183
Solutions: 13, 42, 136, 549, 686, 741, 789, 817, 953, 961, 962, 974
Sorrow: 679
Sources: 269, 909
Speaking: 712, 841
Specifics: 726, 796
Speech: 84, 158, 444, 546, 705, 713, 896, 897
Speed: 25, 169, 837
Spelling: 885, 937
Spending: 246
Spiritual Battle: 976
Spirituality: 363
Sports: 55, 59, 70, 72, 139, 141, 191, 224, 252, 374, 467, 600, 740, 768, 838, 970
Stamina: 29
Standards: 307, 526
Statistics: 163, 377, 508, 670
Status: 455, 521, 981
Stereotypes: 728
Stewardship: 297, 298, 403, 565, 637, 666
Stories: 184
Strategy: 170
Stress: 9, 140, 260, 273, 551, 913, 999
Stubborn: 262
Students: 112, 314
Study: 729
Style: 149, 621, 687
Subjectivity: 680, 739
Substitution: 135
Subtlety: 283, 288
Success: 59, 315, 325, 337, 359, 411, 557, 819, 820, 844, 903, 979
Suffering: 766
Sunday School: 798
Superiority: 731
Support: 313, 451
Surprise: 407, 656
Surrender: 12
Survival: 215
Suspicion: 813
Symbols: 118, 425
Sympathy: 258

Talents: 40, 55, 422
Talk: 105, 322, 544, 545, 579, 639, 790, 840, 841, 876
Tardy: 526
Taxes: 240, 451, 903

Teaching: 112, 165, 270, 306, 314, 346, 503, 946, 952
Teamwork: 210, 212, 252, 828
Technology: 182, 814
Teens: 4, 147, 227, 230, 327, 462, 576, 621, 632, 635, 653, 780, 824, 870, 986
Television: 343
Temporality: 49, 307, 574, 763
Temptation: 197, 417, 560, 561, 692, 993
Tenacity: 672
Testimony: 126
Tests: 139, 187, 271, 304, 540, 547, 857
Thanksgiving: 96, 459, 726, 929
Theft: 194, 201, 218, 340, 406, 564, 592, 951
Theology: 86, 140, 306
Therapy: 520
Thief: 254
Thinking: 498, 518
Thought: 28, 518
Time: 9, 17, 25, 103, 256, 260, 356, 441, 453, 626, 640, 668, 669, 715, 756, 762, 781, 849, 850, 899, 900, 934, 935
Timing: 13, 216, 864
Titles: 558, 666
Tomb: 797
Tongue: 35, 423, 546, 705, 841, 874, 875, 876, 877
Tools: 550, 710
Toothbrush: 693
Tough: 672
Tours: 441, 940
Toys: 137
Tradition: 402
Traffic: 175, 959
Tragedy: 643
Training: 270, 497, 714, 1000
Transformation: 66, 206
Travel: 414, 958
Trials: 162, 324, 496, 643, 820, 947, 976
Troubles: 53, 162, 295, 324, 368, 475, 492, 496, 556, 648, 765, 943, 944
Trust: 18, 222, 247, 310, 344, 363, 413, 583, 592, 661, 753, 813, 814, 854, 942

Truth: 27, 179, 219, 222, 253, 288, 307, 424, 524, 534, 536, 537, 772, 901
Turkeys: 927

Understanding: 131, 321, 509, 550, 805, 898
Undertakers: 869
Unity: 313, 591, 659, 863, 958
Unwillingness: 599
Urgency: 256, 317, 532, 657, 667, 723, 760, 778, 837

Vacations: 755, 944
Value: 218, 308, 317, 372, 700, 980
Values: 203, 338, 436, 461, 524, 573, 574, 624, 730, 737, 832, 956
Vanity: 706
Vices: 477
Victory: 259
Violence: 55, 491
Virtues: 477

Vision: 481, 649, 907, 920, 948
Visitation: 460, 469
Visitors: 236
Vocabulary: 13
Vocations: 957
Vows: 152

Wages: 600
Waiting: 17, 849
War: 513, 722
Warnings: 290
Waste: 935
Weakness: 993
Wealth: 161, 406, 421, 471, 557, 600, 882, 963
Weddings: 181, 220, 466, 730, 988
Weeds: 205, 692
Weight: 276, 277, 280, 281
Willingness: 80, 784
Wills: 989
Winning: 72, 190, 259, 360, 858

Wisdom: 24, 49, 91, 111, 198, 256, 354, 384, 498, 518, 528, 546, 548, 576, 577, 639, 640, 785, 822, 837, 875, 876, 877, 921, 952, 974
Wishes: 525, 919
Wit: 136, 584, 675, 887
Wives: 159, 342, 460, 586, 768, 848
Women: 375, 376, 628, 858
Words: 282, 593, 757, 896, 933, 991
Work: 1, 315, 323, 347, 379, 382, 396, 529, 530, 557, 598, 710, 742, 756, 762, 764, 793, 899, 900, 964, 971, 988
Worldliness: 573
Worry: 678, 793, 931
Worship: 415, 1001
Worth: 44

Youth: 20, 22, 327, 577, 734, 808, 921

Zeal: 373, 773

Alphabetical Index of Titles

(Several titles have been abbreviated for convenience.
Numbers indicate entry number, not page.)

Abstract Art: 57
Abundant Entreaties: 426
Accidents: 335
Accountant's Maxim: 7
Acquaintance: 387
Act of Applause: 712
Act Your Wage: 244
Adam Was a Foreigner: 221
Adjusting to Reality: 181
Adjusting to Realities: 526
Admitting Mistakes: 186
Advice on Marriage: 477
African Proverb: 192
Age Discrimination: 26
Aging: 444
Aging Poem: 28
Agree for Jobs: 615
Alibi: 341
All About Bees: 33
All Goes Wrong: 344
All Is Well: 844
All-Purpose Verses: 967
Almost Expressed Thanks: 54
Almost Persuaded: 882
Almost the Same: 792
Always a Little More: 432
Amazing or Baloney: 707
Amazing Virtuosity: 895
An Acceptable Diet: 278
An Adaptable Fiction: 854
An Easter Rose: 306
An Easy Hug: 217
An Explosive Situation: 816
An Extra Squeeze: 941
An F in Sex: 857
Animal Crackers Thanks: 726
Another Miracle: 587
Another Opinion: 623
Applied Learning: 51
Art of Apology: 40
Ask Him: 791
Asking Her Age: 505
Asleep at Last: 718
Aspects of Aging: 581
Asserting Leadership: 187
Assistance or Respect: 80

Assumptions Cost: 62
Atomic Prayer: 722
Attempting Failure: 315
Authoritative Advice: 357
Autumn Rituals: 476
Avenging Enemies: 806
Awareness Is the Key: 285

Back Seat Driver: 273
Backward Obedience: 636
Bad Bulb: 763
Bad Day When: 496
Bad-Luck Wife: 159
Bad Timing: 354
Battle of the Sexes: 858
Bayonet the Wounded: 78
Be Careful What You Pray: 721
Be Specific: 577
Bearded Christmas: 147
Beatitude Exceptions: 811
Become Possible: 434
Beetle in the Hand: 935
Believe It to See It: 363
Belly-Achers: 173
Best Alibi: 333
Better Boston Prayers: 724
Better Business: 956
Better Day: 734
Better Speaker: 164
Better Than Lame: 303
Better Than Latin: 843
Better Than Nothing: 15
Better Way: 332
Better Year: 970
Beyond Satisfied: 268
Beyond Vale of Tears: 695
Big Bad Grass: 692
Big Black Door: 815
Bike Before Christmas: 137
Bird Catchers: 757
Birth of a Cynic: 227
Blow First: 532
Blown Opportunity: 641
Body Designs: 5
Bogus Wisdom: 905
Boring Sermons: 102
Born a Turkey: 930
Both Drunk: 319

Bottom Dollar: 98
Brain Weight: 499
Branded: 180
Break Retraining: 497
Bridge the Gap: 829
Brief Message of Hot Air: 105
Brilliant Conversation: 390
Bring out Your Bibles: 101
Bubble Gum Return: 43
Buffalo Shuttle: 938
Buried Potatoes: 764
Busted Smiles: 842
But Hurry: 9
Buying Better Treatment: 982
Buying Friends: 768
BZZZZZZZ: 710

Can't Be Helped: 60
Can't Say Enough: 178
Can't Talk about Love: 553
Canine Limits: 709
Canyon or Confusion: 681
Careful Choice: 594
Careful How You Put It: 994
Careful Tracking: 353
Careless Appearance: 48
Careless Conclusion: 728
Carpet Cleanout: 592
Carry the Load: 793
Carry-Outs: 8
Cats and Love Return: 696
Cat's Habit: 439
Catching Monkeys: 572
Catholic Baths: 265
Catholic Grocery Beads: 118
Caught: 521
Change and Perspective: 803
Change for a Reward: 810
Change the Answers: 307
Change the Light: 514
Changing the Odds: 817
Character Crisis: 311
Chasing Shadows: 49
Check Your Wallet, Sir?: 600
Child Manipulator: 563

Child's Candor: 464
Child's Play: 654
Children Ask God: 124
Children's Paraphrase: 122
Chip off the Profane Block: 519
Choose Any Two: 107
Christian Shoppers: 574
Christmas Caution: 132
Christmas Corsage: 308
Christmas Lore: 131
Christmas Shopping: 406
Church Chain Letter: 660
Church Daffynitions:: 991
Churchill's Gratitude: 790
Classy Mutt: 751
Clear Coffee: 73
Clearing Conscience: 196
Clever Disguise: 466
Close to Perfect: 845
Clothes Make a Church: 146
Clout—Who Has It?: 39
Cold Feet: 454
Cold Test: 271
Collect Calls: 370
Colson's Change: 263
Communicating Jargon: 142
Communicating Poverty: 986
Communication: 503
Communication Flow: 81
Company You Keep: 61
Comparative Values: 980
Complexity: 156
Computers: 751
Condensed Viewpoint: 75
Confidence in Experts: 295
Confused: 551
Confusion Begins: 823
Confusion Class: 996
Congregation Immunity: 236
Consistent Lives: 203
Conversational Grace: 427
Converts or Traitors: 995
Corn on the Palm: 117
Cost of Giving: 488
Cost of Peace: 978
Cost of Short Sight: 527
Costly Catch: 377
Counting the Years: 21
Country Persuasion: 688
Creating Chaos: 702
Credit for Long Life: 380
Cries for Mercy: 516
Crisis in Sports: 740

Critical Imperfection: 223
Criticizing: 225
Croaking Frogs: 631
Crowd Control: 638
Cry-Babies: 104
Cure for Hatred: 206
Cynic in All of Us: 222
Cynical View of History: 456

Dated by Computers: 183
Day After Christmas: 127
Day Eight Complaints: 176
Dead or Forgotten: 234
Deadly Dog Biscuits: 209
Deadly Experience: 359
Death from Kids' Views: 233
Decisive Moment: 457
Deep Sacrifice: 893
Deferred Decisions: 255
Deficit Spending: 246
Degrees of Happiness: 997
Denomination Credit: 942
Deserves to Forgive: 386
Designated Giving: 969
Desire for Peace: 481
Devil Dad: 274
Dilemma for the Humble: 472
Direct Message: 729
Disgusting: 560
Disputed Prayer Power: 720
Do As You're Told: 270
Dog Doesn't Know: 779
Dogs Welcome: 601
Don't Explain: 394
Don't Give Up: 302
Don't Go Too Far!: 437
Don't Learn to Do: 261
Don't Let Get Away: 655
Don't Turn Off Jesus: 130
Drink for a Dime: 510

Easy Duz It: 884
Easy Objectivity: 968
Eating Words: 896
Economic Clarity: 509
Effective Strategy: 617
Ego Time: 534
Egocentric Steering: 706
Einstein's Analogy: 771
Embarrassing Snoring: 872
Emotive Friends: 318
End of Ideas: 974
Endearment: 393
Enemies Accumulate: 326
Ennies or Nuns: 593
Entertaining Exercise: 343

Entry Requirement: 446
Episcopal Liturgy: 267
Equal Time: 374
Equal Time: 460
Esoteric Cheating: 113
Established or Stuck: 69
Eternal Epitaph: 328
Evangelism Methods: 330
Events That Reveal: 197
Ever Draw a Blank?: 100
Ever Met a Christian?: 126
Exhilarating Pause: 482
Expecting the Worst: 949
Experience Mistakes: 349
Experience Not Needed: 921
Explain Thanksgiving: 459
Explanations: 358

Face the Facts Boldly: 288
Fair Price: 629
Faithful to the End: 67
False Hopes: 287
Family Resemblance: 145
Famous Humble Doctor: 471
Famous Mothers: 846
Far from Everything: 739
Fatal Blow: 960
Fear of Zeal: 373
Fearful Wisdom: 198
Fearless Timing: 216
Fencing In Is More Credible: 948
Feeling at Home: 470
Fertile Nativity: 128
Fighting on the Ice: 207
Figuring the Profit: 892
Fill the Void: 498
Finally Alone: 148
Finally Satisfied: 836
First Confessional: 479
First Impressions: 50
First in Line: 887
First Priority: 272
Fish Story: 151
Fit to Kill: 388
Flexible Building: 381
Flight Patterns: 337
Foot Doctor: 294
Foot-in-Mouth Disease: 99
Football Fans and Church: 141
Forced Truth: 179
Forgetful Borrowers: 247
Forgetful Middle Years: 580
Forgive Us Both: 733
Formidable Dilemma: 492

383

Formula for Success: 979
Four Men Needed: 628
Four-By-Twos: 154
Franklin on Prayer: 715
Frantic Frog: 215
Free Advice: 14
Free Roses: 606
Fresh Perspective: 139
Friend: 389
Friend for Sale: 106
Friend to the End: 450
Friends: 392
Frog's Perspective: 934
Frugal Rules: 528
Fruit of Hard Work: 396
Fun Anticipation: 984
Futile Call for Unity: 591
Futile Shots: 550
Future: 931

Generation of Mules: 329
Genetic Apparel: 47
Genetic Miracle: 493
Get Even: 807
Get Rid of Your Pastor: 659
Get the Smile Over: 440
Get the Story Straight: 304
Get the Whole Story: 953
Getting Hugs: 167
Getting into Heaven: 448
Getting Organized: 933
Getting Ready to Win: 673
Getting Rid of Daddy: 371
Getty's Success: 557
Gift Exchange with Jesus: 409
Gift of Imagination: 691
Gift of Imagination: 965
Gift of Motivation: 611
Gift You Don't Need: 408
Glorious Send-Off: 686
Go First: 512
Goalie's Rejection: 224
God's Not in a Hurry!: 668
Going Out of Business: 830
Going to Get Help: 316
Golden Bargains: 622
Golf Clubs with Pools: 421
Golfer's Timing: 418
Golfing Tips: 191
Good and Original: 430
Good Bet: 401
Good Day: 53
Good from Bad: 640
Good Manners: 616
Good with the Bad: 83
Great Title: 612
Greatest Pitcher: 77

Greedy Giving: 599
Growing Family: 366
Growing Objects: 115
Guess What They Did: 860
Guidance on Dieting: 417
Guilty Party Exposed: 436

Hair-Raising Sermon: 850
Happiness: 570
Happy Ending: 305
Happy Formula: 452
Hard Winter: 297
Harvey Firestone: 750
Have Your Way: 701
Healthy Circulation: 20
Help from Experience: 350
Help You Honk: 175
Help Yourself: 759
Helpful Adjustment: 999
Helping Others Learn: 805
Hero Not Braver: 453
Hidden Joy: 869
Hide: No; Win: Yes: 976
High Cost of Love: 292
Historical Perspective: 240
History Revisited: 121
Hitch-Hiker Religion: 689
Hold the Twinkies: 276
Honest Outlaws: 494
Honesty Pays: 465
Honking Parent: 34
Hope of Dying: 237
Housing in Heaven: 665
How It's Explained: 880
How Long Can It Take?: 256
How So Stories: 458
How to Get a Car: 780
How to Live: 111
How's That Again?: 582
Human Dilemma: 951
Human Thinking: 184
Humor, Etc.: 474
Hung Jury: 200
Hunting Husband: 973

Identity Crisis: 44
Identity Crisis: 847
If God Were Alive: 109
If Sermon Offends Thee: 848
If Shoe Fits, Sell It: 642
Ignorance: 92
Ignorance and Apathy: 485
I'll Alter Him: 345
Immersed in the Scenery: 86
Immutable Presbyterian: 555
Impact Is What Matters: 738

Impregnable Bias: 885
In Front of Ourselves: 144
In Need of Police: 517
In Time We Look Sillier: 821
Independent Teen: 462
Individual Commuter: 957
Individualism: 27
Infatuation or Love: 2
Inflated Water: 487
Initial Taste of Power: 79
Inside and Out: 441
Insincere Warning: 290
Intellectual Limits: 384
Interpretive Bias: 504
IRS Foxholes: 904
It Won't Happen!: 110
It's a Gift: 55
It's a Puzzle: 992
It's All How You View It: 556
It's Going to Be a Bad Day: 943
It's in the Bag: 201
It's Relative!: 382

Jesus Understands: 663
Jewish Advantage: 513
Join the Crowd: 735
Joy or Fear: 678
Joyous Imperfection: 168
Jump-Start: 30
Jungle Wisdom: 837
Just a Minute: 927
Just Can't Catch Up: 605
Just Counting: 64
Just in Case: 379
Just in Time: 667
Just Like Family: 231

Keep Jumping: 888
Keep Your Pants On: 589
Keeping Problems Away: 743
Keeping Up: 169
Kept Secrets: 423
Kid's Candid Responses: 228
Kid's Concerns: 123
Kidding Aside: 372
Kitchen Accidents: 208
Know the Letters: 500
Know Your Blessings: 753
Know Your Customer: 831
Know Your Place: 972
Knowing Hush: 897

Last Word on Comet: 683
Late Advice: 230
Laugh Cure: 520
Law of Clothes Life: 369

Law of Parenting: 618
Laws of Computing: 182
Lawyer's Brief: 523
Lawyers and Rabbits: 522
Learn from the Past: 243
Left Hand of God: 119
Let Him In: 834
Let Jesus Get It: 413
Let Me In!: 775
Let Them Go: 4
Let's Get Practical: 134
Levels of Love: 699
Liberace's Line: 45
Life Goals: 410
Life Happens: 697
Life in New England: 675
Life Is Tough, But: 162
Life's Deeper Meaning: 42
Light to Light: 543
Like a Son: 786
Limited Atonement: 331
Limits to Life: 442
Limp Understanding: 321
Lions and Lambs: 961
Liquid Courage: 378
Little Voice Inside: 194
Long Film: 103
Long-Term Driving: 17
Long-Term Marriage: 152
Long-Winded Driving: 849
Look of Success: 890
Looking for Loopholes: 652
Looking Out for Mom: 395
Looks Like Trouble: 958
Loose Leaf: 633
Lost Cause: 286
Lost in Translation: 90
Lost Last Two: 399
Love at Second Sight: 822
Love It In: 165
Low Presence: 414
Loyalty to the End: 554

Make Requests Specific: 783
Make Your Eternity: 449
Making a Baby Brother: 93
Making Something: 338
Man Needs a Wife: 342
Man We Want: 59
Marital Gamblers: 818
Married Secretaries: 647
Masked Mom: 602
Measure of a Mom: 603
Mental Health: 163
Middle-Aged Action: 19
Mindless Messages: 851
Misdirected Comfort: 150
Miser's Money: 490

Misplaced Experts: 761
Missing God: 415
Mixed Message: 894
Mixed Motives: 172
Mixed Motives: 291
Model Motivation: 323
Modern Marketing: 10
Modern Music: 621
Modern Scene: 140
Modern Woman: 375
Mom Is the Light: 608
More Careful Thought: 277
More Humble Pie: 664
More Light Bulbs: 1
More Than a Spot: 677
More to Keep Quiet About: 24
Most Neglected Men: 455
Mother Knows: 125
Mother the Cook: 578
Mother's Day Break: 596
Mother's Day Sound: 610
Motivation: 690
Motivation That Works: 760
Motive for Courage: 218
Mouse's Bathing Suit: 135
Mouth Not a Door: 875
Mouth of Babes: 120
Mouth Trap: 874
Movie Cue: 320
Moving Dirt: 425
Much Responsibility: 314
Muddled Note: 767
Mule-Team Scenery: 542
Murphy's Shoes: 620
Music Lover: 624
Musical Clock: 626
Mutual Recognition: 252
My Father Speaking: 539
My Name Is: 595

Nature's Wisdom: 915
Near Miss: 428
Needs: 990
Needs and Wants: 716
Nerd Dad: 368
Never Changed His Mind: 552
Never Satisfied: 174
Never Too Early: 52
New Baby: 598
New Blessings: 325
New Sources of Funds: 298
No Conversation: 155
No God, No Food: 826
No Need to Share: 859
No Old Flames: 987
No One to Tell: 865
No Problem Too Big: 741

No Real Confession: 185
No Searching: 824
No Soap: 928
Noise Tolerance: 630
Normal & Oblong: 680
Not All Is Possible: 871
Not As They Seem: 41
Not Long Ago: 445
Not Meant to Fly: 939
Not Much Missed: 855
Not Ready for Aging: 89
Not Really Suitable: 239
Not Too Subtle Signs: 283
Not What They Seem: 469
Not What You Pay for: 700
Notable Excuses: 339
Now I See!: 266
Now the Good Part: 799
Number Seven Rejection: 336
Nun and the Bed Pan: 588

Obedience: 509
Objective Party: 886
Oblivious Award: 82
Offense of Life: 483
Old Expressions: 226
Old Is Now New: 912
Old Sins: 868
Old Temptations: 561
Omniproblem: 412
On a Shaky Limb: 952
On Second Thought: 537
One Commandment at a Time: 925
One for Johnny: 232
One Last Fling: 420
One Man's Logic: 262
One Up: 789
One Who Is Seen: 383
Only Take What You Can Eat: 275
Only the Tough Grow Old: 16
Open to the Future: 23
Opening Line: 644
Opinions or Thoughts: 639
Opportunity of Lifetime: 576
Optimist and the Fly: 648
Optimistic Planning: 650
Optimistic Whaler: 649
Order of Repentance: 777
Our Inheritance: 489
Our Recital: 909
Our Varied Roles: 214
Out of Order: 754
Out of this Hole!: 798
Outstanding Legs: 926

Overly Helpful: 13
Overpriced Puppy: 832

Paid in Like Currency: 971
Pain in the Neck: 906
Pain of Perfection: 671
Painful Choices: 404
Painless Way to Give: 403
Paneful Target: 6
Parenting Teens: 923
Parrot's Prayer Answered: 719
Part-Time Idiots: 301
Part-Time Tomb: 797
Partial Commitment: 229
Partial Commitment: 451
Partial Forgiveness: 385
Partial Repentance: 438
Parting Shot: 533
Pastor Dad: 657
Pastor Pig: 666
Patience of Noah: 669
Pay or Get off: 637
Peace, Peace: 977
Peaceful Shifting: 742
Pedal Together: 212
People Need People: 213
Perennial Pledges: 296
Perfect Pastor Found: 662
Perhaps a New Vocation: 745
Persistent Liar: 536
Persisting Unbelief: 299
Personal Directions: 484
Personal Touch: 138
Personalized Hymns: 870
Perspective: 258
Perspective: 71
Perspective Puzzler: 676
Phoneless Cord: 913
Picture of God: 188
Pit-Stop Momma: 607
Plan B: 293
Planning for Misery: 76
Plans: 356
Play Like the Pros: 878
Plot Thickens: 136
Point of Purchase: 804
Point of Reference: 58
Poise: 348
Poverty Perspective: 985
Power Crowd: 473
Power of Television: 68
Powerful Positions: 725
Practical Gift for Dad: 405
Practical Present: 597
Prayer Principles: 619
Preacher's Prayer: 364

Predetermined Affirmation: 711
Prejudice Unites: 114
Prepare or Rely: 852
Preparing Perspective: 431
Presents Fill Temple: 1001
Previous Pastor: 347
Price of Experience: 351
Priorities: 254
Priorities for Success: 903
Profit from Failure: 352
Profit in Sermons: 853
Profitable Venture: 433
Profound Warning: 199
Progress In Doctrine: 916
Progressive Delays: 750
Proof Is In: 713
Property Rights: 794
Prophetic Boasting: 736
Prove It Yourself: 983
Puppy Punishment: 614
Purpose: 758
Purpose of Poison Ivy: 108
Pushing Boats: 682
Put the Bones Back: 674

Quick Action: 245
Quick Count: 355
Quick Sincere Choice: 257

Rabbit Resurrection: 251
Raffle Baffle: 400
Raising Boys: 1000
Raising Problem Kids: 924
Rapid Transit: 260
Raw Furniture: 646
Reading Priorities: 91
Ready Excuse: 340
Reality and Otherwise: 72
Really Fast: 25
Really Lucky: 559
Really Sick: 864
Really???: 898
Reason to Die: 495
Reason to Listen: 546
Reason to Sing: 625
Reasons for Marriage: 571
Recipe for Mothers: 604
Recognized Her Laugh: 491
Red Alert: 981
Reduce the Steps: 549
Regretful Speech: 35
Regrettable Actions: 651
Relative Wealth: 161
Remove the Pressure: 531
Repent!: 776
Requirements to Drive: 635
Retirement Breaks: 801
Retirement Plans: 802

Revealed Secrets: 376
Rich Isn't: 963
Right Man: 398
Right Nice Tribute: 467
Right Song: 565
Right Track: 529
Rights: 158
Risky Comparison: 160
Rope's End: 788
Round John Virgin: 129
Row It or Rock It: 211
Rubbed Wrong Way: 515
Ruin It Again: 204
Ruined by Praise: 714
Run Like Crazy: 945

Sampler on Thanks: 929
Saturday Night Live: 97
Say It As If You Mean It: 687
Say Something Funny: 584
Say the Magic Word: 562
Scales of Justice: 249
Scat Cat: 634
Second-Guessing God: 784
Second Opinion: 950
Second Place: 190
Second Time Around: 468
Secret of Progress: 248
Secret of Shorter Days: 899
Secure Mediocrity: 171
Secured Position: 566
Seeds of Marriage: 569
Seeing the Future: 310
Selective Perception: 737
Self-Concern: 708
Self-Made Mess: 189
Self-Perspective: 475
Selfish Grief: 238
Selfish Optimist: 839
Selling Insurance: 833
Senate Prayers: 703
Serve Both Ways: 883
Set up for Life: 698
Severe Judgment: 747
Shameful Students: 861
Share a Brush: 693
Share Troubles: 324
Sharing Experiences: 772
Sharing with Whom?: 862
Shoot the Wounded: 166
Short Route: 250
Short Term Goals: 411
Short-Sighted Memory: 907
Short-Sighted Pig: 966
Shorter Story: 424
Shrink Resistant: 993
Shut out the Truth: 538
Siding with the Devil: 867

Sign in a Bank: 84
Sign of Growing Up: 918
Silent Fool: 841
Silent Suffering: 766
Silver Lining: 429
Simple Immortality: 235
Simple Solutions: 590
Simplified Taxes: 902
Sin Will Find a Way Out: 289
Sinners and Saints: 478
Sinning Is the Best: 116
Sins of Omission: 866
Skunk Removal: 744
Smile!: 873
So Far So Good!: 749
So Many Answers: 547
Some Baby: 508
Something of Nothing: 480
Sons All Look the Same: 732
Sorrow Abounds: 679
Sound Advice: 653
Source of Success: 889
Space-Age Mustard Seed: 814
Speak Clearly: 157
Special Request: 782
Specific Job: 796
Sporting Excuses: 70
Sporting Golf: 202
Sports Job Security: 838
Sportsmanlike Conduct: 419
Stages of a Cold: 37
Stained-Glass Fame: 365
Start out Right: 756
State of Education: 149
Stay Alert: 856
Stay Out of the Way!: 800
Stay Young: 22
Step One: 835
Stewardship Note: 989
Stick Together: 210
Stork Babies: 94
Strategy of Listening: 545
Stretchin' It a Little: 280
Subsidized Farming: 367
Success: 170
Success of the Ruthless: 891
Sudden Skills: 613
Suicidal Businesses: 820
Summer Scene: 461
Superbowl Wisdom: 88
Sure Thing: 727
Sure-Fire Test for Lying: 705
Surgical Advice: 684
Surrendered Advisor: 12

Sweet Revenge: 808
Sympathetic Ear: 954
Synchronized Wallets: 863

Take out the Bones: 241
Take the Truck: 284
Tale of Two Virgins: 502
Talents: 422
Talk to George: 46
Talkers and Walkers: 322
Talking to Oneself: 544
Talking Too Fast: 876
Teacher Jargon: 112
Teaching a Pig to Sing: 785
Teen's Poor Eyesight: 920
Teen-Free Car: 919
Teenage Awareness: 917
Teenage Reason: 922
Teenagers' Demise: 575
Temporal Generation Gap: 327
Ten-Year Drain: 825
Tenacity: 672
Thanks for the Help: 609
That's More Like It: 317
That's the Only Problem: 548
That's the Spirit: 910
Thieves Don't Give: 564
Things Could Be Worse: 881
Third-Time Charm: 774
Thoughtful Thanks: 96
Three Cheers!: 264
Three Shoestrings: 819
Time for Teeth: 31
Time Spent: 932
Timely Repentance: 778
Timing Eggs: 770
Timing Is Everything: 962
Timing Problem: 507
Tired of You: 38
Tiring Test: 540
To Die Like Jesus: 525
To Fix the World: 795
To Get or Not to Get: 95
To Make a Buck: 645
To Tell a Lie: 535
To the Essence: 506
To the Point: 143
Too Full a Quiver: 656
Too Good: 813
Too Late: 32
Too Late to Tell: 900
Too Many Pastors: 661
Too Much Work: 988
Tough to Be a Saint: 435
Tough to Hide Feelings: 694

Tours to Israel: 940
Tradition Ended: 402
Trash-Basket Forgiveness: 717
Trick to Marriage: 567
Trinity: 946
Trouble Changes: 944
True Clout: 193
True Humility: 670
Trust in God: 901
Turn Off the Sound: 877
Turn out the Light: 787
Turnabout: 153
Turtle Top: 908
Two Cards in One: 36
Two Different Words: 11

Ugly to the Bone: 87
Unaware: 911
Uncertain Accounting: 85
Unconditional Love: 3
Understandably Brave: 219
Unexpected Gift: 407
Ungrateful Child: 279
Uniqueness of Snoopy: 959
United Kingdom: 447
Unlucky Marriages: 568
Unspoiled Motivation: 312
Up or Down: 501
Urgent Prayer: 723
Used to Dandelions: 205
Using Your Head: 518

Vacation Is: 964
Valley Version: 746
Value of a Marriage: 242
Valued Wives: 56
Very Pious Thinking: 346
Volume of Maturity: 632

Wait for an Earthquake: 530
Waiting for God: 781
Waiting on God: 658
Wake up Grumpy: 74
Watch Out: 300
Watch the Wreck: 643
Watch Your Words: 748
Ways of God: 752
Ways to Shop: 685
We All Have Our Jobs: 828
We're Gonna Be in a Big Mess: 583
We're Talking Tough: 936
Weaker Conscience: 195
Weasel Word: 253
Weight Loss: 281
What Are They Making?: 762
What Doesn't Count: 66
What Money Can't Buy: 486
What You Want It to Be: 524

What's in a Name?: 558
When God Answers: 585
When It Happens Twice: 463
When Life Begins: 541
When Losing Is Good: 879
When Push Comes to Love: 937
Where's the Paint Can?: 269
Which Side: 704
Whitewashing Sheep: 282
Who Beats Whom?: 259
Who Rubs off on Whom?: 391
Whole Sad Story: 947
Who's Blamed?: 361
Why of Fun: 755

Why We Listen: 840
Wife Is Born: 586
Win or Lose: 360
Within Limits: 812
Woody Allen Wisdom: 914
Words and Actions: 579
Work with People: 955
Working on Sunday: 827
Worn-Out Water: 397
Worst Alibi: 334
Worst-Case Scenario: 65
Worth More Than a Locket: 769
Wright Vision: 975
Wrong Checks: 133
Wrong Egg: 177
Wrong Horse Won: 362

Wrong Machine: 63
Wrong Questions: 765
Wrong Scarecrow: 220
Wrong Verse: 627
Wrong Work Is Better: 998

You Know You're Older: 29
You're in a Small Town: 511
You, Me, and We: 313
Young Enough to Make It: 443
Young Get No Respect: 18
Your Way or God's Way: 416
Yuppies' Prayer: 573

Zealous Evangelism: 773
Zipper Vengeance: 809

Numerical Index of Titles

1: More Light Bulbs
2: Infatuation or Love
3: Unconditional Love
4: Let Them Go
5: Body Designs
6: A Paneful Target
7: Accountant's Maxim
8: Carry-Outs
9: But Hurry
10: Modern Marketing
11: Two Different Words
12: Surrendered Advisor
13: Overly Helpful
14: Free Advice
15: Better Than Nothing
16: Only Tough Grow Old
17: Long-Term Driving
18: The Young Get No Respect
19: Middle-Aged Action
20: Healthy Circulation
21: Counting the Years
22: Stay Young
23: Open to the Future
24: More to Keep Quiet About
25: Really Fast
26: Age Discrimination
27: Individualism
28: Aging Poem
29: You Know You're Older
30: Jump-Start
31: Time for Teeth
32: Too Late
33: All About Bees
34: A Honking Parent
35: Regretful Speech
36: Two Cards in One
37: Stages of a Cold
38: Tired of You
39: Clout—Who Has It?
40: Art of Apology
41: Not As They Seem

42: Life's Deeper Meaning
43: Bubble Gum Return
44: Identity Crisis
45: Liberace's Line
46: Talk to George
47: Genetic Apparel
48: Careless Appearance
49: Chasing Shadows
50: First Impressions
51: Applied Learning
52: Never Too Early
53: A Good Day
54: Almost Expressed Thanks
55: It's a Gift
56: Valued Wives
57: Abstract Art
58: A Point of Reference
59: The Man We Want
60: Can't Be Helped
61: The Company You Keep
62: Assumptions Cost
63: Wrong Machine
64: Just Counting
65: Worst-Case Scenario
66: What Doesn't Count
67: Faithful to the End
68: Power of Television
69: Established or Stuck
70: Sporting Excuses
71: Perspective
72: Reality and Otherwise
73: Clear Coffee
74: Wake up Grumpy
75: Condensed Viewpoint
76: Planning for Misery
77: Greatest Pitcher
78: Bayonet the Wounded
79: Initial Taste of Power
80: Assistance or Respect

81: Communication Flow
82: Oblivious Award
83: The Good with the Bad
84: Sign in a Bank
85: Uncertain Accounting
86: Immersed in the Scenery
87: Ugly to the Bone
88: Superbowl Wisdom
89: Not Ready for Aging
90: Lost in Translation
91: Reading Priorities
92: Ignorance
93: Making a Baby Brother
94: The Stork Babies
95: To Get or Not to Get
96: Thoughtful Thanks
97: Saturday Night Live
98: Bottom Dollar
99: Foot-in-Mouth Disease
100: Ever Draw a Blank?
101: Bring Out Your Bibles
102: Boring Sermons
103: A Long Film
104: Cry-Babies
105: A Brief Message of Hot Air
106: Friend for Sale
107: Choose Any Two
108: Purpose of Poison Ivy
109: If God Were Alive
110: It Won't Happen!
111: How to Live
112: Teacher Jargon
113: Esoteric Cheating
114: Prejudice Unites
115: Growing Objects
116: Sinning Is the Best
117: Corn on the Palm
118: Catholic Grocery Beads

119: The Left Hand of God
120: The Mouth of Babes
121: History Revisited
122: Children's Paraphrase
123: Kid's Concerns
124: Children Ask God
125: Mother Knows
126: Ever Met a Christian?
127: Day After Christmas
128: A Fertile Nativity
129: Round John Virgin
130: Don't Turn Off Jesus
131: Christmas Lore
132: Christmas Caution
133: Wrong Checks
134: Let's Get Practical
135: Mouse's Bathing Suit
136: The Plot Thickens
137: Bike Before Christmas
138: Personal Touch
139: Fresh Perspective
140: The Modern Scene
141: Football Fans and Church
142: Communicating Jargon
143: To the Point
144: In Front of Ourselves
145: Family Resemblance
146: Clothes Make a Church
147: Bearded Christmas
148: Finally Alone
149: The State of Education
150: Misdirected Comfort
151: A Fish Story
152: Long-Term Marriage
153: Turnabout
154: Four-by-Twos
155: No Conversation
156: Complexity
157: Speak Clearly
158: Rights
159: Bad-Luck Wife
160: Risky Comparison
161: Relative Wealth
162: Life Is Tough, But
163: Mental Health

164: A Better Speaker
165: Love It In
166: Shoot the Wounded
167: Getting Hugs
168: Joyous Imperfection
169: Keeping Up
170: Success
171: Secure Mediocrity
172: Mixed Motives
173: Belly-Achers
174: Never Satisfied
175: Help You Honk
176: Day Eight Complaints
177: Wrong Egg
178: Can't Say Enough
179: The Forced Truth
180: Branded
181: Adjusting to Reality
182: Laws of Computing
183: Dated by Computers
184: Human Thinking
185: No Real Confession
186: Admitting Mistakes
187: Asserting Leadership
188: A Picture of God
189: The Self-Made Mess
190: Second Place
191: Golfing Tips
192: African Proverb
193: True Clout
194: Little Voice Inside
195: Weaker Conscience
196: Clearing Conscience
197: Events That Reveal
198: Fearful Wisdom
199: Profound Warning
200: Hung Jury
201: It's in the Bag
202: Sporting Golf
203: Consistent Lives
204: Ruin It Again
205: Used to Dandelions
206: A Cure for Hatred
207: Fighting on the Ice
208: Kitchen Accidents
209: Deadly Dog Biscuits
210: Stick Together
211: Row It or Rock It
212: Pedal Together
213: People Need People
214: Our Varied Roles
215: Frantic Frog
216: Fearless Timing
217: An Easy Hug
218: Motive for Courage

219: Understandably Brave
220: Wrong Scarecrow
221: Adam Was a Foreigner
222: The Cynic in All of Us
223: Critical Imperfection
224: A Goalie's Rejection
225: Criticizing
226: Old Expressions
227: Birth of a Cynic
228: Kids' Candid Responses
229: Partial Commitment
230: Late Advice
231: Just Like Family
232: One for Johnny
233: Death from Kids' Views
234: Dead or Forgotten
235: Simple Immortality
236: Congregation Immunity
237: The Hope of Dying
238: Selfish Grief
239: Not Really Suitable
240: Historical Perspective
241: Take out the Bones
242: The Value of a Marriage
243: Learn from the Past
244: Act Your Wage
245: Quick Action
246: Deficit Spending
247: Forgetful Borrowers
248: The Secret of Progress
249: The Scales of Justice
250: The Short Route
251: Rabbit Resurrection
252: Mutual Recognition
253: The Weasel Word
254: Priorities
255: Deferred Decisions
256: How Long Can It Take?
257: Quick Sincere Choice
258: Perspective
259: Who Beats Whom?
260: Rapid Transit
261: Don't Learn to Do
262: One Man's Logic
263: Colson's Change
264: Three Cheers!

265: Catholic Baths
266: Now I See!
267: Episcopal Lethargy
268: Beyond Satisfied
269: Where's the Paint Can?
270: Do As You're Told
271: A Cold Test
272: First Priority
273: Back Seat Driver
274: Devil Dad
275: Only What You Can Eat
276: Hold the Twinkies
277: More Careful Thought
278: An Acceptable Diet
279: The Ungrateful Child
280: Stretchin' It a Little
281: Weight Loss
282: Whitewashing Sheep
283: Not Too Subtle Signs
284: Take the Truck
285: Awareness Is the Key
286: Lost Cause
287: False Hopes
288: Face the Facts Boldly
289: Sin Will Find a Way Out
290: Insincere Warning
291: Mixed Motives
292: The High Cost of Love
293: Plan B
294: Foot Doctor
295: Confidence in Experts
296: Perennial Pledges
297: A Hard Winter
298: New Sources Of Funds
299: Persisting Unbelief
300: Watch Out
301: Part Time Idiots
302: Don't Give Up
303: Better Than Lame
304: Get the Story Straight
305: Happy Ending
306: An Easter Rose
307: Change the Answers
308: Christmas Corsage
309: Economic Clarity
310: Seeing the Future

311: Character Crisis
312: Unspoiled Motivation
313: You, Me, and We
314: Much Responsibility
315: Attempting Failure
316: Going to Get Help
317: That's More Like It
318: Emotive Friends
319: Both Drunk
320: Movie Cue
321: Limp Understanding
322: Talkers and Walkers
323: Model Motivation
324: Share Troubles
325: New Blessings
326: Enemies Accumulate
327: Temporal Generation Gap
328: Eternal Epitaph
329: Generation of Mules
330: Evangelism Methods
331: Limited Atonement
332: A Better Way
333: Best Alibi
334: Worst Alibi
335: Accidents
336: Number Seven Rejection
337: Flight Patterns
338: Making Something
339: Notable Excuses
340: A Ready Excuse
341: Alibi
342: Man Needs a Wife
343: Entertaining Exercise
344: All Goes Wrong
345: I'll Alter Him
346: Very Pious Thinking
347: The Previous Pastor
348: Poise
349: Experience Mistakes
350: Help from Experience
351: Price of Experience
352: Profit from Failure
353: Careful Tracking
354: Bad Timing
355: A Quick Count
356: Plans
357: Authoritative Advice
358: Explanations

359: Deadly Experience
360: Win or Lose
361: Who's Blamed?
362: Wrong Horse Won
363: Believe It to See It
364: Preacher's Prayer
365: Name That Fame
366: Stained-Glass Fame
367: Subsidized Farming
368: Nerd Dad
369: Law of Clothes Life
370: Collect Calls
371: Getting Rid of Daddy
372: Kidding Aside
373: Fear of Zeal
374: Equal Time
375: The Modern Woman
376: Revealed Secrets
377: Costly Catch
378: Liquid Courage
379: Just in Case
380: Credit for Long Life
381: Flexible Building
382: It's Relative!
383: The One Who Is Seen
384: Intellectual Limits
385: Partial Forgiveness
386: Deserves to Forgive
387: Acquaintance
388: Fit to Kill
389: A Friend
390: Brilliant Conversation
391: Who Rubs Off on Whom?
392: Friends
393: Endearment
394: Don't Explain
395: Looking Out for Mom
396: Fruit of Hard Work
397: Worn-Out Water
398: The Right Man
399: Lost Last Two
400: Raffle Baffle
401: A Good Bet
402: A Tradition Ended
403: A Painless Way to Give
404: Painful Choices
405: Practical Gift for Dad
406: Christmas Shopping
407: The Unexpected Gift
408: Gift You Don't Need

409: Gift Exchange with Jesus
410: Life Goals
411: Short Term Goals
412: Omniproblem
413: Let Jesus Get It
414: Low Presence
415: Missing God
416: Your Way or God's Way
417: Guidance on Dieting
418: Golfer's Timing
419: Sportsmanlike Conduct
420: One Last Fling
421: Golf Clubs with Pools
422: Talents
423: Kept Secrets
424: A Shorter Story
425: Moving Dirt
426: Abundant Entreaties
427: Conversational Grace
428: Near Miss
429: A Silver Lining
430: Good and Original
431: Preparing Perspective
432: Always a Little More
433: A Profitable Venture
434: Become Possible
435: Tough to Be a Saint
436: Guilty Party Exposed
437: Don't Go Too Far!
438: Partial Repentance
439: The Cat's Habit
440: Get the Smile Over
441: Inside and Out
442: Limits to Life
443: Young Enough to Make It
444: Aging
445: Not Long Ago
446: Entry Requirement
447: United Kingdom
448: Getting into Heaven
449: Make Your Eternity
450: A Friend to the End
451: Partial Commitment
452: Happy Formula
453: A Hero Not Braver
454: Cold Feet
455: Most Neglected Men

456: Cynical View of History
457: A Decisive Moment
458: How So Stories
459: Explain Thanksgiving
460: Equal Time
461: Summer Scene
462: Independent Teen
463: When It Happens Twice
464: A Child's Candor
465: Honesty Pays
466: Clever Disguise
467: A Right Nice Tribute
468: Second Time Around
469: Not What They Seem
470: Feeling at Home
471: Famous Humble Doctor
472: Dilemma for the Humble
473: The Power Crowd
474: Humor, Etc.
475: Self-Perspective
476: Autumn Rituals
477: Advice on Marriage
478: Sinners and Saints
479: The First Confessional
480: Something of Nothing
481: The Desire for Peace
482: Exhilarating Pause
483: The Offense of Life
484: Personal Directions
485: Ignorance and Apathy
486: What Money Can't Buy
487: Inflated Water
488: The Cost of Giving
489: Our Inheritance
490: A Miser's Money
491: Recognized Her Laugh
492: Formidable Dilemma
493: Genetic Miracle
494: Honest Outlaws
495: A Reason to Die
496: A Bad Day When
497: Break Retraining
498: Fill the Void
499: Brain Weight
500: Know the Letters

501: Up or Down
502: Tale of Two Virgins
503: Communication
504: Interpretive Bias
505: Asking Her Age
506: To the Essence
507: Timing Problem
508: Some Baby
509: Obedience
510: Drink for a Dime
511: You're in a Small Town
512: Go First
513: Jewish Advantage
514: Change the Light
515: Rubbed Wrong Way
516: Cries for Mercy
517: In Need of Police
518: Using Your Head
519: Chip off the Profane Block
520: Laugh Cure
521: Caught
522: Lawyers and Rabbits
523: A Lawyer's Brief
524: What You Want It to Be
525: To Die Like Jesus
526: Adjusting to the Realities
527: The Cost of Short Sight
528: Frugal Rules
529: Right Track
530: Wait for an Earthquake
531: Remove the Pressure
532: Blow First
533: Parting Shot
534: Ego Time
535: To Tell a Lie
536: Persistent Liar
537: On Second Thought
538: Shut out the Truth
539: My Father Speaking
540: Tiring Test
541: When Life Begins
542: Mule-Team Scenery
543: Light to Light
544: Talking to Oneself
545: Strategy of Listening
546: Reason to Listen
547: So Many Answers
548: That's the Only Problem
549: Reduce the Steps

550: Futile Shots
551: Confused
552: Never Changed His Mind
553: Can't Talk about Love
554: Loyalty to the End
555: Immutable Presbyterian
556: It's All How You View It
557: Getty's Success
558: What's in a Name?
559: Really Lucky
560: Disgusting
561: Old Temptations
562: Say the Magic Word
563: Child Manipulator
564: Thieves Don't Give
565: The Right Song
566: Secured Position
567: The Trick to Marriage
568: Unlucky Marriages
569: Seeds of Marriage
570: Happiness
571: Reasons for Marriage
572: Catching Monkeys
573: Yuppies' Prayer
574: Christian Shoppers
575: Teenagers' Demise
576: Opportunity of Lifetime
577: Be Specific
578: Mother the Cook
579: Words and Actions
580: Forgetful Middle Years
581: Aspects of Aging
582: How's That Again?
583: We're Gonna Be in a Big Mess
584: Say Something Funny
585: When God Answers
586: A Wife Is Born
587: Another Miracle
588: Nun and the Bed Pan
589: Keep Your Pants On
590: Simple Solutions
591: Futile Call for Unity
592: Carpet Cleanout
593: Ennies or Nuns
594: A Careful Choice
595: My Name Is
596: Mother's Day Break

597: Practical Present
598: The New Baby
599: Greedy Giving
600: Check Your Wallet, Sir?
601: Dogs Welcome
602: Masked Mom
603: Measure of a Mom
604: Recipe for Mothers
605: Just Can't Catch up
606: Free Roses
607: Pit-Stop Momma
608: Mom Is the Light
609: Thanks for the Help
610: Mother's Day Sound
611: Gift of Motivation
612: Great Title
613: Sudden Skills
614: Puppy Punishment
615: Agree for Jobs
616: Good Manners
617: Effective Strategy
618: Law of Parenting
619: Prayer Principles
620: Murphy's Shoes
621: Modern Music
622: The Golden Bargains
623: Another Opinion
624: Music Lover
625: A Reason to Sing
626: A Musical Clock
627: Wrong Verse
628: Four Men Needed
629: A Fair Price
630: Noise Tolerance
631: Croaking Frogs
632: Volume of Maturity
633: A Loose Leaf
634: Scat Cat
635: Requirements to Drive
636: Backward Obedience
637: Pay or Get off
638: Crowd Control
639: Opinions or Thoughts
640: Good from Bad
641: Blown Opportunity
642: If Shoe Fits, Sell It
643: Watch the Wreck
644: Opening Line
645: To Make a Buck
646: Raw Furniture
647: Married Secretaries
648: Optimist and the Fly
649: Optimistic Whaler

650: Optimistic Planning
651: Regrettable Actions
652: Looking for Loopholes
653: Sound Advice
654: Child's Play
655: Don't Let Them Get Away
656: Too Full a Quiver
657: Pastor Dad
658: Waiting on God
659: Get Rid of Your Pastor
660: Church Chain Letter
661: Too Many Pastors
662: Perfect Pastor Found
663: Jesus Understands
664: More Humble Pie
665: Housing in Heaven
666: Pastor Pig
667: Just in Time
668: God's Not in a Hurry!
669: The Patience of Noah
670: True Humility
671: Pain of Perfection
672: Tenacity
673: Getting Ready to Win
674: Put the Bones Back
675: Life in New England
676: Perspective Puzzler
677: More Than a Spot
678: Joy or Fear
679: Sorrow Abounds
680: Normal & Oblong
681: Canyon or Confusion
682: Pushing Boats
683: Last Word on Comet
684: Surgical Advice
685: Ways to Shop
686: A Glorious Send-Off
687: Say It As If You Mean It
688: Country Persuasion
689: Hitch-Hiker Religion
690: Motivation
691: Gift of Imagination
692: Big Bad Grass
693: Share a Brush
694: Tough to Hide Feelings
695: Beyond This Vale of Tears

696: Cats and Love Return
697: Life Happens
698: Set up for Life
699: Levels of Love
700: Not What You Pay For
701: Have Your Way
702: Creating Chaos
703: Senate Prayers
704: Which Side
705: Sure-Fire Test for Lying
706: Egocentric Steering
707: Amazing or Baloney
708: Self-Concern
709: Canine Limits
710: BZZZZZZZ
711: Predetermined Affirmation
712: Act of Applause
713: The Proof Is In
714: Ruined by Praise
715: Franklin on Prayer
716: Needs and Wants
717: Trash-Basket Forgiveness
718: Asleep at Last
719: Parrot's Prayer Answered
720: Disputed Power of Prayer
721: Be Careful What You Pray
722: Atomic Prayer
723: Urgent Prayer
724: Better Boston Prayers
725: Powerful Positions
726: Animal Crackers Thanks
727: Sure Thing
728: Careless Conclusion
729: The Direct Message
730: Harvey Firestone
731: Classy Mutt
732: Sons All Look the Same
733: Forgive Us Both
734: A Better Day
735: Join the Crowd
736: Prophetic Boasting
737: Selective Perception
738: Impact Is What Matters
739: Far from Everything
740: Crisis in Sports
741: No Problem Too Big

742: Peaceful Shifting
743: Keeping Problems Away
744: Skunk Removal
745: Perhaps a New Vocation
746: The Valley Version
747: Severe Judgment
748: Watch Your Words
749: So Far So Good!
750: Progressive Delays
751: Computers
752: The Ways of God
753: Know Your Blessings
754: Out of Order
755: The Why of Fun
756: Start out Right
757: Bird Catchers
758: Purpose
759: Help Yourself
760: Motivation That Works
761: Misplaced Experts
762: What Are You Making?
763: A Bad Bulb
764: Buried Potatoes
765: The Wrong Questions
766: Silent Suffering
767: Muddled Note
768: Buying Friends
769: Worth More Than a Locket
770: Timing Eggs
771: Einstein's Analogy
772: Sharing Experiences
773: Zealous Evangelism
774: Third-Time Charm
775: Let Me In!
776: Repent!
777: Order of Repentance
778: Timely Repentance
779: The Dog Doesn't Know
780: How to Get a Car
781: Waiting for God
782: A Special Request
783: Make Requests Specific
784: Second-Guessing God
785: Teaching a Pig to Sing
786: Like a Son

787: Turn out the Light
788: Rope's End
789: One Up
790: Churchill's Gratitude
791: Ask Him
792: Almost the Same
793: Carry the Load
794: Property Rights
795: To Fix the World
796: A Specific Job
797: Part-Time Tomb
798: Out of this Hole!
799: Now the Good Part
800: Stay out of Way!
801: Retirement Breaks
802: Retirement Plans
803: Change and Perspective
804: Point of Purchase
805: Helping Others Learn
806: Avenging Enemies
807: Get Even
808: Sweet Revenge
809: Zipper Vengeance
810: Change for a Reward
811: Beatitude Exceptions
812: Deserving within Limits
813: Too Good
814: Space-Age Mustard Seed
815: The Big Black Door
816: An Explosive Situation
817: Changing the Odds
818: Marital Gamblers
819: Three Shoestrings
820: Suicidal Businesses
821: In Time We Look Sillier
822: Love at Second Sight
823: The Confusion Begins
824: No Searching
825: A Ten-Year Drain
826: No God, No Food
827: Working on Sunday
828: We All Have Our Jobs
829: Bridge the Gap
830: Going Out of Business
831: Know Your Customer

832: Overpriced Puppy
833: Selling Insurance
834: Let Him In
835: Step One
836: Finally Satisfied
837: Jungle Wisdom
838: Sports Job Security
839: Selfish Optimist
840: Why We Listen
841: Silent Fool
842: Busted Smiles
843: Better Than Latin
844: All Is Well
845: Close to Perfect
846: Famous Mothers
847: Identity Crisis
848: If Sermon Offends Thee
849: Long-Winded Driving
850: A Hair-Raising Sermon
851: Mindless Messages
852: Prepare or Rely
853: The Profit in Sermons
854: An Adaptable Fiction
855: Not Much Missed
856: Stay Alert
857: An F in Sex
858: Battle of the Sexes
859: No Need to Share
860: Guess What They Did
861: Shameful Students
862: Sharing with Whom?
863: Synchronized Wallets
864: Really Sick
865: No One to Tell
866: Sins of Omission
867: Siding with the Devil
868: Old Sins
869: Hidden Joy
870: Personalized Hymns
871: Not All Is Possible
872: Embarrassing Snoring
873: Smile!
874: The Mouth Trap
875: Mouth Not a Door
876: Talking Too Fast
877: Turn Off the Sound
878: Play Like the Pros

879: When Losing Is Good
880: How It's Explained
881: Things Could Be Worse
882: Almost Persuaded
883: Serve Both Ways
884: Easy Duz It
885: Impregnable Bias
886: Objective Party
887: First in Line
888: Keep Jumping
889: The Source of Success
890: The Look of Success
891: Success of the Ruthless
892: Figuring the Profit
893: Deep Sacrifice
894: Mixed Message
895: Amazing Virtuosity
896: Eating Words
897: A Knowing Hush
898: Really???
899: Secret of Shorter Days
900: Too Late to Tell
901: Trust in God
902: Simplified Taxes
903: Priorities for Success
904: IRS Foxholes
905: Bogus Wisdom
906: Pain in the Neck
907: Short-Sighted Memory
908: Turtle Top
909: Our Recital
910: That's the Spirit
911: Unaware
912: The Old Is Now New
913: Phoneless Cord
914: Woody Allen Wisdom
915: Nature's Wisdom
916: Progress In Doctrine
917: Teenage Awareness
918: A Sign of Growing Up
919: Teen-Free Car
920: Teen's Poor Eyesight
921: Experience Not Needed
922: Teenage Reason
923: Parenting Teens
924: Raising Problem Kids

925: One Commandment at at Time
926: Outstanding Legs
927: Just a Minute
928: No Soap
929: Sampler on Thanks
930: Born a Turkey
931: The Future
932: Time Spent
933: Getting Organized
934: Frog's Perspective
935: Beetle in Hand
936: We're Talking Tough
937: When Push Comes to Love
938: Buffalo Shuttle
939: Not Meant to Fly
940: Tours to Israel
941: An Extra Squeeze
942: Denomination Credit
943: It's Going to Be a Bad Day
944: Trouble Changes
945: Run Like Crazy
946: Trinity
947: Whole Sad Story
948: Fencing In Is More Credible
949: Expecting the Worst
950: Second Opinion
951: The Human Dilemma
952: On a Shaky Limb
953: Get the Whole Story
954: Sympathetic Ear
955: Work with People
956: Better Business
957: Individual Commuter
958: Looks Like Trouble
959: Uniqueness of Snoopy
960: The Fatal Blow
961: Lions and Lambs
962: Timing Is Everything
963: Rich Isn't
964: Vacation Is
965: The Gift of Imagination
966: Short-Sighted Pig
967: All-Purpose Verses
968: Easy Objectivity
969: Designated Giving
970: A Better Year

971: Paid in Like
      Currency
972: Know Your Place
973: Hunting Husband
974: The End of Ideas
975: The Wright Vision
976: Hide—No; Win—Yes
977: Peace, Peace
978: Cost of Peace
979: Formula for Success
980: Comparative Values
981: Red Alert

982: Buying Better
      Treatment
983: Prove It Yourself
984: Fun Anticipation
985: Poverty Perspective
986: Communicating
      Poverty
987: No Old Flames
988: Too Much Work
989: Stewardship Note
990: Needs
991: Church
      Daffynitions:

992: It's a Puzzle
993: Shrink Resistant
994: Careful How You
      Put It
995: Converts or Traitors
996: Confusion Class
997: Degrees of
      Happiness
998: Wrong Work Is
      Better
999: Helpful Adjustment
1000: Raising Boys
1001: Presents Fill Temple

List of Sources

Brackets contain date of use in Saratoga Press Publications:
[PEMay87] indicates *Parables, Etc.*, May 1987;
[SFJun85] indicates *The Pastor's Story File*, June 1985.

1: No source available [PEMay87]
2: Judith Viorst, "What Is This Thing Called Love?" *Redbook*, February 1975 [PEMay90]
3: Submitted by George Price [PEMay90]
4: *Sunday Sermons*, vol. 18, no. 3, p. 43 [PEJul88]
5: Adapted [PENov85]
6: Submitted by Steve Hodgin [PENov90]
7: No source available [PENov87]
8: Submitted by John H. Hampsch [PESep90]
9: Submitted by Joe Schmitt [PEMar84]
10: Submitted by William Hamilton [PEJan84]
11: Submitted by Doug Vernon [PEMar88]
12: From the devotional book *Forward* as reported in *Context* [PEJul85]
13: Adapted [PEJul87]
14: Adapted [PEOct84]
15: No source available [PEApr82]
16: Submitted by Carl Ericson [PEApr91]
17: No source available [PEJul90]
18: No source available [PEMay82]
19: Patricia Leimbach, *Woman's Day* [SFJun87]
20: Logan Pearsall Smith (1865–1946), submitted by Robert Strand [PEDec86]
21: *Ladies Home Journal,* March 1990 [PEAug90]
22: Submitted by Jack Lee [PEMay87]
23: *Sunday Sermons*, vol. 15, no. 6, November-December 1985, published by Voicings, p. 44 [PEMar87]
24: Adapted [PEApr87]
25: *Fortune*, April 11, 1988, p. 33 [PEJun88]
26: Harold Churman, *All People Are Famous* [PEJul82]
27: Adapted [PEJan87]
28: Submitted by William McConnell [PENov82]
29: No source available [PEJul82]

30: Submitted by Rich Hardison [PENov86]
31: Submitted by Mac Fulcher [PEOct93]
32: Adapted [PEApr86]
33: *Corner Stones* [PEMay88]
34: Submitted by Douglas Sabin [PEApr91]
35: Adapted from *Dynamic Preaching* [PENov87]
36: Robert Smith [PEMar89]
37: No source available [PEFeb84]
38: Submitted by Jeff Callender [SFJul87]
39: No source available [PEMay82]
40: No source available [PEOct84]
41: Submitted by Kim J. Wilson [PEMay90]
42: Submitted by Keith Kendall, from Tom Mullen's *Laughing Out Loud And Other Religious Experiences* [PEJan84]
43: Submitted by William Carrington, Jr. [PENov82]
44: No source available [PEJan85]
45: From Tom Shea's article in the May 21, 1984 issue of *InfoWorld* [PEAug84]
46: Submitted by William Northcott [PEJul87]
47: Chaplain P. A. Merubia [PEJul87]
48: Robert Dalke [PEFeb84]
49: Thad Collier [SFMar92]
50: Adapted [PEMay85]
51: Submitted by Kay Bartlett [PEJun90]
52: No source available [PEJul90]
53: Patrick White [PESep85]
54: Leslie Flynn, submitted by Steve Schoepf [SFNov85]
55: Submitted by Ronnie Patton, from *Sports Illustrated* [PEApr83]
56: Agatha Christie, submitted by Jeff Callender [SFJul87]
57: Al Capp [PEJul88]
58: *Funny, Funny World* [PEMay85]
59: No source available [PEApr83]
60: Submitted by Jack Lee of Arcadia, California [PENov84]

61: *Swim with the Sharks,* by Harvey MacKay (New York: William Morrow, 1988) [PEFeb91]

62: Adapted from *Leadership,* submitted by Tim Purcell [PEJun88]

63: *On The Upbeat* [PESep84]

64: Submitted by James Ankerberg [PEJun87]

65: *Bits & Pieces,* published by Economics Press, Inc., 12 Daniel Road, Fairfield, NJ [PEFeb86]

66: Billy Sunday, submitted by M. E. Hutchinson [PEApr86]

67: No source available [PEDec86]

68: Adapted from a column by Armfield Coffey that appeared in the *Watauga Democrat,* March 12, 1986, reported in *Campbell's Notebook,* January 1988 [PEAug88]

69: Max Hickerson, *Pulpit Digest,* submitted by Dave Gerbrandt [SFApr88]

70: *Moody Monthly,* submitted by Steve Schoepf [PEFeb86]

71: No source available [PEOct86]

72: From a story in the *Los Angeles Times,* as submitted by David Bolton [PEMar86]

73: *Chestnuts,* 1981 [PEMay81]

74: No source available [PEAug81]

75: No source available [PESep88]

76: No source available [PEJan82]

77: No source available [PEJan83]

78: P. Rubin, *The Great Business Quotations* [PENov87]

79: *Funny, Funny World* [PEDec85]

80: *On The Upbeat* [PEAug83]

81: No source available [SFFeb85]

82: Sent in by Marty Youngkin [PEJun83]

83: *Healing Grace,* by David A. Seamands, submitted by Dave Rushton [PEJun90]

84: No source available [PEAug90]

85: John J. Creedon, quoted in the *Wall Street Journal* [PEDec88]

86: "On Top of the World News," from *Catholic Digest,* May 1988 [PENov90]

87: Chuck Swindoll speaking at the Pastor's Conference at Mt. Hermon Conference Center [PEMar82]

88: No source available [PEMar90]

89: As reported in *Christian Communications Laboratory* [SFJun87]

90: No source available [PEMar82]

91: No source available [PEAug82]

92: Submitted by Elizabeth Towers [PEMay81]

93: No source available [SFMay87]

94: Howard Hendricks, *Heaven Help The Home* (Wheaton, Ill.: Victor Books, 1974) [SFMay87]

95: No source available [PEMar91]

96: Submitted by Robert Strand [SFNov85]

97: Michael Hodgin [PEMar90]

98: *Sunshine Magazine,* June 1973 [PEMar91]

99: No source available [PEMay85]

100: No source available [PENov82]

101: Michael Hodgin [PEAug90]

102: No source available [PEOct88]

103: No source available [PENov82]

104: Burton Hillis, in *Better Homes and Gardens,* May 1989 [PEDec90]

105: Submitted by Alan Thompson [PEMar88]

106: *Sermons Illustrated,* submitted by Bob Kabat [SFJun84]

107: Ralph Dunagan, Field Syndicate [PEOct81]

108: *Sunday Sermons,* vol. 14, no. 5, p. 45 [PENov84]

109: *Christian Leadership Letter* by World Vision, February 1982 [PEApr82]

110: Submitted by Richard Bersett, First Christian Church, Belleville, IL [PEOct86]

111: No source available [PEOct86]

112: No source available [PEAug82]

113: No source available [PEDec85]

114: No source available [PEOct81]

115: No source available [PENov83]

116: Submitted by Robert Hutchinson [PEJan85]

117: Margaret M. Sevigny, Sanford, Minnesota in *Redbook,* April 1990 [PEMar91]

118: Submitted by John H. Hampsch [PESep90]

119: Submitted by Kent Anderson [PESep90]

120: Submitted by John D. Gondol [PEMay90]

121: Submitted by Bernard Brunsting [PEMar90]

122: Submitted by Christine Oscar [PEJul90]

123: Submitted by Bruce Rowlison [PEJun90]

124: No source available [SFMay87]

125: *Wright's Secrets of Successful Humor,* submitted by Don Cheadle [SFMay86]
126: *Seasonings for Sermons,* by John Krahn, submitted by Gene Sikkink [PEApr88]
127: Marguerite Gode, submitted by John Bristol [PEDec83]
128: Submitted by Walter Lauster [PEDec84]
129: Aurora, Minnesota [SFDec84]
130: Submitted by William Stehr [PEDec84]
131: Submitted by Charles Krieg [PEDec88]
132: Submitted by Charles Krieg [PEDec88]
133: Adapted from an item in the *Louisville Courier-Journal Magazine* [PEDec88]
134: Submitted by G. Patrick White [SFDec85]
135: Submitted by J. Vanden Busch [SFDec85]
136: John Timpson's *Early Morning Book* (London: Collins) [PEMay88]
137: P. R. Van Buskirk [SFDec85]
138: Adapted [PEDec84]
139: No source available [PEJun88]
140: No source available [PEDec84]
141: Submitted by Dr. John D. Walden, Sr. [PESep90]
142: Received at General Foods, submitted by Curry Pikkaart [PEMay88]
143: Zig Ziglar, *Top Performance* (Old Tappan, NJ: Revell, 1986), submitted by Stan Buck [PEFeb88]
144: *Now to Live,* by Dr. Ralph W. Sockman, submitted by Palmer B. Wold, edited by Michael Hodgin [SFMar91]
145: Victoria Ryan, Hamilton, Ohio, from *Ladies Home Journal,* April 1990 [PENov90]
146: Submitted by Bernard Brunsting [PEJun90]
147: Submitted by David Palm [PEDec83]
148: *Stripped Gears,* a Rotary publication [PENov87]
149: Adapted [PEAug84]
150: Adapted from an item in the *Danbury News-Times,* Danbury, CT [PEJun88]
151: Submitted by Richard Risser [PEJul83]
152: No source available [PEMay90]
153: Adapted [PEJul84]
154: No source available [PEApr88]
155: Submitted by Jeff Meaney [PEAug82]
156: Submitted by Charles Cooper [PEJan87]
157: Ethel Fried, as quoted in the *Hartford Courant,* Hartford, CT [SFJul87]
158: Jim Vorsas, Saratoga, California [PEAug84]
159: Submitted by Bernard Brunsting [PEMay88]
160: Adapted [PEApr87]
161: Adapted [PEFeb83]
162: No source available [PESep84]
163: Ann Landers [PESep81]
164: *Dynamic Preaching,* April 1987, p. 7 [PEJun87]
165: R.J. Hastings in the Illinois Baptist, Springfield, IL, submitted by Donald G. Shoff [PEMar91]
166: Chuck Swindoll speaking at the Pastor's Conference at Mt. Hermon Conference Center [PEMar82]
167: No source available [PENov84]
168: Submitted by Douglas Sabin [PEApr91]
169: Submitted by Steve Hodgin [PEApr91]
170: Wendell Wilkie, submitted by Gene Sikkink [PEMay90]
171: *Christian Clippings,* submitted by Micheal Kelley [PEOct88]
172: Submitted by Eugene Barron [PEJul83]
173: Submitted by Don Maddox [PEAug90]
174: Submitted by J. D. Cooper [PEJun88]
175: Submitted by Bruce Rowlison [PEDec86]
176: Adapted [PEOct85]
177: Pastor Roy Knight [PENov82]
178: Adapted [PEJun87]
179: Harry Emerson Fosdick, *Living Under Tension* (London: Student Christian Movement Press, 1941) [SFJul85]
180: Submitted by Alan Thompson [PEJul90]
181: Submitted by Don Cheadle [PEJun86]
182: *Personal Computers, A to Z,* by Joel Makower (Washington, DC), submitted by Bruce Rowlison [PEAug90]
183: No source available [PEDec83]

184: No source available [PEMar83]
185: Adapted [SFFeb86]
186: No source available [SFJan88]
187: Submitted by Robert Smith [PEDec85]
188: No source available [PEAug82]
189: *Sunday Sermons*, November–December 1987 [SFJan88]
190: Paul Ziegler in *Bits & Pieces* [PEJan83]
191: No source available [PEMar85]
192: *Kingdom Quarterly*, Summer 1990 [PENov90]
193: No source available [PENov82]
194: *Sunday Sermons Treasury of Illustrations*, vol. 1, p. 232 (no. 438) [PENov84]
195: Adapted [PEAug84]
196: No source available [PEFeb85]
197: No source available [PEFeb83]
198: Adapted [PEDec86]
199: William Jones [PEJun87]
200: No source available [PEFeb86]
201: Submitted by Gary Graff [PEJan85]
202: Mark Twain [PEJan87]
203: Submitted by Kay Bartlett [PEJun90]
204: *Bits & Pieces* [PEMar83]
205: No source available [PEMar85]
206: From an account by Norton Mockridge, submitted by Thomas Holdcroft [SFJan86]
207: Submitted by Dick Underdahl-Pierce [PEDec87]
208: Submitted by James Ankerberg [PENov85]
209: Submitted by Bruce Rowlison [PEMar86]
210: From a sermon by Dr. Joe Harding, submitted by Dave Baldridge [PESep90]
211: No source available [PEJul87]
212: *Laughsville, USA*, Scholastic Books, submitted by Mark Graves [PEFeb87]
213: *Creative Sermon Resources*, vol. 7, Summer 1986, p. 294 [PEOct86]
214: H. V. Adolt, *Forbes* [PEDec81]
215: Picture supplied by Ernest Angel, commentary by Michael Hodgin [SFJul93]
216: Adapted [PEApr88]
217: *Funny, Funny World* [PENov83]
218: Submitted by Dave Mote [SFMar86]
219: No source available [SFMar86]
220: *Progressive Farmer*, January 1991, Birmingham, AL [SFJun93]

221: *2500 Anecdotes for All Occasions*, edited by Edmund Fuller. [SFAug87]
222: George F. Will, *The Pursuit of Happiness and Other Sobering Thoughts* [PEJul82]
223: Submitted by Dennis Kamper [PEJul92]
224: Former hockey goalie, Jacques Plante [PEAug82]
225: *Pulpit Helps*, November 1981 [PEMay91]
226: Adapted [PEAug87]
227: Joe Taylor Ford, *The Executive Speechwriter Newsletter*, St. Johnsbury, VT [PENov88]
228: Submitted by the Rev. D. R. Jackson [SFSep85]
229: Charles Krieg [PEMar87]
230: Mell Lazarus, author of *Momma* [PEJun83]
231: Adapted [PESep84]
232: *It's God's World*, Asheville, NC [PEMar90]
233: *Good Housekeeping*, submitted by Dick Underdahl-Pierce [SFMay84]
234: Submitted by Dick Underdahl-Pierce [SFMay84]
235: Woody Allen, submitted by Dick Underdahl-Pierce [SFMay84]
236: Submitted by G. Patrick White [PEAug85]
237: No source available [PESep83]
238: No source available [PEAug83]
239: Submitted by Kent Anderson, taken from *Quote Unquote*, compiled by Lloyd Cory (Wheaton, IL: Victor Books), p. 81 [SFMar88]
240: Submitted by Rich Hardison [SFMar88]
241: Submitted by Naomi Breedlove [SFMay86]
242: Sent in by Joseph Winston [PEMay84]
243: Dean Head [PEMay87]
244: No source available [PEMar82 & PESep91]
245: No source available [PEAug88]
246: *Bits & Pieces*, May 1985 [PESep85]
247: Adapted [PEJan86]
248: Samuel Butler [PEAug82]
249: Brigid Bourgeois, submitted by Joe Barone [PESep88]
250: Saki [PEMar88]
251: Mark Twain, submitted by Joe Murphy [PEMar84]
252: Taken from *Mize Outlook*, Mize, MS, July 6, 1905 [PEMay91]

START WITH YOURSELF

The following words were were
written on the tomb of an Anglican
bishop in the crypts of Westminister
Abbey:
"When I was yong and free
and my imagination had no limits, I dreamed of changin g the
world. As I grew older and wiser, I
discovered the world would not
change, so I shortened my sights
somewhat and decided to change
only my country. But it too seemed
immovable.

As I grew into my twilight
years, in one last desperate attempt, I settled for changing only
family, those closest to me, but
alas, they would have none of it.

And now as I lay on my
deathbed, I suddenly realize if I
had only changed myself first, then
by example I would have changed
my family. From their inspiration
and encouragement, I would then
have been able to better my country and, who knows, I may have
even changed the world.
By anonymous.

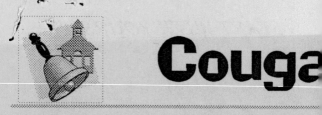

ACS AUCTION MARCH 5!!!

A 1920's theme has been selected by the auction committee for this year's Evening of Elegance III March 5th auction to be held at the Eureka Inn on March 5th. Much help is needed. New families please feel free to get involved in this fun event. Contact Kathe Robinson at 822-9555 for more information.

ACS
THURS

Student pic
grades on Th
Attached to
mational pa
made out to
not ACS! E
separate env
Oct.15

F

The 8th gra
fundraiser for t
fir and alder
senior citizens
5986. We wil

253: Adapted [PENov86]
254: No source available [PEJan82]
255: No source available [PEApr90]
256: Robert Sarpalius [PEOct87]
257: Quoted by Martin Marty in *Sports Illustrated* [PEMar86]
258: No source available [PENov85]
259: Submitted by the Rev. G. Patrick White [PESep85]
260: Adapted [PEJan85]
261: Submitted by Gene Sikkink [PEJul90]
262: No source available [PEFeb85]
263: No source available [PEJun90]
264: Adapted, April 1990 [PEAug90]
265: No source available [PEJul84]
266: Cathedral Press's EXCHANGE, vol. 25, no. 3, 1983, p. 8, submitted by James A. Lang [SFNov84]
267: Submitted by Bruce Rowlinson [PEMar93]
268: Adapted [PEJul83]
269: *Christian Clippings,* submitted by Micheal Kelley [PENov90]
270: *10,000 Jokes, Toasts & Stories,* edited by Lewis and Faye Copeland, (Garden City, NJ: Garden City Books [PEOct90]
271: *Christian Clippings,* submitted by Michael Kelley [PESep88]
272: No source available [PEFeb85]
273: No source available [PEAug82]
274: No source available [PEAug81]
275: Submitted by Kenneth L. Dodge [PEJan91]
276: Adapted [PEOct88]
277: Adapted [PEJul88]
278: Adapted from material submitted by Gary Sturni [PESep87]
279: Eleanor Doan, ed., *Kid Stuff* (1970), submitted by Bruce Welander [SFNov85]
280: Submitted by Don Cheadle [PEMar86]
281: *Chestnuts, Freshly Roasted* [PEAug82]
282: No source available [SFMar85]
283: *Funny, Funny World* [PESep87]
284: Larry Ballenger [PEApr82]
285: *Sunday Sermons* [SFFeb86]
286: Adapted [PEMar86]
287: No source available [PEAug84]
288: Told by Sister Rhoda, Society of St. Margaret, submitted by the Rev. Wade A. Renn [SFFeb85]
289: No source available [SFMay85]
290: Adapted [PEJan84]
291: No source available [PEMar86]

292: *Farm and Ranch Living,* June-July 1984 [PEMay90]
293: Henny Youngman, submitted by Douglas Ehrlich [PEFeb85]
294: Henny Youngman, submitted by Douglas Ehrlich [PEFeb85]
295: Bill Hoest, King Features [PEDec81]
296: Submitted by Jim Vorsas [PENov87]
297: Submitted by Kirk Neeley [SFSep87]
298: Adapted [PEAug84]
299: No source available [PEMar83]
300: *Jest-In-Time* [PESep88]
301: Jim LeShana [SFMay87]
302: Marie Schwalbe [PEApr88]
303: *Man of the House: The Life and Political Memoirs of Speaker Tip O'Neill* [PEApr88]
304: Submitted by Don Cheadle, from a book by Ben Haden [PEMar85]
305: Submitted by Bruce Welander [SFJan85]
306: Randall Tschotter [PEApr87]
307: *Stripped Gears,* a Rotary publication [PEDec87]
308: *Sunday Sermons Treasury of Illustrations* [SFDec84]
309: "Now Hear this," *Fortune,* August 15, 1988, p. 16 [PEOct88]
310: *Cincinnati Enquirer,* submitted by Bruce Rowlison [PEJan88]
311: *Ladies Home Journal,* quoted in *Catholic Digest,* December 1987 [PEMar91]
312: No source available [PEApr82]
313: Submitted by Marie Schwalbe, Longwood, FL [PEJan88]
314: Adapted [PENov87]
315: No source available [PEMar91]
316: No source available [SFApr94]
317: No source available [PENov87]
318: Submitted by Chris Thore [PEFeb91]
319: Submitted by John H. Hampsch [PESep90]
320: Harold Helfer, from *Catholic Digest,* December 1987 [PEFeb91]
321: *On the Upbeat* [SFJun87]
322: No source available [SFAug93]
323: No source available [PEFeb85]
324: No source available [PEJul84]
325: No source available [PEJan82]
326: Chuck Swindoll speaking at the Pastor's Conference at Mt. Hermon Conference Center [PEMar82]
327: No source available [PEJan84]

328: J. M. Kennedy, Morning Sun, Iowa [SFJan85]
329: Source Unknown [PEOct90]
330: *Christian Communications Laboratory* [PEOct84]
331: Submitted by Steve Espamer [SFSep85]
332: No source available [PEJun87]
333: No source available [PEMar86]
334: No source available [PEMar86]
335: No source available [PESep82]
336: No source available [PENov87]
337: No source available [SFJun87]
338: No source available [PEMar91]
339: No source available [PEMay87]
340: Adapted from Herb Caen, *San Francisco Chronicle* [PEApr87]
341: Submitted by Edward Beckwith, Jr. [PEDec81]
342: Adapted [PEJan86]
343: *Corner Stones* [PEMay88]
344: Submitted by Bernard Brunsting [PEMay88]
345: Donald Strobe, submitted by Wayne Rouse [PEMay93]
346: Adapted [PEMay85]
347: No source available [PEAug84]
348: No source available [PEFeb85]
349: No source available [PEMar91]
350: Walter Johnson, Rotarian, Amarillo, Texas [PEJan85]
351: Leonard Lauder, president of Estee Lauder, taken from *Men's Life*, published by Church Development Resources, Grand Rapids, MI, submitted to Stan Buck [PEMay91]
352: Thanks to the Rev. John G. Blewitt [PENov82]
353: No source available [PEJul82]
354: Adapted [PEAug87]
355: S. A. Edmiston in *The Rotarian* [PEApr88]
356: No source available [PENov82]
357: *Bits & Pieces* [PEDec86]
358: Political commentator Mark Shields, reported in *Psychology Today,* November 1984. [PEJan85]
359: *Christian Communications Laboratory* [PEMay81]
360: Snoopy, in "Peanuts" by Charles Schultz [PENov87]
361: Submitted by Dr. Harold Friesen [PEMar85]
362: Herb Miller, *Actions Speak Louder Than Verbs* (Nashville: Abingdon Press, 1989), submitted by Rich Thornton [SFApr91]
363: Adapted [PEFeb85]
364: Submitted by Pastor Douglas [PEMay84]
365: Sbumitted by Alan C. Thompson [PESep93]
366: No source available [PESep81]
367: No source available [PEApr88]
368: Submitted by Bruce Rowlison [PEOct86]
369: Kim Hubbard [PEMar87]
370: Submitted by David Michel [SFMar85]
371: Robert Sarpalius [PEOct87]
372: Adapted from a story by Elizabeth Leyda [PEJan89]
373: David McCullough, *Mornings on Horseback* (New York: Simon & Schuster, 1981), p. 103 [PENov86]
374: *Motherhood: It Helps If You Smile,* by James Dobson (Colorado Springs: Focus on the Family) [SFMay87]
375: Cotham in *Cosmopolitan* [PEApr88]
376: Quote from Anita Loos [PEAug90]
377: Submitted by Carl Ericson [PEMay91]
378: No source available [PEMay82]
379: No source available
380: No source available [SFJul85]
381: No source available [PEAug82]
382: Submitted by Gene Sikkink [PEApr91]
383: Adapted [SFJun87]
384: No source available [PEApr87]
385: Submitted by Thomas Holdcroft, Sumas, WA [SFJan86]
386: *The Little, Brown Book of Anecdotes,* edited by Clifton Fadiman, p. 371 [SFFeb88]
387: Ambrose Bierce [PEJul88]
388: No source available [PEMar88]
389: Submitted by Gene Sikkink [PEMay90]
390: Submitted by Gene Sikkink [PEMay90]
391: Submitted by Jerry Hickson [PENov90]
392: Andy Rooney [PEMar90]
393: Submitted by Kay Bartlett [PEJun90]
394: No source available [PEMar91]
395: Marvin Crow, International Christian Center Church [SFMay90]
396: *Bits & Pieces* [PESep84]
397: Submitted by Phil Hines [PEDec85]
398: *National Motorist,* submitted by Clint Frank [SFJan85]

399: Submitted by Charles Krieg [PEAug88]
400: Submitted by John H. Hampsch [PESep90]
401: Submitted by Bernard Brunsting [PEMar90]
402: Credited to Hal Brady by Frank Harrington, submitted by Don Maddox [PEFeb91]
403: Submitted by Ben Hurley [SFSep87]
404: *Friends/Enemies* [PEJan82]
405: No source available [SFJun93]
406: No source available [PEDec81]
407: *Nothing But Winners,* Williams and Hussar [SFDec88]
408: No source available [SFDec88]
409: No source available [SFDec88]
410: Adapted [PESep84]
411: From "Peanuts" by Charles Schultz [PEJul81]
412: From a sermon by the late Dr. Robert T. Ketchum [PEMay90]
413: Submitted by Cal Hiebert, Holdrege, NE [PENov88]
414: No source available [PEJun81]
415: No source available [PEOct90]
416: Submitted by Lawrence Guzowski [PEDec84]
417: No source available [PEJun84]
418: No source available [PEDec81]
419: As told by Don Houchen [PEMar90]
420: Submitted by Stephen L. Donat [PEAug92]
421: No source available [PEOct88]
422: *Christian Communications Laboratory* [PEJan85]
423: *On the Upbeat* [PEMar86]
424: *On the Upbeat* [PEJun87]
425: *Contact,* submitted by Jerry Sebranke [PEOct87]
426: Steven Cole [PENov82]
427: *Chestnuts, Freshly Roasted* [PEJun85]
428: *Funny, Funny World* [PEApr87]
429: Bruce Rowlison [PEFeb87]
430: *Funny, Funny World* [PESep87]
431: Submitted by Jeff Dietrich [PEOct82]
432: Source Unknown [SFJan94]
433: No source available [PEMay90]
434: Submitted by Thomas Sublett [SFMar85]
435: Submitted by Donald Fogelsanger [SFMar85]
436: *The Rotarian,* October 1985 [PEDec85]
437: Charles Krieg [SFJul84]

438: Les Schultz, quoted by Alex Thien, submitted by Dicky Love [SFAug91]
439: Submitted by Verle Brubaker [PENov84]
440: Submitted by Bernard Brunsting [PEMay88]
441: No source available [PEJul90]
442: No source available [PEApr86]
443: *Sunday Sermons* [PEDec87]
444: No source available [PEAug82]
445: David Mote [SFFeb87]
446: Garrison Keilor, *The Prairie Home Companion Radio Show,* submitted by Terry Morgan [SFFeb87]
447: No source available [PESep87]
448: Submitted by William Pile [PEOct88]
449: Adapted from various sources [SFMar93]
450: Submitted by Father Emmet O'Neill [PEApr91]
451: Adapted [PESep87]
452: No source available [SFJan87]
453: Attributed to Ralph Waldo Emerson by Dick Underdahl-Pierce [SFMar86]
454: *Context* by Martin Marty, submitted by Don Maddox [PEJun90]
455: No source available [PEJan85]
456: Ambrose Bierce [PEFeb83]
457: Adapted from a story told by Dr. Kenneth Gangel at a G.L.A.S.S. Conference in 1986, submitted by David Bolton [PEMar87]
458: Tommy La Sorda, as quoted in *Me and DiMaggio,* by Christopher Lehmann-Haupt (New York: Simon & Schuster) [PEMay87]
459: Comic strip by Hank Ketcham [SFNov85]
460: Submitted by Jeff Callender [SFJul87]
461: No source available [PEJul84]
462: No source available [PEApr87]
463: No source available [PEJul88]
464: Steve Wing [PEOct88]
465: *Christian Clippings,* submitted by Michael Kelley [PEJul90]
466: Submitted by Byron Erixon [PEMar88]
467: No source available [PEDec88]
468: *2500 Anecdotes for All Occasions,* edited by Edmund Fuller, Avenal, NY, 1980 [SFSep84]
469: Submitted by Sherwin Brantsen [PEJul85]
470: No source available [PESep91]

471: No source available [PEApr81]
472: Bob Thaves, Newspaper Enterprise Association [PEMay88]
473: No source available [PEMar88]
474: *Chicago Tribune* [PEJan82]
475: Submitted by Richard Moore [PEApr82]
476: *Bits & Pieces* [PEOct83]
477: No source available [PEApr81]
478: No source available [PEMay82]
479: *Christian Clippings,* submitted by Michael Kelley [PEOct90]
480: Submitted by Bob Moyer [PEJan91]
481: Submitted by David Rockhill [PEJun83]
482: No source available [PEJul84]
483: Reul Howe, submitted by Gene Sikkink, Glendorado Lutheran Church [PEMay90]
484: *Leadership,* vol. 10, no. 4, submitted by Dave Baldridge [PEDec90]
485: Submitted by Stan Buck [PEMar88]
486: Adapted [PEFeb86]
487: Adapted [PEAug83]
488: American Legion [SFSep87]
489: No source available [PEApr82]
490: *On the Upbeat* [PEJan86]
491: No source available [PEFeb85]
492: No source available [PEApr83]
493: No source available [PENov84]
494: Submitted by Douglas Sabin [PEApr91]
495: Submitted by Grant Darling [PEApr91]
496: Adapted from a cartoon in *Have a Good Day* [PESep85]
497: No source available [PESep88]
498: Submitted by Wayne Rouse [PEOct90]
499: No source available [PEMay90]
500: Vanna White (co-host of *Wheel of Fortune*), from *Campus Life,* March 1990 [PEFeb91]
501: Submitted by Billy D. Strayhorn [PEFeb91]
502: Submitted by Jerry D. Ruff [SFAug92]
503: Submitted by Robert Strand [PEMay86]
504: No source available [PEFeb83]
505: Submitted by Charles Krieg [PEJul88]
506: Submitted by Jim Vorsas, Saratoga, CA [PEJul84]
507: Submitted by Thomas Sublett [SFMar85]
508: Submitted by Charles Krieg [PEDec88]
509: Mark Twain, submitted by Gene Sikkink [PEMay90]
510: No source available [PEMar90]
511: Submitted by Don Cheadle [PEMar86]
512: No source available [PEOct82]
513: Submitted by Rabbi Samuel M. Silver [PEJan91]
514: Submitted by Rabbi Samuel M. Silver [PEMay91]
515: Submitted by John Bristol [PEMay87]
516: Richard J. Needham [PEJul90]
517: No source available [PEJul82]
518: Claire Morrow [PEMay81]
519: No source available [SFJun93]
520: Charles Davis [PEApr87]
521: *Jokes Un-Ltd.,* Hollywood, CA [PEJul86]
522: No source available [PEJan91]
523: Alfred E. Neuman [PEJul90]
524: No source available [PENov81]
525: From Steve Hodgin by Leslie Flann [SFMar91]
526: No source available [PESep84]
527: Submitted by Robert Strand [PEJan89]
528: *Sunday Sermons,* November-December 1986 [PEJan89]
529: No source available [PEDec85]
530: W. A. Poovey, *The Prayer He Taught,* submitted by Lance Kittleson [PEJun87]
531: No source available [PEApr83]
532: Proclaim, January 1984 [PEFeb85]
533: Herm Albright, *Perry Township Weekly* [SFJun87]
534: Submitted by James R. Dyke [PESep92]
535: Submitted by David Rockhill [PEOct85]
536: *Sunday Sermons Treasury of Illustrations,* vol. 2, p. 320 [SFJul85]
537: Adapted [SFJul87]
538: No source available [PEAug88]
539: No source available [PEAug81]
540: No source available [SFMay85]
541: No source available [PEAug83]
542: Submitted by Jeff Chandler [SFOct88]
543: No source available [SFApr91]
544: Submitted by Tim Purcell [PEJan87]
545: Kin Hubbard, as quoted in *Forbes* [PENov86]
546: Adapted [PEFeb87]
547: Adapted from *The Teaching of Elementary Science and*

Mathematics by Alexander Collandra, submitted by Byron Swash [PENov87]

548: Submitted by Robert Strand [PEJan88]
549: Submitted by John H. Hampsch [PESep90]
550: Adapted [PESep88]
551: No source available [PEFeb83]
552: *40 Ways to Say I Love You,* James Bjorge, submitted by Pastor Vernal G. Anderson [SFFeb85]
553: Submitted by Rick Hardison [SFFeb85]
554: No source available [PEMar86]
555: Submitted by Rabbi Samuel M. Silver [PESep90]
556: Submitted by Charles Krieg [PEAug88]
557: No source available [PEApr81]
558: Submitted by Dick Underdahl-Pierce [PENov86]
559: Doyal Van Gelder [SFApr88]
560: No source available [PEMay90]
561: President Ronald Reagan [PESep81]
562: *Chestnuts* [PESep85]
563: Submitted by Hoyt Johnson [SFMar85]
564: Submitted by Barry Wineroth [SFSep87]
565: Submitted by Marie B. Schwalbe [PEJun90]
566: Submitted by John H. Hampsch [PESep90]
567: Helen Roland, submitted by Jeff Callender [SFJul87]
568: No source available [PEApr83]
569: James Wharton, submitted by Jeff Callender [SFJul87]
570: Michael Meaney [PEApr81]
571: Told by Lanson Ross, Planned Living Seminar, Yakima, WA [PEDec90]
572: *Faith Planning,* Bruce Cook, p. 111, submitted by Alan Thompson [PEMar90]
573: *Washington Post,* submitted by Byron Neufeld [PESep90]
574: Submitted by Ken Langley [PEDec90]
575: Adapted [PEJun85]
576: No source available [PEMar82]
577: Adapted [PENov87]
578: Calvin Trillin [PEAug88]
579: No source available [PEApr82]
580: No source available [PENov82]
581: No source available [PEJul82]

582: No source available [PEDec81]
583: No source available [SFJun93]
584: *Funny, Funny World* [PEAug83]
585: *Parables from Outside Paradise,* by James Cammack [PEJan87]
586: No source available [PEMay87]
587: Adapted [PEMar88]
588: Submitted by Emmett O'Neill [PEMar91]
589: Submitted by Wayne W. Eisbrenner [SFMay93]
590: H. L. Mencken [SFSep91]
591: No source available [PENov88]
592: No source available [SFApr91]
593: Submitted by Pastor Fred D. Musser [SFFeb85]
594: Adapted [PENov86]
595: Charles Krieg [SFMay87]
596: Adapted from Leslie Flynn, *Humorous Notes, Quotes, and Anecdotes,* p. 111, submitted by Charles Krieg [SFMay87]
597: Submitted by Charles Krieg [SFMay87]
598: No source available [PEMay87]
599: Submitted by Kay Bartlett [PEJun90]
600: *Sports Illustrated,* March 5, 1990 [PEAug90]
601: Submitted by James Ankerberg [PENov85]
602: No source available [SFMay93]
603: Submitted by Dick Underdahl-Pierce [SFMay86]
604: Submitted by Steve Schoept [SFMay86]
605: "A Funny Thing Happened . . .," *Church Administration,* January 1990, by Mark Edworthy [SFMay91]
606: Bea Alexandrovich, from *Catholic Digest,* May 1988 [SFMay91]
607: Submitted by Dick Underdahl-Pierce [SFMay86]
608: Submitted by Arnold Nelson [SFMay86]
609: Submitted by Bart Conner [SFMay86]
610: Condensed from *Motherhood: The Second Oldest Profession,* submitted by Rich Hardison [SFMay86]
611: No source available [PEJun81]
612: Submitted by Jay Bartow [PEFeb87]
613: No source available [PEJul86]
614: Adapted [PEFeb88]
615: *Illustration Digest,* March-April 1990 [PEAug90]
616: No source available [PEAug84]

617: No source available [SFFeb85]
618: Submitted by Gene Sikkink [PEMay91]
619: *Wittenburg Door,* December 1982, submitted by Jerry Ableidinger [SFOct87]
620: No source available [PEFeb85]
621: Submitted by Jim Vorsas [PEAug84]
622: Burton Hillis, *Better Homes and Gardens,* May 1989 [PEAug90]
623: Coleridge, from *4800 Wise-Cracks, Witty Remarks and Epigrams for All Occasions,* edited by Edmund Fuller, published by Avenel Books [PEAug90]
624: Adapted. [PEJan85]
625: Submitted by William Jennings [PEMar84]
626: No source available [PEAug90]
627: No source available [PEAug90]
628: Charles Kinyon [PEJun83]
629: *News of the Weird,* p. 110 (New York: Penguin Books, 1989) [PEMar91]
630: Arthur Schopenhauer [PENov86]
631: *Pulpit Helps,* February 1990, submitted by Don Julian [PEMay90]
632: No source available [PEJul90]
633: Submitted by Stan Buck [PEMar88]
634: No source available [PEMay82]
635: Submitted by Al Earley [PEOct84]
636: *Funny, Funny World* [PEOct84]
637: *Journal of Religious Speaking for Christ,* submitted by R.L. Bersett [SFNov84]
638: Adapted [PESep87]
639: Andy Rooney [PEMar90]
640: Submitted by Lee Griess [PEAug88]
641: "Personal Glimpses," in *Reader's Digest,* attributed to Herb Caen, submitted by Steven Cole [SFDec84]
642: Adapted from George Jessel, *The Toastmaster General's Guide to Successful Public Speaking,* submitted by Charles Krieg [PEJul87]
643: Submitted by Dale Bean [PEDec82]
644: No source available [PENov83]
645: No source available [PESep83]
646: Submitted by Ryan Hodgin [PEMay90]
647: Submitted by Robert Strand [PEMay91]
648: George Jean Nathan [PEMar85]
649: Zig Ziglar [PEApr81]
650: No source available [PEJul81]
651: Submitted by Robert Dalke [PEAug90]
652: *300 Seed Thoughts* by Miller and Moore (Lubbock, TX: Net Press, 198) [PEAug90]
653: Submitted by C. Richard Stone [SFMay91]
654: No source available [SFMay87]
655: Submitted by the Rev. Robert Smith [PEAug84]
656: Submitted by Ron Watts [SFMay91]
657: Submitted by Carl Ericson [PEDec93]
658: No source available [PEMar90]
659: Richard De Haan, submitted by Jack Ritsema [PENov88]
660: No source available [PEMay81]
661: Submitted by Dick Underdahl-Pierce [PEOct87]
662: Submitted by Malcolm MacPhail [SFOct88]
663: Phil Hines [PEFeb87]
664: No source available [PEJan87]
665: Submitted by the Rev. William Trickett [SFJan85]
666: Submitted by James Swanson [SFSep86]
667: *Scottish Rite Bulletin,* submitted by Bruce Rowlison [PEMay90]
668: Ronald Dunn, *Any Christian Can!* (Kalamazoo, MI: Master's Press, 1976) [PEJul90]
669: Stephen Wing [PEMar86]
670: Adapted [PEDec83]
671: Adapted [PEDec86]
672: No source available [PEApr90]
673: Submitted by Charles Coggins [SFNov87]
674: Submitted by Michael Hodgin [PEJun91]
675: "In Search of New England's Humor: A Few Familiar Faces," *The Yankee,* September 1987 [PEMay90]
676: Submitted by the Rev. Danny Hensley [PENov81]
677: *Bits & Pieces* [PEMay87]
678: Submitted by Bruce Rowlison [PEDec86]
679: *Preaching,* July-August 1986 [PENov86]
680: Keith Miller, *The Becomers,* submitted by Frank Barker [PEMar88]
681: Submitted by Rae Holt [PEJan86]
682: Submitted by Ron Kerr [PENov84]
683: *Forbes,* May 19, 1986, p. 19 [PEOct86]
684: Adapted [PENov84]

685: No source available [SFDec87]
686: Submitted by H. Mitchell, adapted [SFJan85]
687: Adapted [PEDec87]
688: *Willard Scott's Down Home Stories,* submitted by Cris Cannon [PEApr87]
689: Submitted by Rabbi Samuel M. Siler, Temple Sinai [PEJan91]
690: From "Peanuts" by Charles Shultz [PEApr84]
691: No source available [PEJun81]
692: *Entrepreneurial Manager's Newsletter* [PEMay81]
693: *Paul Harvey News,* March 3, 1988, submitted by Mark Shepard [PEApr91]
694: *Bits & Pieces* [PEOct84]
695: Adapted from *Funny, Funny World* [PENov85]
696: No source available [PEMay93]
697: No source available [PEDec81]
698: No source available [PEApr86]
699: Adapted from *Rotary Magazine* [PEJul86]
700: *Modern Maturity* [PEJul88]
701: *Campbell's Notebook,* January 1988 [PEJul88]
702: *Modern Maturity* [PEJun88]
703: No source available [PEJul87]
704: Submitted by Rabbi Samuel M. Siler [PEJan91]
705: Submitted by William Moyer [PEMay87]
706: No source available [PESep83]
707: *Capper's Weekly,* submitted by Charles Krieg [SFJun84]
708: Submitted by Kay Bartlett [PEJun90]
709: Adapted [PENov86]
710: Adapted from *Jest-In-Time* [PESep88]
711: Adapted *Bits & Pieces,* December 1984, p. 15 [PEMar85]
712: Submitted by Lester Weeks [PEJan87]
713: Submitted by Robert Strand [PEMay86]
714: Norman Vincent Peale [PEMar81]
715: No source available [SFOct87]
716: Submitted by Yeprem Kelegian [PEJan89]
717: Submitted by Robert Strand [SFJun91]
718: No source available [SFJun91]
719: Kit Hoag [PEJan83]
720: No source available [SFSep85]
721: *Corner Stones* [PEApr88]

722: No source available [SFOct87]
723: James Colaianni, *The Giant Book of Sunday Sermons* (Voicings Publ., 1984), p. 1093 [SFOct87]
724: *Chestnuts, Freshly Roasted* [PESep84]
725: No source available [PEFeb87]
726: Submitted by Ken Young [SFSep85]
727: Adapted [PEMay87]
728: Submitted by Robert Smith [PEFeb88]
729: No source available [PEAug81]
730: *Uncommon Friends,* p. 78 [PEAug88]
731: Submitted by Dale Steele [PEApr82]
732: Suzanne Wray, submitted by Dicky Love [SFJun91]
733: Submitted by Robert Strand [PEDec87]
734: Adapted from *The Little, Brown Book of Anecdotes,* edited by Clifton Fadiman, p. 9 [SFJan88]
735: Adapted from *The Little, Brown Book of Anecdotes,* edited by Clifton Fadiman, p. 228 [SFJan88]
736: No source available [SFJan88]
737: *Young America,* Minnesota [PEMar87]
738: No source available [PEJun82]
739: *Fairbanks News-Miner,* Fairbanks, AK, submitted by Jeff Callender [PEFeb87]
740: Duffy Daugherty, Michigan State football coach [PEJan87]
741: Submitted by Gene Sikkink [PEMay88]
742: No source available [PEJan82]
743: No source available [PEJun91]
744: No source available [PEFeb85]
745: Adapted [PEMay85]
746: Submitted by Dr. William Paterson [PENov87]
747: Submitted by Wesley Payne [PEFeb85]
748: Submitted by Robert Smith, from *Preaching,* July-August 1987 [PEOct87]
749: Randy Marshall [PEJan91]
750: Adapted [PEMay87]
751: No source available [PEApr85]
752: Submitted by Carolyn M. Kendrick [PEJan91]
753: Submitted by David Palmer [SFOct87]
754: Submitted by Ed Rutherford [PENov86]
755: Adapted [PENov84]

756: No source available [PEOct86]
757: No source available [PEDec85]
758: John Henry Cardinal Newman, submitted by Gene Sikkink [PEMay90]
759: No source available [PEJul90]
760: *Bits & Pieces* [PEJul86]
761: George Burns [PEAug82]
762: Adapted [PEMay90]
763: *Funny, Funny World* [PEFeb86]
764: *Sunshine Magazine,* August 1973 [PEFeb91]
765: Submitted by Bernard Brunsting [PEAug88]
766: No source available [PEMay87]
767: No source available [PEOct82]
768: Adapted [PEFeb86]
769: *Theological Worlds: Understanding the Alternative Rhythms of Christian Belief* (Nashville: Abingdon, 1989), p. 36, submitted by Billy D. Strayhorn [PEFeb92]
770: "Mule Eggs and Topknots," *Seven Worlds,* submitted by Dave Gerbrandt [SFApr88]
771: Submitted by Curry Pikkaart [PEMay88]
772: *On the Upbeat* [SFFeb86]
773: No source available [PEDec82]
774: No source available [PEApr87]
775: Submitted by Michael Hodgin [SFJun91]
776: Submitted by Aaron Nagel [PEOct92]
777: *Mac's Giant Book of Quips and Quotes* [SFJul84]
778: Submitted by Charles Krieg [SFJul84]
779: No source available [PEJun91]
780: Submitted by Jim Vorsas [PEJun87]
781: Submitted by Phil Hines [PEDec86]
782: Ellen Hammonds, as reported in *Partnership* [SFOct86]
783: No source available [PEApr82]
784: Adapted [PESep87]
785: No source available [PESep87]
786: No source available [PEAug81]
787: Submitted by James Swanson [SFNov87]
788: Submitted by Larry and Ann Menschel [PEJun91]
789: No source available [PEJun90]
790: Adapted [PEOct88]
791: *On the Upbeat* [PEMar85]
792: Billy D. Strayhorn [SFMay91]
793: Adapted [PEDec82]
794: *Pulpit Helps* [PESep81]

795: *Christmas Rhapsody,* by Phil Brower (Grand Rapids: Singspiration) [PEDec90]
796: No source available [PEMay87]
797: Robert Carrington [SFMar91]
798: Submitted by Judy Meyers [PEMar90]
799: Submitted by Charles Krieg [PEMar90]
800: No source available [PEAug90]
801: No source available [PEApr88]
802: *On the Upbeat* [PESep84]
803: No source available [PEAug82]
804: Adapted [PEDec88]
805: *Bits & Pieces* [PEJan82]
806: Chinese proverb, quoted in *Christian Communication Laboratory* [PEOct83]
807: No source available [PEApr83]
808: No source available [PEApr84]
809: Submitted by the Rev. Byron Edwards [PEMay84]
810: *Jest-In-Time* [PESep88]
811: *Context,* as reported by Martin Marty [PEMay85]
812: From "Peanuts" by Charles Shultz [PEOct84]
813: *Chestnuts, Freshly Roasted* [PEAug84]
814: No source available [PEMar90]
815: Submitted by Timothy J. Helm [PEJun90]
816: Submitted by Ron Yates [PEJan91]
817: Submitted by Michael Colvin, from Dr. Jerome Frank, Professor of Psychiatry at Johns Hopkins University [PEMar83]
818: Mme. De Rieux [SFJul87]
819: No source available [PEOct82]
820: Jon Cornell, head of the semiconductor sector of Harris Corporation, as quoted in *Fortune* [PEJan86]
821: No source available [PEMar83]
822: Sam Levenson, submitted by Pastor Rowlison [PEOct90]
823: No source available [PEDec88]
824: *Funny, Funny World* [PENov86]
825: No source available [PEFeb88]
826: No source available [PEFeb88]
827: No source available [PEMay90]
828: Submitted by Charles Krieg [PESep90]
829: Submitted by Dennis Fast [PESep90]
830: No source available [PESep84]
831: *On the Upbeat* [PEJul85]

832: Adapted from Tyndale House, 1968, Charles E. Jones [PEApr81]
833: Adapted [PESep84]
834: Submitted by Karl Ingersoll, Falconer, NY [PEFeb84]
835: No source available [SFFeb87]
836: No source available [PENov82]
837: Robert Strand [PEJan89]
838: Lou Holtz, football coach, from *Sports Quotes* [PEJan87]
839: No source available [PEMar91]
840: Ed Howe, *Forbes* [PEFeb87]
841: Author unknown, submitted by the Rev. Ronald Albertson [SFApr91]
842: Submitted by the Rev. Lynn Jost [PEJan85]
843: Charles Spurgeon [PEMay86]
844: From "Peanuts" by Charles Shultz [PEJul83]
845: No source available [PEJun81]
846: Submitted by Steve Schoept [SFMay86]
847: Submitted by Robert Smith [PESep84]
848: Submitted by Carolyn M. Kendrick [PEJan91]
849: Submitted by Daniel Koehler [PEJul90]
850: Told by Pastor Todd Renegar, submitted by Paul Forbes [PEMar88]
851: Submitted by Robert Strand [PEJun91]
852: No source available [PEJun82]
853: Dr. Pierce Harris, as submitted by Dean Head [PEJan88]
854: No source available [PEApr87]
855: Submitted by John Herman [PEJan87]
856: No source available [PESep84]
857: *Sales Upbeat,* August 1, 1986 [PENov86]
858: Henry Kissinger [PEJul90]
859: Marsha Smith, *Redbook,* April 1990
860: Submitted by Robert J. Strand [PESep92]
861: Adapted from *Christian Clippings,* submitted by Micheal Kelley [PESep88]
862: Tom Payton, submitted by Robert Thompson [SFNov84]
863: Adapted [SFDec84]
864: No source available [PEAug88]
865: No source available [PEOct90]
866: No source available [PEMay83]
867: Submitted by Mark English [PEJan88]
868: Told by Edith Robertson, submitted by Rick Willis [PEJul92]
869: No source available [SFJan87]
870: Michael Hodgin [PEAug90]
871: Adapted [PEFeb83]
872: Submitted by Robert Strand [PEMay88]
873: Adapted [PEApr86]
874: *Sunshine Magazine,* August 1973 [PEDec90]
875: Adapted [PEFeb86]
876: Stephen Fast [PEMar87]
877: *Quote* [PEApr87]
878: *Paul Harvey, News and Comments,* December 11, 1989, submitted by Mark Shepard [PEAug90]
879: Submitted by Larry and Ann Menschel [PEJun91]
880: Joe Taylor Ford, *The Executive Speechwriter Newsletter,* St. Johnsbury, VT [PENov88]
881: Robert Sarpalius, DeSoto, TX [PEOct87]
882: Submitted by Calvin Van Kirk Hoyt [PEMay83]
883: *My Little Salesman Truck Catalog* [PEJun88]
884: No source available [PEDec81]
885: *Funny, Funny World* [PEAug83]
886: No source available [PENov86]
887: Submitted by Bruce Rowlison [PEOct86]
888: No source available [SFJun87]
889: *Jokes Priests Can Tell,* by Arthur Tonne, vol. 1., submitted by Dennis Fast [PEJan87]
890: No source available [PEAug84]
891: No source available [PESep81]
892: No source available [PEMay83]
893: Submitted by Dick Underdahl-Pierce [SFFeb88]
894: Submitted Bruce Welander [SFJan85]
895: Adapted [PEOct86]
896: Adlai Stevenson [PEJul90]
897: Sir Alan Herbert, *Sunday Times,* London, submitted by Robert Strand [PEDec86]
898: Submitted by Gene Sikkink [SFMay91]
899: Submitted by Kenneth L. Dodge [PEFeb91]
900: Submitted by Kenneth L. Dodge [PEFeb91]
901: Submitted by Bill Winch [PEMar84]
902: Submitted by Gene Barron [PEApr83]

903: No source available [PEFeb85]

904: No source available [PEApr82]

905: Submitted by Mark Martin, adapted [PEMay85]

906: Submitted by Elwin Collom [PESep90]

907: Submitted by Alan Kraft [PESep92]

908: Submitted by Dennis Fast [PESep90]

909: *Stories for Sermons,* vol. 5, by Arthur Tonne, submitted by Charles Krieg [PESep90]

910: Submitted by J. D. Cooper [PEJun88]

911: No source available [PEJul82]

912: Submitted by Dave Gerbrandt [PEApr88]

913: No source available [PENov87]

914: As quoted by Dianne McKenna, Santa Clara County Supervisor [PESep87]

915: Karen Savage and Patricia Adams, *The Good Stepmother* (New York: Crown) [PEDec88]

916: Submitted by Bernard Brunsting [PEJan89]

917: Submitted by Dick Underdahl-Pierce [SFMay86]

918: *Corner Stones* [PEDec87]

919: No source available [SFMay87]

920: Adapted [PEJun87]

921: No source available [PEApr87]

922: No source available [PENov85]

923: Submitted by Rich Hardison [SFMar85]

924: *Chestnuts, Freshly Roasted* [PENov83]

925: No source available [PEDec91]

926: No source available [PEJan85]

927: *Sunshine Magazine,* June 1973 [PENov90]

928: No source available [PENov83]

929: Adapted from *Mac's Giant Book of Quips and Quotes* by E. C. McKenzie (Eugene, OR: Harvest House) [PENov82]

930: Submitted by Bruce Welander [SFNov85]

931: Abraham Lincoln, submitted by Kay Bartlett [PEJun90]

932: William E. Thorn, *Catch the Little Foxes That Spoil the Vine* (Old Tappan, NJ: Revell, 1980) [PEJul90]

933: Submitted by Robert Strand [PESep87]

934: Adapted from Beryl Pfizer, *Bits & Pieces* [PEJan83]

935: No source available [PEAug82]

936: Submitted by Doyal Van Gelder [PEFeb86]

937: Adapted [SFMay91]

938: Submitted by Michael Jackson [PEJun94]

939: Submitted by Bob Mendelsohn [PENov87]

940: George Winters, submitted by Jon Honda [PENov86]

941: Submitted by Ken Davidson [SFSep87]

942: Submitted by Kenneth Dodge [PEFeb85]

943: No source available [PEAug81]

944: David Lloyd George [PEAug82]

945: Submitted by Kenneth Winter [PEMar84]

946: No source available [PEApr82]

947: No source available [SFAug93]

948: Submitted by Don Elmore [SFOct92]

949: Submitted by Charles Krieg [SFApr88]

950: No source available [PEJun82]

951: *Funny, Funny World* [PESep84]

952: *The Quest for Character,* by Charles R. Swindoll (Portland, OR: Multnomah Press), p. 183 [PEMar91]

953: *Funny, Funny World* [PEMay85]

954: Submitted by Richard Breusch [PEOct84]

955: *San Francisco Chronicle* [SFMar88]

956: No source available [PESep81]

957: Michael Meaney [PEApr81]

958: Submitted by Michael Brooks [PEJun81]

959: Submitted by Michael Brooks [PEJun81]

960: *Context,* October 15, 1982, submitted by Dick Daniels [PESep90]

961: Robert Strand [PESep87]

962: No source available [PESep87]

963: Adapted [PEMar86]

964: Submitted by Jim Vorsas [PEAug84]

965: No source available [PEJun81]

966: *On the Upbeat* [PEJun85]

967: Submitted by Dennis Fast [PENov83]

968: *Parables from Outside Paradise,* by James Cammack [PEJan87]

969: Submitted by Jay Martin [SFNov84]

970: No source available [PEJan85]

971: No source available [PENov84]

972: Submitted by Jim Vorsas [PENov87]

973: *10,000 Jokes, Toasts & Stories,* edited by Copeland (New York: Garden City Books) [PENov90]

974: Submittedby Marie Schwalbe [PEJan88]

975: No source available [PEAug82]

976: *Preaching,* March-April 1990, p. 46 [SFMar91]

977: A true story, submitted by Lee Prong [PEDec82]

978: Adapted [PEMar85]

979: Submitted by David Sell [PEAug88]

980: Submitted by Tim McLemore [PEApr87]

981: "Other Comments," in *Forbes,* May 19, 1986, p. 20 [PEOct86]

982: No source available [PEAug84]

983: No source available [PEAug84]

984: Submitted by Jim Vorsas [PEJun83]

985: Submitted by Larry Kineman [SFNov84]

986: No source available [PEFeb85]

987: Adapted [SFJul87]

988: Virginia Myers, *Saturday Evening Post,* April 1990, submitted by Rich Thornton [SFMay91]

989: No source available [PEMay83]

990: Sophie Tucker, quoted by R. Russell in *Life Is a Banquet* [PEApr81]

991: Steve Hodgin [PEAug90]

992: Mary H. Waldrip in *Dawson County Advertise,* Georgia [PEApr88]

993: *Sunday Sermons,* vol. 18, no. 3, p. 16 [PEJul88]

994: Pastor's wife in Enterprise, OR [PEApr84]

995: Submitted by Randall Tschetter [SFJul84]

996: Submitted by Travis T. Schmidt [SFOct92]

997: Submitted by Jim Vorsas [PEMay85]

998: Robert Benchley [PENov87]

999: No source available [PEAug83]

1000: Marvin Hein, *The Christian,* submitted by Dicky Love [SFJun91]

1001: Submitted by Ann Menschel [PEJun91]